People under three

As economic pressures and the desire for equal opportunities propel mothers into the workforce, more and more young children spend at least part of their day away from home. With social services day nurseries and family centres catering mainly for 'children in need', the number of private and work-based child care centres is rapidly increasing. *People Under Three* focuses on the group day care of very young children and is designed specifically for those who look after them day by day, as well as for policy makers, administrators and the managers of child care services. The authors, both well known for their work on child welfare and child care services, show how the theoretical advances we have made in understanding children's minds and the influences on their behaviour and development can be translated into everyday practice.

All the practical ideas in the book have been developed and tested in nurseries and family centres in Britain and elsewhere. They include detailed guidance on educational play for babies and toddlers; the 'key person' system, caring for children's emotional needs; and how to transform the outdoor area. The book also explores the difficult area of child protection and working with parents and children with a variety of problems, and includes a chapter on the staff group.

Based on the authors' enormous range of experience and expertise, *People Under Three* will be essential reading for managers of child care and family centres and private nurseries, for people responsible for registering and inspecting day care facilities, and for all those training to work with young children. Parents, too, will find the book helpful in evaluating the care available for their children.

Elinor Goldschmied is one of Europe's acknowledged experts on the management of day care services. She now works as a consultant in day care services for children in the UK, Italy and Spain. **Sonia Jackson** is a leading figure in the social work world and internationally known for her research on child welfare. She is Professor of Applied Social Studies at University College, Swansea.

People under three
Young children in day care

Elinor Goldschmicd and
Sonia Jackson

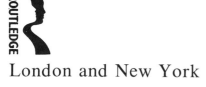
London and New York

First published 1994
by Routledge
11 New Fetter Lane, London EC4P 4EE

Simultaneously published in the USA and Canada
by Routledge
29 West 35th Street, New York, NY 10001

Extract from 'To My Friends', by Primo Levi, from *Collected Poems*,
translated by R. Feldman and B. Swann, Faber & Faber Ltd, reprinted
with permission.

Typeset in Times by Except*detail* Ltd, Southport

Printed and bound in Great Britain by
Biddles Ltd, Guildford and King's Lynn

British Library Cataloguing in Publication Data
A catalogue record for this book is available from the British Library.

Library of Congress Cataloguing in Publication Data
Goldschmied, Elinor.
  People under three: young children in day care/by Elinor Goldschmied
and Sonia Jackson.
    p. cm.
  Includes bibliographical references and index.
  1. Day care centers. 2. Day care centers–Great Britain.
  3. Infants–Care. I. Jackson, Sonia. II. Title.
  HV851.G65 1993
  362–7'12'0941–dc20   93-7401
                                                            CIP

ISBN 0–415–10188–3 (hbk)
ISBN 0–415–05976–3 (pbk)

To our grandchildren and their parents

We are guilty of many errors and many faults, but our worst crime is abandoning the children, neglecting the fountain of life. Many of the things we need can wait. The child cannot. Right now is the time his bones are being formed, his blood is being made and his senses are being developed. To him we cannot answer 'Tomorrow'. His name is 'Today'.

Gabriela Mistral

Contents

Illustrations

Acknowledgements

Over the years that this book has evolved and finally come to be written, very many people have given us ideas and influenced our thinking, some of them no longer here to receive our thanks, in particular Susan Isaacs, Donald Winnicott, Anna Freud, Jack Tizard and Brian Jackson. Thanks also for thought-stirring conversations to Leonard Davis, Kay Carmichael, Thelma Robinson, Katrine Stroh, Anita Hughes, Denise Hevey, Sue Dowling, Miriam David and Michael Duane.

We have drawn examples of good practice from many different day care settings where we have worked or acted as consultants, in Britain and overseas. These include nurseries in thirty-five Italian cities, especially Milan, Arezzo, San Giovanni Valdarno and Cinisello Balsamo. Among others, Mima Noziglia, Mara Mattesini, Anna Mallardi, Luciana Nissim and Elda Scrazella in Italy, Ethel Roberts, Pat Coe and Linda Osborn in England and Irene McIntyre in Scotland, have made it possible to try out on the ground ideas which often involved a considerable departure from accepted practice.

Another important source of new ideas, proved in action, has been the development projects carried out over nearly ten years by students on the University of Bristol interprofessional Diploma in Work with Young Children and Families. They showed what could be done with tiny resources provided they were combined with conviction and enthusiasm. All course members are organizers or managers of early childhood services with many years experience. Their contributions to this book cannot now be disentangled, but special thanks are due to Peter Fanshawe, Chris Leaves, Marion Taylor, Sylvia McCollin, Phil Lyons, Judith Chinnery, Fiona Stuart and Val Bean.

The course owed its origins to a conversation in Copenhagen with Bill Utting, and its realization to the support of colleagues at the University of Bristol Social Work Department, above all Annette

Holman, and later Renee Daines, Walter Barker, Roger Clough, Allan Brown and Cherry Rowlings. Thanks, too, to Christopher Beedell, who supervised Elinor's Personal Social Services Fellowship at Bristol, during which the first version of the *Treasure Basket* video, *Infants at Work*, was made.

Brenda Wright and John Robinson were among the first social services managers to see the need for appropriate, interdisciplinary training for senior nursery workers. This led to a long-term collaboration to the great benefit of students, the course and the day care service in Leicestershire. Many of the ideas worked out in that partnership have found their way into this book.

We have drawn directly for specific chapters on the work of Judy Hackett, Sue Finch, Veronica Sherborne and Christine Leaves. We are also grateful for general advice and comments on drafts to Dorothy Rouse, Mary Fawcett, Rebecca Abrams, Diane Ryken, Linda Osborn, Sophie Levitt, Pat Coe, Brenda Wright, Diane Houston, Dominic Abrams and Natasha Burchardt, and to Ellen Jackson for help with the index.

Apart from professional contacts, much of what we have put into this book comes from our personal experience as working mothers and grandparents. We thank our children and grandchildren for the pleasures and anxieties they have brought us. Perhaps the mind of a child is lost forever to adults, but it is in the intimacy of family life that one can get closest to it.

Producing a book also involves a good deal of domestic disruption – the kitchen table covered with papers for weeks on end, word processors bleeping and printers chuntering at unreasonable hours of the night and morning, long telephone calls at inconvenient moments. Derek Greenwood and Seth Jackson, the main sufferers, have shown unfailing tolerance, and provided much practical help.

Our greatest debt is to each other: neither of us would have thought of writing this book alone, and if we had known what a commitment we were making we might have thought again!

Sonia Jackson
Elinor Goldschmied

Introduction

A society can be judged by its attitude to its youngest children, not only in what is said about them but how this attitude is expressed in what is offered to them as they grow up.

Despite the great advances in our knowledge of how an infant develops from before birth to maturity, in this country we are far from giving serious recognition to the importance of the first three years. The absence in Britain of any coherent policy for early childhood care and education places almost the entire burden of bringing up the next generation upon the shoulders of young parents, in social conditions which create high levels of stress, both economic and psychological. The low value set on this vital task is reflected in the status, salaries, working conditions and lack of career opportunities and training for those who share the daily care of children in a variety of services and institutions.

In all European countries it is increasingly common for young children to spend at least part of the day away from their own homes. In Britain this may mean a local authority day nursery or children's centre, a family centre, workplace creche, the home of a child minder or day foster parent, or a community, voluntary or private nursery.

Though the variety of facilities may sound impressive, the reality is that parents usually have little choice about which form of care they use since such services are patchy and in many areas non-existent. Women are increasingly claiming the right to take paid employment and there is good evidence, that contrary to some popular impressions, this is often beneficial both to themselves and to their families. Yet local authority nurseries now cater almost exclusively for 'priority cases', children identified as being at risk of abuse and neglect or those defined as 'in need' under the Children Act, 1989.

There is surely no excuse for the failure of successive British governments to invest in the young children who are our future, the 'fountain of life' in Gabriela Mistral's phrase. In common with almost everybody who has written about pre-school services in the past fifteen years, we believe that major policy changes are necessary. However, we argue here that the experience of very small children in day care could be transformed even within the existing unsatisfactory framework and limited available resources if full use were made of the knowledge which now exists about early childhood development.

This book focuses on under threes in day care because so little has been written about them by comparison with the extensive literature on nursery education for 3- and 4-year-olds. It is also concerned with their parents, because in our view no distinction can be drawn between the wellbeing of parents and that of their young children.

The book is intended to be of practical use to people, at a variety of levels: to those who look after other people's children day by day in centres or in their own homes, to managers and organizers of day care services, and to those whose job is to establish and maintain standards. The book will also be relevant to administrators, community workers and to the wide range of specialists involved with young children and their families. We believe that it is essential for these people, who normally work at one remove from children, to understand how a child's daily experience is affected by managerial and resource decisions beyond the control of face-to-face workers. Parents, too, will find the book helpful in evaluating the care available, both for their child's happiness and their own peace of mind. As parents become better informed, we hope that they will press for more sensitive and stimulating care and more say in what is offered to their children.

Our knowledge of how children learn and develop has increased at an enormous rate in recent years as psychologists develop ever more sophisticated ways of observing and measuring the behaviour of babies from their very first moments in the world. Much research on early child development and learning highly relevant to nursery workers remains buried in academic journals and textbooks. Until now child care workers have been given rather little guidance on how they should change what they do in the light of this knowledge. We aim to make it more accessible by showing how it relates to everyday practice in child care settings, both at management level and in face-to-face contact with children and parents.

In the following chapters we put forward the view that every aspect of the nursery environment can make a significant contribution both to the emotional wellbeing and to the cognitive development of the young child. Now that we have good evidence that babies learn even in the womb, what justification can there be for the artificial division between care and education which has dominated our under-fives facilities for so long?

But knowledge alone is not enough. Good care must be not only educational but sensitive and responsive; it needs to be informed by an imaginative understanding of the experiences and feelings of young children, especially when they are separated from their parents. That is why we emphasize throughout the book the need for workers to observe the children they care for closely and systematically, to reflect on their observations and to share and discuss them with parents and each other. Whenever possible we draw analogies between things that happen to children and those that we commonly experience as adults. As memories before the age of three are mostly lost, this is one of the few ways available to us of attempting to understand the sensations and feelings of a small child.

We describe and explain three particular innovations derived from the principles outlined above: the key person system, the 'Treasure Basket' and heuristic play. All have been successfully introduced in day care centres in Britain and overseas, but will be new to many readers. We have also included a substantial chapter on the use of outdoor space, with detailed proposals for transforming the typical flat rectangular plot into an extended learning area.

We agree with the Commission for Racial Equality (1990) that the seeds of prejudice and discrimination are sown in infancy. This idea has been slow to penetrate pre-school services, but is as relevant to under threes as to older children and as important in all-white areas as in settings where many different cultures mingle. Throughout the book we emphasize the need to be aware of the messages we convey to children, through our actions as well as words and in the environment we create for them. We hope that our readers will be, like us, opposed to all forms of discrimination. The problem is to find ways of expressing those beliefs in everyday practice.

It is seldom easy. For example, the sexist nature of the English language presents difficulties to authors. 'He or she' becomes irritating when often repeated, but 'they', often used as a way out of the problem, has a depersonalizing effect. We wanted to refer to individual children, stressing their individuality. In this book we have come to the solution of imagining the child to be a girl or boy in alternate chapters (except where a specific child is described). In principle we should have used the same device in referring to staff, but it seemed unnecessary since we know that the vast majority of carers are women and there is little prospect that this will change in the near future. Of course, that makes it all the more important for women who work with young children to be aware of how they have themselves been influenced by traditional gender stereotypes so that they can avoid passing on attitudes which perpetuate disadvantage.

Young children and their parents have the right to expect that the extensive knowledge that we possess today about child development should shape the services that they so greatly need. Attitudes to children are changing. We have moved on from the view that simply because people are very young their thoughts and feelings do not matter, but we still often feel frustrated and mystified in our efforts to understand what little children are trying to say to us. In the same way many of the things we adults do and say must seem very puzzling to them. We would like to think that this book may in some small measure help to bridge that gap in our understanding of each other.

1 Values and principles

He who would do good to another must do it in Minute Particulars.
William Blake, 1804

This is a book for practitioners, and rather than clutter our text with references to theoretical discussions and research findings, which might seem irrelevant to readers who are more interested in applying ideas in their own work contexts, we have generally allowed the theory to remain implicit. However, it will be evident that the whole argument of this book rests on a particular set of values and point of view.

To start at the beginning, we accept that babies are born with their own genetic make-up and distinctive predispositions and personalities. However, we believe that what happens to them after birth is more significant in determining what sort of people they will become. That puts a heavy responsibility on those who care for them in their most formative years.

POLICY AND PRACTICE

This responsibility extends beyond the daily concerns of the work-place; people who work with young children need to understand how their particular job fits into the overall framework of services for families. In order to provide the best possible experience for the children in their care, they also need to be able to step outside their immediate work setting and see things from a wider viewpoint.

The underlying reason why services for children under school age in Britain are so inadequate and fragmented is that their care and upbringing are seen as the private concern of parents rather than the shared responsibility of our whole society (Jackson, 1992). As a result no government since the war has been prepared to make spending on child care and support for parenting a high priority.

Early years workers now have access to detailed factual information about day care and education in other countries (Melhuish and Moss, 1991; Sylva and Moss, 1992). The comparison makes it clear how far behind we have fallen as a result of the short-sighted policies of successive governments. In Sweden, Denmark, France and Italy, parents are supported in numerous ways in the task of child rearing. In this country parents are helped only when they are already seen to be failing, and have perhaps in the process done considerable harm to their children.

This is a self-defeating policy in which the absence of affordable child care plays a major part. A third of all children under five are living in poverty, many as a result of the unavailability of day care which would enable their mothers to work (Cohen, 1988). In turn, the pressures of poverty make it very difficult for parents to meet their children's needs (Gill, 1992).

As well as children and parents, both public and private day care providers suffer from this situation. As social services day care becomes more than ever an arm of child protection, nursery workers find themselves, often with little support or extra resources, caring for a group of children who are all from families in difficulties and show symptoms of disturbance and developmental delay.

Private centres, on the other hand, face the dilemma of how to provide good quality care without charging fees that few parents can afford. The Children Act, 1989, requires local authorities to monitor, regulate and review private services, but as Gillian Pugh has pointed out (1992a), inspection on its own will neither create new services nor produce quality in those that exist. Our discussions with organizers of private nurseries suggest that it is more likely to produce severe irritation.

It is important for early years workers to be aware of these policy issues if they are not to become overwhelmed, and direct their frustrations at the wrong targets – parents, colleagues or managers. They need rather to join forces with other professionals to speak more effectively on behalf of young children who have no voice of their own. In Chapter 4 we suggest that this kind of awareness is an essential aspect of staff development and training, as well as the understanding of children's cognitive, social and emotional development which we now go on to discuss.

FREEDOM AND STRUCTURE

Most books on child development start from the eighteenth century philosophers, Rousseau and Locke. The first believed that children should enjoy maximum freedom so that their natural ability and creativeness could flourish, the second that a child's mind is a tabula rasa, a blank screen on which everything he or she learns has to be written. The pioneers of early childhood education, Froebel, the Macmillan sisters, Susan Isaacs, were strongly influenced by Rousseau's point of view, which made its way into the British nursery school tradition and the playgroup movement, and until recently dominated thinking and practice in all early years work.

To some extent we incline to the Rousseau camp. For example, we think that an important part of the work of an adult caring for a small child is to see that for as much of the time as possible he or she is *happy*. Life holds quite enough pain and frustration without deliberately adding to it by strict, punitive or intrusive child-rearing practices. On the other hand, we don't think that unlimited freedom is at all likely to lead either to happiness or optimal development. Therefore, though we may appear to take a typically non-interventionist position in urging that wherever possible the adult acts as facilitator rather than director of the child's activities, we do so in the context of a carefully planned and organized environment.

Adults play an important part in shaping children's behaviour, but they can choose to do it in authoritarian or co-operative ways, by dictation or negotiation. There is good evidence that the second way is by far the more effective, as well as leading to less conflict and distress. We therefore put much emphasis both on caregivers negotiating with children rather than coercing them, and also on the need for adults to help children to negotiate with each other.

THE IMPORTANCE OF PLAY

The contribution of play to children's development is a subject which well illustrates the pendulum effect. The attitudes parodied by Dickens in *Hard Times*, which characterized play as a frivolous activity of no value compared with the learning of useful information, persisted in a modified form well into the postwar period. Play was what children did when not under the immediate control of adults, at best time-filling and always in potential conflict with 'sitting still and being good' or with more useful kinds of activity. However, as Meadows (1986) describes, the opposing view that 'play is children's work' has enjoyed a period of considerable dominance in psychological and educational theory.

Recently, there have been signs of a more critical assessment of the function of play and how it relates to learning and adult achievement. Smith (1984) has pointed out that experimental studies have not produced any conclusive evidence that more play leads to enhanced language development, problem-solving, creativity or social adjustment.

One problem for nursery and infant teachers and playgroup leaders has always been to convince parents that their child is well occupied 'just playing'. It could be that parents have some reason to resist the prevailing orthodoxy. In many cultures play is given little importance; no attempt is made to provide children with elaborate playthings, and although one can see that children do play spontaneously, their activities are not accorded any particular adult attention. Yet the children appear to develop perfectly normally and may do well at school. It does seem that, at least for academic and occupational success, other qualities of the environment may be more important than the opportunity to play freely in early childhood.

If we look at ethnic groups which seem to be successful in promoting their children's development despite adverse socio-economic conditions, such as, for example, the Jews of New York or Asian immigrants to Britain, we might identify as significant a high level of adult–child interaction, the inclusion of the child in home-based adult activities, the open expression of affection, a respect for learning and literacy and the recognition of educational success as a key factor in determining life chances.

What this illustrates is that play is only one element in child development; much more crucial is adult concern and attention. Nevertheless, as will be obvious, we do consider play to be of great importance in any child care setting. There are good pragmatic reasons for this. The long hours that children spend in day care centres have to be occupied. Bored children are fractious and miserable. The better the quality of the play opportunities offered to them, the more pleasurable the experience, both for adults and children.

The other reason is that, although the research evidence in favour of learning through play may not be conclusive, there is certainly no better evidence *against* it to conflict with fifty years of practice experience. What we are learning to do, perhaps, is to discriminate better between different types of play, rediscovering the truth of John Stuart Mill's assertion that push-pin is not as good as poetry. It is, in other words, right and reasonable to value some kinds of play more highly than others, to create conditions in which children are more likely to choose particular activities, to encourage complex, concentrated play in preference to aimless flitting from one thing to another. To do this without introducing constraint and coercion is a highly skilled task, requiring detailed personal knowledge of each individual child, and an adequate number of adults in proportion to children.

The quality of play we have observed in British day care centres is notably inferior to that seen in nursery schools. Where the children are under three there is not even an established body of knowledge to call on, and this is one reason why we have devoted a major part of this book to the provision and organization of play opportunities for these very young children.

CARE AND EDUCATION

The discussion of play is set in the context of the day care centre as a total environment in which every aspect of organization and every activity offered makes a contribution to the child's development and learning.

Britain is not the only country to have inherited a split between care provided by health professionals, primarily for poor children, and education provided as a general service, staffed by teachers. However, it is the only country where the distinction has continued to the present day, indeed intensified. This is partly because of the curious idea that children don't really learn anything until they start compulsory schooling – before that they are just filling in time – and partly because local authority day nurseries are controlled by social services departments which do not see education as their business. (This split is even more obviously reflected in the service provided to children in residential or foster care (Jackson, 1988).)

In the case of day nurseries and child minders, this has meant that the very children who most urgently need care with a high educational content are least likely to get it (Jackson and Jackson, 1979; Osborn and Milbank, 1987). Combined centres, which were set up to provide integrated care and education, continue to reflect established professional divisions (Ferri, 1981). We have even heard children categorized as 'social' or 'educational', as if the acutely deprived children occupying 'priority' day care places were not in need of education.

Unfortunately, this perception is only too accurately reflected in what is provided for them. Curiously enough, though pre-school provision for disadvantaged children in the United States is dominated by the idea of compensatory education and the prevention of later school failure (the whole Head Start programme for example), this never really took hold in Britain, and has now virtually disappeared. It is perhaps not accidental that an American, Kathy Sylva, is one of the few to restate this position strongly (Sylva, 1991).

We entirely agree with her view that the educational content of care for disadvantaged children requires particular emphasis and that the staff group should include people with educational qualifications. All day care staff need to understand the educational importance of their work and be familiar with the early requirements of the National Curriculum so that the experiences of the young children they look after are not only satisfying in themselves but foster the qualities, such as concentration and persistence in the face of difficulties, which will stand them in good stead in later years at school.

In our culture the key to educational success is literacy (to a lesser extent numeracy). For this reason, if no other, children need to be introduced to books at a very early age and helped to see them as a source of interest and pleasure. There is clear evidence that learning to read easily is closely linked with being read to early and often (Wells, 1985). One of the most useful things nurseries can do with parents is to encourage them to read and talk about stories with their children from infancy, and show them how to help children read for themselves as soon as they are interested in doing so.

RELATIONSHIPS IN DAY CARE

If day nurseries have fallen short in providing a stimulating educational environment, so have they often failed to meet the emotional needs of young children. Here our theoretical position has its origins in Bowlby's seminal work on attachment and loss (Bowlby, 1969/82). That is, we give great importance and value to attachments between individual children and adults, and acknowledge the acute pain caused by their insensitive disruption, or alternatively by the absence of such attachments. This is the basis for the key person system described in Chapter 3, which is designed to promote a special relationship between a child, his family and a particular caregiver.

The citing of Bowlby's work as an argument against provision of day care for young children has been discredited both by Schaffer's research on multiple attachments (Schaffer, 1977), and by more recent evidence on the effects of day care (Moss and Melhuish, 1991), but that does not mean that all his original insights were invalid. It is worth noting that Rutter (1972), who more than anyone else was responsible for the re-evaluation of Bowlby's original thesis, qualified his view that it was not harmful for a child under three to spend time away from his mother by specifying the need for the child to be enabled to form secure, stable relationships with a substitute caregiver. However, studies of day nurseries as currently organized suggest that they generally fail to provide such opportunities. A number of research reports (Bain and Barnett, 1980; Mayall and Petrie, 1983; Van der Eyken, 1984) have found high staff turnover leading to many changes of caregiver for the child, and a low level of adult–child interaction. Similar observations have been made in day care settings in the United States, and Clyde comments on the situation in Australia:

> It would be alarming to tally the numbers of centres which make few provisions for adults and toddlers to form special relationships of attachment and friendship, or do not recognize this as a critical part of the daily programme.

> (Clyde, 1988)

Tizard (1991) identifies a high staff–child ratio as the key ingredient of good quality day care, but we suggest that this is not a sufficient condition unless the organization of the care setting ensures regular occasions when concentrated attention is given by a particular caregiver to a particular child.

This is especially important for very young children for two reasons: their recurrent need for intimate bodily care, and their developing capacity for communication. American research shows that children enrolled in day care programmes with more responsive caregivers are likely to have better cognitive and language development and be more socially competent. But responsiveness depends on familiarity. Young children begin to communicate with idiosyncratic speech or gestures which may be meaningless except to a caregiver who knows them well.

The evidence in favour of fostering individual attachments in day care is strong but not undisputed. As Rouse and Griffin (1992) point out, child development workers in other countries, for example Japan, China and Italy, see group care as offering a positive antidote to smothering maternal attention and over-attachment. Without disputing this proposition, though we suspect it is less relevant in the British cultural context, it is certainly not a valid argument against the key person system advocated here, which aims only to ensure loving and responsive attention from a significant adult at certain times of the day.

However, our reasons are grounded less in research than in

subjective experience: the observation that throughout our lives we seek individual relationships and like to feel ourselves of particular importance to one person. This is especially so in stressful situations. If we are concerned with children's happiness now as well as their future development, we need to pay attention to this kind of knowledge.

PARENTS AND CHILDREN

Parents are by far the most important people in the lives of their children, a fact which schools and nurseries have only slowly come to recognize. Until a few years ago there was an almost complete split in the way people thought and wrote about young children. Psychology textbooks and child care guides addressed to parents laid great emphasis on the importance of the interaction between mother and child, almost to the exclusion of other relationships, while the training of teachers and nursery nurses virtually ignored the child's family.

In recent years the job of the nursery worker in Britain has changed dramatically, so that at least in local authority nurseries and family centres, there is an expectation that the unit will undertake active work with parents, and this is usually specified in its statement of aims. A whole new vocabulary has grown up to describe the relationship between caregivers and parents, but these terms often conceal a good deal of wishful thinking.

For example, although 'partnership with parents' is a popular aspiration, appearing in many statements of aims and objectives and promotional literature, the reality is elusive. Gillian Pugh and Erica De'Ath visited 120 centres to explore the extent to which services were planned, implemented and delivered in partnership with families, but as the project progressed 'so little was identifed that could truly be described as partnership' that in order to continue the work at all it was necessary to extend the brief to the whole area of parent involvement (Pugh and De'Ath, 1989). Daines and colleagues (1990) came to a similar conclusion in their study of Barnardo's family centres with an explicit commitment to partnership. They concluded that the power relationship between professionals and parents was so unequal that partnership in the sense of mutuality of support, alliance and shared control was not achievable and should be replaced as an objective by 'maximum feasible participation'.

But involvement and participation are also words which can mean many different things. There is a danger of putting all families in the position of social work clients rather than people using a service. Involvement is not seen as a way of enabling parents to have more influence over how their child is cared for in the nursery but rather as a means of changing the way they behave towards the child, 'improving their parenting skills'. Too often, as New and David argued (1986), this can mean imposing staff attitudes and values on people whose class and culture lead them to have quite different priorities and concerns. When every child in a centre has been referred explicitly because the care they receive from their family is considered by somebody to be inadequate, it is difficult for staff to avoid developing a stereotyped notion of parents, which is one reason why we are strongly opposed to such segregated provision.

The model we prefer emphasizes the importance of good working relations with parents in the interests of the child's wellbeing, but fully acknowledges the family's primacy in the child's world. The aim is to achieve continuity and consistency for the child, so that the important thing is to secure the best possible communication and understanding between the nursery workers and those who will still provide most of the child's care. Building good relationships is essential, but it is easy for 'involvement' to become an aim in itself, siphoning off staff energy which would be better spent improving the daily experience of the children.

This is in no way to devalue the work of family centres which provide a variety of services to a local community. The Pen Green Centre, which flourishes in the left-behind industrial town of Corby, demonstrates how the needs of parents and children can be held in balance without either being subordinated to the other (Whalley, 1992).

It is a matter both of resources and attitudes. A nursery where the staffing takes no account of anything but the direct care of children will have difficulty in going through the necessary processes of consultation, discussion and training, and time given to work with parents must mean less time for the children. On the other hand a child or family centre does provide a natural focus for a whole range of facilities for adult education and recreation which may improve the quality of life of the parents and thus, indirectly, of the children. The danger lies in trying to do too much without appropriate resources, and perhaps also in trying to impose a single pattern on people with a whole range of different needs and life styles on whom the label 'parents' confers a spurious uniformity.

COMBATING DISCRIMINATION

The term 'parent' in practice means 'mother' nine times out of ten. We are torn between wanting to write of things as they are and our strong belief that fathers need to share the upbringing of children equally with mothers. Early years professionals must bear some of the responsibility for reinforcing the assumption that the mother is the primary carer. An example comes to mind of the health visitor quoted by Brian Jackson (1984), who exclaimed when a father opened the door with the baby on his shoulder, 'What are you doing with the baby? Where's your wife?'

However, we should recognize that the desire to draw men into the world of early childhood reflects a value position which the majority of writers in the field implicitly share, but many other people do not.

In Chapter 9 we have included a discussion of approaches to anti-discriminatory practice in day care. It is probably true to say that in social services and education at the time of writing there is a wide consensus on this subject, a point of view that might be called politically correct. Moreover anti-racism is given legislative backing by the Race Relations Act, 1976, and the Children Act, 1989, which acknowledge and offer measures for counteracting racism in early years provision (Lane, 1990). The difficulty is that, as with the role of fathers, these views are often not shared by the population in general, or even by the people who are victims of discrimination. How does our commitment to equal opportunities and undifferentiated gender roles mesh with our commitment to respect parents' views and wishes for their children? What do we do when a central aspect of their culture is to distinguish very clearly between the roles and responsibilities of men and women and the behaviour considered appropriate in boys and girls?

We do not believe it possible to take a neutral position because in our view that simply perpetuates discrimination. An active anti-discriminatory policy must involve compensating for the images which constantly surround children in the world outside the nursery (Siraj-Blatchford, 1992).

Yet we must acknowledge that what we propose does represent an assertion of our own values, which may be in conflict with those of others. There is little doubt that racism and sexism, with the stunting of opportunities they entail, have their roots in children's earliest experiences, and that this is the best time to address them (Derman-Sparks, 1989). At the same time the nursery must recognize its educational role and enter into a dialogue with parents, not simply override their views. Our own ideas, as professionals, have evolved over many years, helped by workshops, discussions and reading. It is unreasonable to expect people to change their whole way of looking at things just because their child is attending a day care centre.

SUMMARY

This chapter sets out some of the ideas and values which underpin the approaches to practice described in the book. At the top of the list we put the shared responsibility of the state and families to use the best knowledge we have in caring for and educating our youngest children. Although the quality of care experienced by children probably depends as much on political and sociological factors as on what is done by their immediate caregivers, we believe that even within an unsatisfactory structure there is much scope for improvement.

The key to high quality care is respect for the child as a person, expressed in detailed daily arrangements. Small children looked after away from home have a right to a loving relationship with a particular caregiver, to be offered the best possible conditions and materials to explore and experiment, appropriate to their age, to see their culture and language valued and their close adults working in harmony with each other. In the next chapter we suggest ways of organizing an environment which will help us move towards these objectives.

2 Organizing space for living, learning and playing

Apparently small details should not be ignored, for it is only through them that large designs are possible.

St Jerome

The physical environment exerts a major influence on how nursery workers feel about the job and on the quality of experience they can offer the children. However we have seen some of the most creative work with under threes going on in very unsuitable buildings, whereas the best-designed centres can have a cold, sterile, institutional feel about them. Whatever the limitations of the building, there is always something that can be done to make it more comfortable and attractive to the adults and children who spend long hours of the day there.

In this chapter we look first at the general organization and appearance of the centre. The next section considers how the use of space relates to the roles of the adult in day care, and the last part of the chapter discusses in more detail equipment and play material for different age groups.

CREATING A SATISFYING ENVIRONMENT

Unlike a nursery school, a day care centre is a place for living as well as working and playing. The physical environment must take account of this dual function. It has to combine comfort and homeliness with the practicality of a well-run nursery classroom. Its overall appearance should offer interest and pleasure to children and adults alike.

Because day care provision has such low priority in funding, nurseries and family centres often have to make do with furnishings accumulated over time, with low cost the main consideration. As a result many rooms have furniture which is not the right shape, cushions and curtains of colours and textures which do not add up to any harmonious scheme and that most of us would not tolerate in our own homes.

Banks, shops and restaurants pay huge sums to interior designers to create a visual environment which is attractive to customers during their brief visits. Yet we are often content for children to spend their most formative years surrounded by ugliness and clutter. It is noticeable that this is not generally true in countries like Italy, which give far more importance to visual and artistic education than we do in Britain.

Take pictures for example. All too often we find nurseries decorated with crude cut-outs of Disney cartoon characters which add nothing to the appearance of the room and hold little interest for children after the first pleasure of recognition. Reproductions of good paintings are rarely seen in British nurseries or child care centres, though in other countries this is regarded as an aspect of introducing children to their cultural heritage.

Of course much of the wall area in a nursery will be needed to display children's work or for notices and information to staff and parents, but there is usually space in entrance areas, passages or the staff room. It is also worth thinking about places where the wall space is usually thrown away, such as kitchens, bathrooms and cloakroom areas.

Some local art galleries run loan schemes, and may have basements full of once-despised Victorian narrative paintings and water-colours, now to be found reproduced in every greeting-card shop. These can be very appealing to children and offer much scope for conversation. Children tend to be eclectic in their tastes and are also intrigued by non-representational art, paintings by twentieth-century artists such as Picasso, Miro and Chagall, for example. Staff members may have favourite pictures which they would be willing to lend on a temporary basis. Chinese, Persian, African and Indian paintings and wall hangings also offer much interest.

Creating a satisfactory visual environment is not a once-for-all job, but something that needs to happen continuously. Just as at home we are constantly making small adjustments and improvements, changing pictures from one room to another, moving a lamp or a plant, a nursery will only look inviting and cared for if the same kind of process is going on.

If a nursery unit is being created or furnished from scratch, it is best to stick to plain colours, not too bright, for basic items, so that nursery workers can exercise their creativity in the wall displays, hangings, mobiles, cushion covers, pictures and other easily removable and replaceable objects. Fitted carpets create the effect of more space, absorb noise and are pleasant to sit on.

Though it seems expensive, hardwearing stain-resistant carpet, with an appropriate machine for cleaning it, is an excellent investment and, properly cared for, will continue to look good for many years. We know too many nurseries which make do with offcuts of assorted garish patterns or tumbletwist rugs which ruckle up. It may be hard to convince managers that expenditure on a new carpet is justified, and raising money for such a purpose sounds a bit mundane compared with, say, a piece of large play equipment or an outing to the seaside, but in the long term it could make a bigger contribution to staff morale and children's comfort.

The entrance area

The space that people come into when they first enter the nursery needs careful thought if it is going to be genuinely welcoming. Coming into a bright, carpeted area with comfortable chairs for waiting, plants, well-displayed photographs and pictures on the walls feels quite different from a dark passage with a narrow bench, prohibitory notices and stacked-up equipment. Careful thought needs to be given to the visual impact of this area, both on those visiting the nursery for the first time and those who enter it every day.

The entrance area is a public statement by the centre about its values and priorities. What messages does it convey? We can see that some nurseries create an artificial child's world with no reference to anything that goes on outside, while others make a positive attempt to create bridges with families and the community. There are blown-up pictures of local neighbourhood and family life, photographs of nursery staff with their names, so that parents and visitors can easily identify them, photographs of children engaged in play activities. There are welcoming messages in the different languages of families using the centre. Notices are carefully designed and non-authoritarian in tone.

The amount of information that staff want to provide in the entrance area may conflict with the aim of keeping it looking visually attractive. Too many notices can give it an institutional feel and create an overcrowded effect. The important thing is to keep examining it with a critical eye.

The impressions we receive on entering a new place do not only come through the eye – we need to give attention to the auditory as well as the visual environment. Anyone who has visited a friend in hospital will know that one of the most distressing aspects is the incessant clatter. We need to do everything possible in a nursery to keep the noise level to a minimum. This means attending immediately to crying babies, no shouting or calling across rooms, music only as part of the planned programme, surfaces designed to be sound-absorbent. Noise creates stress for staff and inhibits children's speech development; we return to some of these points later.

THE ORGANIZATION OF THE NURSERY

A few purpose-built centres have adopted an open-plan design, with children free to use the whole floorspace but with 'home' areas enclosed on three sides. We have seen this working very well, allowing different play activities to be concentrated in separate areas and avoiding isolation of staff. On the other hand, if not well managed, it can be a recipe for chaos.

In most countries children in day care are grouped by age, like school children, as they used to be in Britain. Here, the majority of day nurseries over the past twenty years have adopted the 'family group' system of organization which places children of mixed ages in the same room in the care of one or two nursery workers. The idea is that a mixed group is more natural, closer to ordinary family life and offers more variety to the nursery worker.

Age grouping and 'family' grouping

There are clear advantages in enabling siblings to remain together or be separated, depending on their personal characteristics and relationship, rather than on some arbitrary rule related to their dates of birth. Children develop at different rates and some may not be ready to move into an older group at the 'right' age. Children with special needs can perhaps be more easily integrated in a family group system. Child minders almost inevitably find themselves looking after an assortment of children at different stages of development and have to accept the particular difficulties that creates.

However, we suggest that it is time to look more critically at the benefits of 'family' grouping. Could it be that the dominance of this form of organization was the product of a particular historical moment which has now passed? In the field of residential child care we have learnt painfully that no institution can do the job of a good parent, only simulate some features of it (Jackson, 1989). The 'family group homes', set up with such good intentions in reaction to the large anonymous children's homes of the past, are disappearing, to be replaced by foster carers who make no attempt to take the place of the child's parents and by residential units which do well what they can, without pretending to be 'just like a family'. Family grouping, as Elsa Ferri pointed out in her study of combined nursery centres (Ferri *et al.*, 1981), similarly carries an element of wishful thinking. What could be less like the average family in the 1990s than up to ten children of different ages spending all day in the same room in the charge of one or two young nursery workers? As Ferri's research showed conclusively, the system does not even produce more one-to-one contact between the child and his 'own' family group worker and may particularly disadvantage 2-year-olds. It seems to be an attempt to gloss over the reality of day care and to counteract its negative image.

The practical advantages of age grouping are substantial. It is almost always easier for a nursery worker to manage a relatively homogeneous group of children than one of the same size where all are at different stages of development. Most importantly, it enables her to give full attention to the play and learning opportunities appropriate to their age without constant disruption by older or younger children whose needs are different. We may see a move back towards age grouping as it comes to be recognized that providing for the cognitive development of even the youngest children is a central aspect of the nursery worker's task. There are already signs that this is happening. Probably the majority of centres where under twos are cared for already have a separate room for them.

THE ROLE OF THE ADULT IN THE GROUP ROOM

Except in centres with open plan arrangements, day care usually involves one or two adults spending large parts of the day in a 'group room' with a number of children. During this time the nursery workers take on a number of distinct but interrelated roles on which the functioning of the unit depends – those of organizer, facilitator and initiator.

As *organizer* the nursery worker is responsible for use of space, ventilation, arrangement of furniture, comfort of seating, storage, the appearance of the room and keeping things clean and in good repair in co-operation with domestic staff. Time for starting and ending activities, for clearing up and putting away, sharing a bathroom with other groups, setting up tables for mealtimes, are all matters for precise organization, while allowing flexibility to accommodate the unpredictable needs of individual children.

Organizing shifts, rest breaks and time to attend to parents or visiting specialists all add to the complexity of the day's events and cannot happen smoothly without detailed planning. For child minders, who have to combine all the functions performed by different staff members in a nursery, and often have also to take and collect older children from school, effective time management is equally essential (Bryant *et al.*, 1980).

Successfully carrying out the second role, that of *facilitator*, depends on this planned organization of time, space and materials. By imaginative provision and arrangement of play equipment, the adult enables children to choose and develop their play, on their own or with others. Her attentive presence provides emotional anchorage to the group of children, who know that, if necessary, she will intervene as referee or comforter.

In the third role, as *initiator*, the adult is more directly in charge of the activity. She may work with a small group which requires her undisturbed attention, giving technical help and encouragement to those who need it in activities such as using clay, baking biscuits, making a collage, footprints with paint, finger painting, making music, reading a story or gardening.

This kind of initiator is not to be confused with acting as what might be called 'ringmaster', which is sometimes necessary when there is a large group to control. Here the worker risks finding herself in the role of entertainer, dominating the group in a charismatic way, and finding herself exhausted in the process. It is important to clarify the difference, because large-group orchestrated activity, is generally inappropriate for children of this age, restricting and distorting their play and learning (see, for example, Sylva *et al.*, 1980).

Balancing the roles

To some extent it is a matter of temperament whether an adult likes to have children under control and gathered around her as opposed to being a secure figure who provides a point of reference for the children while they play. In a stable staff group the workers will complement each other, with different members giving more emphasis to one of the three roles.

When there are two staff present, they need to work out how best to divide their responsibilities. In this situation one adult can give total attention to a small group while the other is able to be available for the overall supervision of the remainder. Managers and supervisors can encourage workers to bring the three roles into better balance by helping them to become aware of their own preferences and work style.

ORGANIZING THE GROUP ROOM

The way in which the group room is planned makes a big difference to how far activity can be child-initiated and self-directed or require constant, exhausting intervention by the adults. All nursery workers have to cope with the daily task of keeping the group room in reasonable order. Lack of floor and storage space and the constant shifting of furniture can make this a very trying aspect of the job.

Careful thought needs to be given to how these problems can be minimized. The unalterable fact that playing, eating and sometimes sleeping must be provided for in the same space brings feelings of stress and restriction which affect both children and adults, but people often put up with avoidable inconvenience simply out of habit.

The appearance of the room

It is important that all staff should feel that their group room is sufficiently attractive and well organized for everyone to experience some pleasure and satisfaction as they enter each day. Unless a really critical eye is maintained, it is easy for people to get used to a room with a chaotic and uncared-for appearance. This can have a profoundly depressing effect without people being consciously aware of it. A useful way of initiating improvement in appearance and organization is to run a meeting, including everyone who uses the room, with the theme, 'What I would like to keep in this room and what I would like to get rid of'. This can result in some energetic throwing out, allowing storage space to be used more efficiently.

Furniture

Effective arrangements for storing play materials in good order are essential. To enable the staff to operate as facilitators, the storage should, as far as possible, be on open shelves so that children can fetch items for themselves or see what is available and ask for what they want.

Another most important point often overlooked, is the need for at least two adult-sized chairs in every room so that a staff member and parent can sit down and talk in comfort. Every group room needs a chair which is suitable for an adult holding or comforting a child. Nursery workers who habitually hold children in their arms while standing up put themselves at serious risk of developing back trouble.

Depending on the size and shape of the group room there will be more or less scope for the arrangement of furniture. For instance, if there is a rather large piece of furniture such as a storage cupboard, it is better to place it so that on entering the room the eye does not encounter it immediately. Smaller pieces of furniture, such as sofas and bookcases, can be used for making partitions.

The most successful kind of group room has the appearance of spaciousness, but with cosy corners. People who design the interior of restaurants and pubs know that their customers prefer comfortable, secluded areas and that no-one likes to sit at tables out in the middle of the floor. Children feel the same way.

It is important to be selective about the number of mobiles, hanging decorations and paintings or drawings that are displayed on the walls. More is not necessarily better. Small children's paintings can look very attractive but only if they are properly mounted, with the background chosen to complement the dominant colour, and if care is taken that they are firmly fixed in place.

Responsibility for wall displays should be clearly allocated to a particular person for an agreed period. Otherwise they can quickly acquire an uncared-for look, creating a kind of visual confusion. Windows also need regular attention. Clean windows make a great difference to the appearance of the room.

Sometimes staff paint or stick pictures on the windows, either in an effort to brighten the place up, or, in the case of private centres, to indicate the function of the building and to attract enquiries. Unfortunately, the result is often to reduce the available light, especially on dull days, and also to give a cluttered effect in a space which may be too small anyway.

In planning the available space to the best advantage, a good exercise is to observe the children's movements carefully during different times of the day. We can often identify a 'dead area' where for some reason children do not go, increasing crowding in other parts. Once this is recognized, the space can be brought into use by making it more accessible or by putting equipment for a popular activity there.

INVOLVING CHILDREN IN CARE AND MAINTENANCE

Maintaining order in the group room is an essential task for the nursery worker in her role as organizer. A constant unobtrusive re-ordering, enlisting the help of individual children whenever possible, works better than the practice sometimes seen in nurseries of allowing the room to become chaotic and having a grand clear-up two or three times a day.

Involving the older children in tidying and cleaning up can mean more effort for the staff as it is usually quicker for the adults to do it themselves. But if we look on everything that happens in the nursery as part of the children's learning, this is a short-sighted approach. There will be some occasions when time pressure is too great, but it is usually possible to organize some of the helping so that both adults and children enjoy it and feel a sense of achievement.

Of course it is particularly important that boys should see clearing up as their job as much as that of the girls. Numerous studies of family life and the division of domestic work between men and women have shown that, even when the woman is working as long hours as the man and in an equally demanding job, she almost always continues to take responsibility for running the household and doing by far the greater part of the routine work (McCrae, 1986; Jackson, 1992). Because staff of day care centres are almost all female, little boys can easily get the idea that clearing up is women's work, especially if that coincides with what they see at home. Nursery staff have an important contribution to make here, both by ensuring that they do not collude with this attitude and by challenging it in others, including the children themselves (Aspinwall, 1984).

When both parents are working, it is quite likely that they will not have time or patience to involve children in domestic tasks, so the nursery can add appreciably to this aspect of children's experience. There is the further point that a shared domestic task can provide an excellent opportunity for close one-to-one contact between the staff member and child.

ORGANIZING A GROUP ROOM FOR UNDER TWOs

A baby room needs to combine a sense of spaciousness with intimacy, allowing free movement for mobile children and a quieter area for babies not yet able to move by themselves. We still sometimes see baby rooms almost entirely taken up with cots. A better solution is to use suitably covered mattresses in one corner, where babies can be put to sleep (or put themselves) when they are tired. The staff member supervising this end of the room can sit on a low, comfortable chair, placed so that she can protect the space from invasion by older, mobile children, but be available to talk to them as they play in the rest of the room. The general layout of the room for this age group needs to give maximum scope for the gross motor activity which occupies so much of the children's energy as they progress from crawling and pulling themselves up to making first steps.

Mattresses are good for babies at the stage of sitting, propped up by cushions or unaided, and rolling or levering themselves about; but as soon as they begin to crawl they need the firm surface of a carpet.

Carpet is essential for children who have begun to stand and take first steps so that they can have bare feet, allowing them to grip in the process of achieving the balance necessary for walking. They also like to sit on a carpeted area to manipulate anything which comes to hand. All-over carpet has the additional advantage of quietness, and the inevitable spilt food at mealtimes can be managed by slipping a nylon sheet under the table which can be removed and washed elsewhere.

Direct access to a covered outdoor area and/or garden is a great advantage, allowing free movement in and out of the room and enabling babies to sleep in prams in the open air (always of course under close supervision). The garden area for under twos should be separated by a low fence from the general outdoor space so that, while this age group is not cut off from the rest of the nursery, they are protected from accidental bumps and knocks by bigger children using tricycles, prams, cars and trolleys in their outdoor play. More suggestions for planning and equipping an outdoor area for under twos are given in Chapter 11.

Adequate, well-planned storage space is just as essential in a room designed for under twos as for older children. This becomes obvious as soon as we start to give real thought to play objects for this age group, as described in Chapters 6 and 8. It is most important that each child's personal cuddly toy or love object has a designated place for when it is temporarily discarded, so that it can be quickly retrieved when wanted.

Baby rooms are too often cluttered up with bulky containers or plastic baskets into which everything is indiscriminately flung at clearing-up time. As well as occupying valuable space, this encourages thoughtless accumulation of mass-produced plastic toys and grubby stuffed animals, sometimes of startling ugliness, which have nothing to contribute to the children's development.

As with a group room for older children, it is best to have

earmarked 'corners' for different types of play material. There is a difference, however, in that as soon as they can move freely, children of this age will roam about, exploring energetically, carrying with them whatever they happen to be holding and dropping it wherever they are when something new catches their interest. They will play with the available material all over the room, not focusing their activity as the older ones do. We have to accept that much of the nursery worker's effort will go into quietly re-ordering the play equipment and maintaining a reasonably attractive appearance to the room rather than allowing it to degenerate into a battlefield. This continuing, but not interfering or obsessive re-ordering, is part of the facilitating role of the worker.

Provided various types of equipment are based (and replaced continually) in specified parts of the room, even very small children will quickly learn to respond to the adult's request to 'put dolly back in her cot' or 'this goes with the other books in that corner'. These simple instructions, related directly to an action, and evoking the smile and thank you of the adult, provide genuine experience in collaboration which need in no way be oppressive. A sense of self and the beginnings of personal autonomy are built up in a myriad small ways by a nursery worker's understanding of such daily opportunities.

LAYOUT AND EQUIPMENT FOR MIXED AND OLDER AGE GROUPS

When long periods are available for free play, the organization of the room needs careful attention to avoid a noisy, restless atmosphere. If the group room provides very well-equipped and maintained activity points, the ability of children to become engrossed in their play is greatly improved.

Once the nursery workers have achieved an arrangement which feels satisfactory it is best to keep the activities in the same position. This gives the children a sense of security and competence. Repositioning activity corners may seem a trivial matter to the organizer but should not be done without a good reason. Think how uncomfortable we feel ourselves when we go into our local supermarket and find that the washing powder has moved to the place where the cereal used to be. Or when our favourite newspaper switches the editorial pages to the back.

We assume as standard practice that a group room for over twos will have most of the following designated areas, though there may not be space for all to be in permanent fixed positions:

The quiet corner

In the long nursery day it is essential to arrange a quiet, enclosed space for resting, daydreaming or looking at books, magazines, catalogues or collections of cards. Reading corners are not always sufficiently protected to provide such a refuge. If there is not an actual corner available, this can be created by placing a sofa or divan at right angles to the wall, combining it with low shelving or the back of a cupboard facing the other way.

Because the staff usually have the opportunity, however limited, to withdraw and be quiet in their staffroom, it may be forgotten that children also need a space away from the pressure of the general activities of the group. The aim should be to create and maintain an atmosphere of cosiness and safety.

The essentials are a proper carpet, and cushions in abundance, large and small. A covered cot mattress on the floor and another placed up against the wall are very welcome for sitting or sprawling, and a low armchair or sofa if there is enough space. These can form part of the protective 'wall' together with a wooden book rack on which a changing selection of books is kept. Alternatively, books can be placed in a wall rack with easy access so that children can take them out and put them away themselves. There must of course be a firm rule that no books are to be thrown about or left on the floor to be trodden on.

When there is an opportunity, a staff member or volunteer can spend time with one or two children seeing that the books are in good order, not torn or with frayed bindings, so that maintenance is a continuous process. It is more effective if a particular member of staff takes responsibility for this. She may be the person who makes contact with the local librarian, arranging to have books on loan or to take a small group of children along to the library, preferably with the help of a volunteer or student.

Mail order catalogues are interesting to small children, but need regular checking so that they can be eliminated before they become grubby or torn. A shoe box or a rectangular wooden box filled with well-chosen postcards, forms a point of interest. The smallest children will enjoy looking at postcards of single subjects, such as animals, flowers, cars and ships. It is useful for staff to have access to small amounts of petty cash so that in the course of their own shopping they can keep an eye out in local newsagents and stationers for cards that will engage the children's attention and stimulate comment and conversation. If there is a suitable shop nearby, a small group can be taken to choose for themselves. Parents and friends can also be invited to contribute to the collection, which needs regular weeding and new additions.

Other items for quiet activities can be stored on shelves out of the children's reach, only for use when there is an adult available to work with a small group. Examples would be a collection of finger puppets, a large assortment of buttons in a decorated cake tin, a box filled with remnants of different materials – bits of lamé, velvet, lace, Indian and Chinese silks, pieces of embroidery, upholstery trimmings. Market stalls and charity shops are a good source for this kind of item. Other possibilities are tropical shells, African beads, coral pieces, shiny pebbles or tiny decorated boxes. All of these can offer scope for fantasy and imagination.

Because such collections are made up of small items which easily become lost, they should only be used under the guidance of a nursery worker who herself has some interest in their care and replenishment. One period of the day when using such collections is especially helpful is towards evening when only a few children are left and some kind of comfort and intimacy is what everybody needs. Similar items will be used by the key person during her special time with her small group before the midday meal, as described in the next chapter.

Imaginative and make-believe play

Such play is very wide-ranging and can occur anywhere, but seems to be particularly stimulated by what is usually called the 'Home Corner'. A 'Wendy house' structure is not essential and may take up too much space in the group room, but it is important that the chosen area should be permanent and that the play in and around it goes on undisturbed. Low, solid screens will suffice, with a curtained 'window' on one side. A curtain can also be used for a door if necessary. The space inside should always be carpeted to create a sense of intimacy and comfort.

Finding detailed items for the Home Corner is a good opportunity for the nursery worker, and her own 'play' in the area is a central factor in developing its full potential. One member of staff in the group room needs to take reponsibility for assembling and replacing items and keeping them in good condition.

The corner needs its own special furniture, a small low table and two chairs, not the standard nursery ones; small wicker chairs are ideal.

Figure 2.1 Make-believe play with real equipment.

The 'cooker' can be an upturned wooden box with hob plates, either painted or represented by glued-on cork or rush table mats. Some nurseries use a real cooker, but it can be confusing for children that they are allowed to turn the knobs in play at the nursery when this is strictly forbidden at home. A small dresser or set of shelves is needed for keeping pots and pans, cutlery, plates, cups and saucers.

Kitchen equipment should consist of real, not toy items, which children can identify with what they know at home (see Figure 2.1). Of course this should reflect the range of cultural diversity in food preparation and eating customs to be found in Britain today. It will often be helpful to ask for advice from parents, or better still to visit them at home. They may also be able to offer packets and jars to stock the shelves and these can be filled with corks or large nuts to represent food.

Above all, the Home Corner needs to be kept looking attractive and orderly (not over-tidy) to encourage enjoyable individual or sociable play.

Table play

The tables in a group room generally have three uses: for mealtimes; for small-scale manipulative play; or when a nursery worker with a small group leads an activity most easily carried out sitting at a table. Examples would be playing with dough, making biscuits or fruit salad for lunch, stamping patterns with potatoes, cutting out and pasting.

An important point for good maintenance of table play materials is that each item should be kept in strong, low wooden boxes, not the cardboard boxes in which they are sold, which will not stand up to the wear and tear of group use. Staff need to be vigilant in seeing that each box is complete and that small pieces do not get carried to other rooms. A puzzle which is missing a piece is better thrown away as the point of it is its completeness.

Some suggested items for table play include:

- Large coloured wooden beads (the younger children find it easier to thread these on plastic-covered electrician's wire which is easy to handle. Older children will use the usual 'boot lace' coloured string with a long metal threader)
- Wooden insets and puzzles
- Peg boards
- Sorting trays with coloured counters
- Soft boards with coloured wooden shapes, hammer and pin nails
- 'Fuzzy-felt' boards
- Deep meat-roasting tins filled with bird seed or lentils for scooping and pouring with small containers and spoons
- Blunt-ended scissors and catalogues or magazines for cutting out and pasting
- Sticky coloured paper shapes for pattern-making (provide a damp sponge pad as found in the Post Office)
- Thick wax crayons and paper for drawing

Floor play

A flat, carpeted area is desirable to make possible tower-building and use of wooden blocks and construction materials of varying sizes. Each type of material should have its own box, kept on the floor space or ranged on open shelves close at hand.

Another useful item for floor play is a car track with painted road and tunnels, bridges, trees and people for arranging. The small metal cars, buses, fire engines, ambulance, tractor, lorries, etc., should all have their own garage units close by into which the vehicles are put away after use. The cars should *not* be lumped together in a box or basket looking like a car cemetery or break-up yard. Cars found about the room should be regularly replaced, with children encouraged to share in keeping the floor play area looking inviting. A farm or zoo with animals can also be located here, with its own storage space on a nearby shelf.

The floor play area should be protected from disturbing incursions by children not engaged in the play, and the number limited to a group of not more than four. 'Turns' need to be negotiated to permit concentrated and extended play.

Painting

A two-sided easel is essential equipment and a plentiful supply of paper securely clipped on. Although the paper can be cheap, it should be properly cut with straight edges and not roughly torn. A guillotine kept safely in the staffroom is a useful piece of equipment for this purpose. If there is no 'wet' area, a sheet of nylon should be laid beneath the easel to limit spills. Paint pots of already mixed powder paint with long-handled broad brushes need regular maintenance. Paintings are best hung to dry on a plastic clothes dryer, clipped on the rungs with clothes pegs. Aprons should be easily accessible.

Finger painting needs a formica-topped table and pieces of cloth for wiping hands.

Sand play

A sand tray may be located in the group room if there is space, though it need not be available to the children all the time if it has a cover which is not too cumbersome to put on and remove. If there is a 'wet' area available, this is obviously the best place to put it. A certain amount of sand will, of course, be spilt, especially if there are younger children, but a sheet of heavy nylon laid underneath the tray will serve to make a boundary and reduce scattering. When sand is spilt, the staff can, by lifting the edges of the nylon sheet, shake the sand gently inwards, making it easier to sweep up. To avoid waste, keep a clearly marked dustpan and soft brush together with a fine wire-mesh kitchen strainer hung up close to the tray. When sand is swept up into the dustpan, it can immediately be sieved and replaced in the tray with any large bits of dirt removed.

Sand needs to be washed regularly as it can become very smelly, and probably unhygienic. This is a task with which even small children (not more than two together) much enjoy helping. Shovel some of the sand into a bucket, take the bucket to the sink, fill the bucket with water and leave the tap running until it overflows the rim. Turn off the water while stirring up the sand lying in the bottom of the bucket to release the dirty bits and accumulated dust. Running the tap again, the dirt coming to the surface will gradually clear away. Some drops of disinfectant can be added.

The equipment for use in the sand tray should be appropriate to its size, that is, not buckets and spades scaled to the outdoor sandpit, which are too large for an indoor tray. The small plastic plant pots from garden centres come in a useful variety of sizes and serve very well for filling and emptying of sand and making 'castles' and 'cakes'. Because the plastic splits easily, it is a good idea to glue one container inside another. Plastic scoops are less satisfactory than the metal ones used in hotel and restaurant kitchens for flour and sugar. Stores specializing in catering equipment are often a better source of items for the sand tray than toyshops.

The sand should sometimes be dry, but more usually kept damp to avoid the risk of it being flicked into eyes or hair. There must be an ample amount of sand if the children are to use it pleasurably; most sand trays have too many implements and too little sand. Staff need to take notice of this and frequently remove the objects which are less used, freeing the sand for other uses, such as making tracks and mounds. Equipment should be taken out of the sand tray at the end of the day and stored in a box beneath or beside the tray.

If the tray is on legs, it is sometimes too high for the youngest children to reach comfortably. Low wooden boxes turned upside down make a helpful platform for them. It is important that the sand play area does not become overcrowded. The adult who is supervising this part of the room needs to decide how many children can be comfortably accommodated at any one time and negotiate this with the children themselves.

Water play

This kind of play can take place throughout the nursery day: helping to wash and wipe toys and tables, washing dolls' clothes, watering plants and above all in the bathroom. The key person with her small group can allow the children unhurried time for experimentation with running water. Only taps provide the experience of trying to catch with finger and thumb the descending column of water and watching the swirl as it disappears down the drain. That experience is impossible in a crowded bathroom when any experiments are likely to lead to squirting and flooding and have to be firmly discouraged by staff.

When a water container is provided in the group room, as with the sand tray, it is desirable to provide a box for the smallest children to stand on, as if they are not at the right height, the water will constantly run down and wet their arms and elbows. Aprons should be hung handily and be long enough to cover shoes, otherwise drips run down the front and soak the child's feet. Care should be taken to see that cuffs and sleeves are rolled up securely as wet woollen jersey sleeves can be very unpleasant and ruin the jumper. The water should be kept at a tepid temperature, with a towel accessible for drying hands.

There should be a variety of equipment, not all in the water container at the same time – it is essential not to overcrowd it. Nursery workers should observe what is the quality of play and experimentation that the items offer and periodically weed them out and add new ones.

One of the most dismal sights in a water tray is a 'drowned' doll floating face down. Bathing dolls should be a quite separate operation with its own equipment, consisting of a bowl, sponge, soap, talcum powder, a changing board and small towels hanging neatly. This will require regular maintenance if it is to present an inviting appearance.

Suggested items for water tray include:

- Cup with handle
- Small containers
- Tin with holes knocked in lower part
- Metal indoor plant watering can with thin spout
- Small metal teapot with hinged lid
- Funnels of different sizes
- Lengths of tubing, transparent and opaque
- Narrow-necked containers for filling and measuring
- Corks and pingpong balls for floating
- Pebbles for sinking
- Small wooden bowl (for filling to sinking point)

SUMMARY

Because of the long hours that adults and children spend in day care centres, it is important to create an environment that is comfortable and visually satisfying to all. When children are grouped by age, it is easier to match the arrangement of the group room to their developmental needs than with a mixed-age system. Careful planning is needed to ensure that space is used to the best advantage and to avoid any unnecessary stress for the nursery workers. Ample, well-chosen materials, readily accessible, encourage child-initiated, self-directed play and enable the adult to choose the role of facilitator instead of always directing the children's activities.

3   The key person

... remember the time
Before the wax hardened,
When every one was like a seal.
Each of us bears the imprint
Of a friend met along the way.

Primo Levi, 1985

Most people who work with young children are well aware that satisfactory growth depends on all aspects of their development being seen as a whole. At one time it was thought that if food and warmth, cleanliness, sleep and safety were adequate, this would ensure healthy early development. In the past the instinctive loving feelings of close adults for babies were often disregarded or actively discouraged, while the feelings of babies were hardly taken into account at all.

Understanding more, as we now do, about how young children feel, has not made our task in day care any easier. In fact it has made the work more difficult, more complex and more demanding. In this chapter we focus on the particular difficulty of satisfying a child's emotional needs – which has implications for all other aspects of development – in a day care centre or nursery.

Research on day nurseries shows that children are typically handled by many different staff members in the course of a day (Bain and Barnett, 1980). Moreover, if we follow an individual child through a nursery day we are likely to find that there is little time, if any, when that child has the close, undivided attention of an adult (Marshall, 1982). This is almost invariably reported by students carrying out child studies at day nurseries, and is especially worrying when the child may be attending the nursery because he or she is not felt to be getting enough attention and stimulation at home.

In the days when very young children were in residential nurseries and children's homes, visitors would often find that children would come round them, ask their names, want to sit on their knees and touch or even kiss them. Frequently, these children were described as being sociable, friendly or 'very affectionate', and such misconceptions still crop up occasionally in reports of social workers or health visitors in child abuse enquiries. We know now that this is not a normal way for children to react to strangers and that such behaviour indicates that they are seriously deprived in their personal relationships, with little or no experience of truly affectionate contact with anyone.

This different way of interpreting what we see comes from the knowledge we have gained through observation and research about the way that a young child develops his ability to make relationships. Real sociability comes through the experience of the reliable affection of a few close people. Human beings have great resilience and some individuals show an amazing capacity to catch up and recover from damaging early experiences, but many do not. There is no excuse for us to repeat the ignorant mistakes of the past in the care we provide for young children today. The denial of close personal relationships is a serious flaw in most group day care, which can partly be overcome by changes in organization. However, it is essential that everyone concerned understands the reasons for such changes and is committed to making them work.

THE IDEA OF A KEY WORKER

In many areas of social work it is a well-established practice to give one person special responsibility for a particular client or service-user. Some family centres have taken up the idea to the extent that each worker is allocated responsibility for a number of named families.

However, this does not necessarily imply a close relationship between individual adults and particular children. We have often seen in nurseries a child's supposed 'key worker' attending to impersonal tasks while he was fed or comforted by another staff member. Unless the key person system is given primacy in the organization of the day, the child may have no more contact with his designated worker than with any of the other adults. In that case the relationship can have no real meaning for him. Very small children can only recognize a special interest if it is expressed in close personal interaction day by day.

THE VALUE OF A KEY PERSON SYSTEM

Why should it be worth the time and trouble to introduce the key person system in a nursery where this has not been the practice? We have to consider the question not only from the point of view of the child, but also from that of the worker who takes on the emotional responsibility. Thinking of our own relationships as adults may give us some answers.

Most of us have, or would like to have, a special relationship with some person on whom we can rely, a relationship which is significant and precious to us. If we are parted from that person we have ways of preserving continuity even through long separations. We use telephones, letters, photographs, recollections, dreams and fantasies to keep alive the comfort which we derive from such human relationships. When we lose them, we experience sadness and often deep feelings of despair. If we look back we may recall important people in our early lives who, though they are not there in person, give continuity and significance to how we conduct our present lives. Often we seek to repeat and to enjoy again the warmth of those relationships in a different form.

The young children with whom we work, and who do not yet have language to express what they are experiencing, need to have these special relationships too, and deeply need to have them in a very immediate and concrete way. It is against this backcloth of what we know from our own experience, that we have to consider the meaning of a key person for a young child. We can never remind ourselves too often that a child, particularly a very young and almost totally dependent one, is the only person in the nursery who cannot understand why he is there. He can only explain it as abandonment, and unless he is helped in a positive and affectionate way, this will mean levels of anxiety greater than he can tolerate.

The relationship which the child develops with his key person is in no sense a substitute for the relationship between child and parent. For a start the arrangement can only be for part of the day. Even then the key person will have to be shared with other children. To the parent we can explain it as our attempt in the nursery to offer children a person to whom they can relate in a special way during *some* of the often long hours which they spend away from home. Staffing ratios for under twos usually allow for a key person to focus on a sub-group of four children for some of the time, though for older children the group may have to be five or six. During the rest of the day the child will be cared for by another or probably two other members of staff, whom, however, he will also know well. The way this can be organized is explained later in the chapter.

OBJECTIONS TO THE KEY PERSON SYSTEM

Problems for nursery workers

All kinds of objections may be put forward to the idea that we should offer a young child some form of special relationship with a member of staff. Some are of a practical organizational kind and others concerned with the emotional impact on nursery workers. An undeniable difficulty lies in the apprehensiveness many people feel about taking on a relationship with a child who is not their own. We need to recognize such fears and not try to pretend that they do not exist.

When the idea of a key person system is first introduced, staff will say 'Yes, it seems a nice idea, but we couldn't do it here because. . .' It is important then for nursery managers not to get caught up in the 'Yes but' game but to respond to the anxiety underlying this reaction. First, it may be necessary to help people recognize that there is a problem. Individual nursery workers might be asked to observe one child in another group for a period and make a systematic recording of the number of different people who handle him. They are likely to be surprised if not shocked by the result (Marshall, 1982).

We also have to recognize that moving to a key person system is not necessarily straightforward for nursery workers. Some will already have suffered the pain of parting from a child whom they have grown to love. They may have found that when attachments develop, children become more demanding and possessive.

Juliet Hopkins, who ran a group for nursery workers designed to help them develop more intimate relationships with children, identified two particular sources of conflict: the ideal of equality and the goal of fostering independence (Hopkins, 1988). The workers believed that children should be treated equally and be given equal attention, but in practice this seemed to mean avoiding any significant involvement with individual children for fear that the others might feel ignored or become jealous. In addition, 'The counterpart of the belief that all children should be treated equally was the apparent belief that all nurses should be equal and therefore interchangeable'.

There was considerable pressure for children to attain early independence, both physical and emotional, under the apparent misapprehension that this can be equated with 'good' development. In fact other research suggests that it is more likely to produce a kind of 'pseudo self-reliance' described by Eva Holmes (1977), which prevents children from seeking appropriate support from adults and inhibits their learning processes. A further point is that infants with strong individual attachments are much more likely to make their feelings known, sometimes in inconvenient ways, so that in the short term the nursery worker's task may appear to be more difficult.

Relations with parents

Another objection often made by staff is that if children are encouraged to develop a special tie with individual nursery workers, parents may become resentful. Parents differ in this respect, and it is those whose own relationship with the child is least secure who are most likely to be uneasy about other attachments. The safeguard which we build into the key person system is that at the same time as developing a relationship with a child, the staff member also deepens her relationship with the child's parent(s).

Some parents may need help to understand that sharing love and affection with another caregiver is not like sharing an apple or a sandwich where the more people the less there is for each. Love is learnt by loving, and we know from the work of Rudolf Schaffer (1977) that by the end of their first year, most children have formed attachments to several different people. Their love for their mothers is in no way diminished by this.

It can be very stressful for a staff member when she is key person to a child whom she feels is neglected or unloved by a parent. The emotions generated are intense. The worker may feel that if only she could replace the inadequate parent, all would be well. 'I wish I could take her home with me' is a phrase that sounds a warning note. The worker's natural sympathy and affection for the child are causing her to confuse her role with that of the parent.

In such a situation the nursery worker needs help to look at her relationship with the parent(s) and to recognize that it is nearly always possible to achieve some understanding and compassion for them even if she does not approve of aspects of their behaviour or necessarily 'like' them as people. If the nursery worker can see her job as working to improve the relationship between parent and child rather than rescuing the child from a 'bad' parent, she may begin to see things differently.

Of course, these issues do not only arise in connection with the key person system, but they are likely to put a greater strain on the carer because of the closeness between individual staff and children which is the whole purpose of the system. It is essential that nursery workers should not be left to deal with this emotionally taxing situation on their own. They need opportunities to talk through their feelings with colleagues and senior staff in a climate of acceptance and understanding, through which they can achieve a better perspective.

ORGANIZING FOR INTIMACY

We now turn to the practical organization which is required for the effective operation of a key person system, emphasizing that it will only 'work' and therefore be maintained if the nursery staff are convinced that it will be of benefit to the children, to the parents and to themselves.

It is usual in nurseries for the maximum number of staff to be present during the middle of the day, approximately from 10.30 a.m. until the early afternoon. In order to put the key person arrangement into practice, this is essential. It may be necessary to consider re-organizing rotas or recruiting volunteers to ensure an adequate number of adults to free nursery staff for this direct work with children.

Personal intimacy is an element which is often lacking in any kind of institutional life, but this has even more serious implications for young children. So much of the subtle communication for children who do not yet have command of language comes through touch and handling. We know from any hospital experience we may have had that a series of strange hands and different voices imposes great stress on us, especially when we are in a state of dependency, as young children always are. Trudy Marshall, in her close observational study of a day nursery, saw a toddler sat on a pot by one nurse, wiped by another and having his pants pulled up by a third (Marshall, 1982). How, then, can we avoid this kind of impersonal 'care' and ensure some moments of intimacy during the nursery day, especially around what are often seen as routine tasks?

Observing nurseries in operation and talking to staff we note that the point in the day which is often described as 'chaotic' is the period at the end of the morning's activities, while the children are using the bathroom, the room is being cleared up and tables set out for the midday meal. This period is the ideal time for each adult in every group room to become the focus for her small group of children until after their meal is finished. In a group of, say, twelve children, there would usually be three staff during the middle of the day. The four children in each group would then be sure that for that part of the day they would have the close attention of their key person.

When play material and various activities have been tidied away, each member of staff, with the small number of children to whom she is the key person, withdraws into a quiet corner. The staff member has her own space which, for this pre-lunch time, is what may be called her 'island of intimacy'. It should always be the same corner, made comfortable with rug and cushions, giving her the opportunity for quiet and unhurried observation and listening time with her group.

During this time, at some point agreed by the staff, each small group in turn goes with their key person to the bathroom. When bathrooms are shared between more than one group it generates a sense of rush and tension which is easily avoided by better planning.

Until the food trolley is actually in the room, the small groups remain with their adult in their own corners. This avoids the bad practice of children being made to sit down at the tables before the food arrives, inevitably creating noise and restlessness. Sometimes children are given books to look at or they sing songs or do finger plays while they wait. This kind of institutional nonsense creates more problems than it solves, besides being exhausting for the adult. Far better to avoid the problem in the first place.

Two points of organization must be agreed: first, that a member of ancillary staff or a volunteer will bring the trolley to the room so that a nursery worker does not have to absent herself from her small group to do this; second, that during this whole span of time, before, during and after the meal, staff members do not receive telephone calls except in real emergency.

The idea behind the creation of the 'island of intimacy' stems from the need to build firmly into the day's programme a period when the key person for each small group of children gives her undivided attention to them. Children require time and space and an available adult to enable them to develop their power of speech. This is especially important in view of the high incidence of language delay among children attending social services day nurseries.

What, then, does the adult do to maintain interest and calm in her group? Recalling our own childhood we can probably bring to mind playing with 'Granny's button box' or with a collection of shells and coloured pebbles. There seems to be a special fascination in containers – small purses, bags or boxes with different things inside them. The adult needs to provide such material to be a focus of conversation (some suggestions were made in Chapter 2). Essentially this is a 'listening time' on her part. Any sort of collection, which she is interested in creating herself will provide interest and amusement.

The activity offered during 'island time' (as we heard one child explain it) should be something special to this short period. When a worker has created her own collections, she should keep them exclusively for her own group, since if they become common property there is a high probability of their being lost or dispersed.

When the food trolley arrives, the key person for each small group goes to the table with her children. Once she is seated everything should be so arranged that she does not have to get up again – essential if she is to get any enjoyment from her own meal.

Our own experience helps us to understand why it is necessary in creating a tranquil atmosphere for both nursery workers and children that the adult should remain seated. Imagine ourselves invited to a friend's house for a meal. If our hostess continually gets up to fetch things she has forgotten, there comes a point when the whole company choruses, 'For heaven's sake come and sit down!' As well as wanting her presence we are also a bit fed up that she hasn't prepared things properly. The feeling of agitation generated by her constant movement interferes with our own digestion. It is just the same in a nursery. Detailed suggestions about how the meal can be arranged to minimize disturbance are given in Chapter 11.

The small-group arrangement should continue until sleeptime or quiet activity begins.

OVERCOMING DIFFICULTIES

It will be pointed out that staff members are quite often absent through holidays or illness. The way to reduce or modify a child's sense of loss when 'his' person is away is to anticipate and plan for such contingencies by having a named alternative person. Take holidays first. The precise dates of these absences are always known beforehand. The key person should explain to her children, however young and seemingly unable to understand, that she will not be there for a while, and name the nursery worker who will look after them. Parents, too, need to be told. When the child arrives at the nursery on a day when his special person is on holiday, the alternative worker will take the initiative in making it clear to him that he is expected and welcome.

When a worker is absent through illness, the nursery is usually not informed until the beginning of a working day. Whoever receives the message in the morning should take responsibility for informing the alternative worker and ensuring that the agreed arrangement works properly. No child should feel in doubt who is standing in for his key person.

In some nurseries the key workers have their photographs taken in a group with their three or four children. The alternative worker can point to the photograph on the wall, saying to the child 'Angela is away today; she's staying at home because she isn't well; she'll be back soon.' Long before they can talk, young children are aware of our mood and our concern for them even if they don't understand our words exactly. Think how well we can get on in a foreign country where we only have a rudimentary knowledge of the language.

It is also interesting to note that Juliet Hopkins (1988) in the study already quoted found that, once nursery workers had formed close attachments, staff absence was much reduced because they felt it was really important for them to be in the nursery for 'their' children.

THE KEY PERSON SYSTEM IN PRACTICE

Initial visits

Going to see children in their own homes used to be considered quite outside the scope of day nursery staff, and there is still some doubt and apprehension about it. However, it is becoming common practice for someone to make a home visit when it is intended to offer a day nursery or family centre place. In the past this was usually done by the head of centre or deputy, sometimes accompanied by the social worker or health visitor. As home visiting becomes generally accepted, the visit is more often made by the member of staff into whose group the child will come on admission. With the system proposed, this would be the key person.

This visit has several important functions. First, it enables the worker to introduce herself to the child and parent(s), so that when they come to the nursery they will see at least one familiar face. Second, she can get some idea of the environment in which the child, even if he attends day care full time, will still spend three-quarters of his life. Without asking intrusive questions, the visitor can encourage any family members present to tell her as much as they would like to about themselves, all of which will help her, as she will explain, to understand and care for the child better.

It is tempting on this kind of visit to offer a lot of information about the nursery which the family are unlikely to take in, being probably too preoccupied at this stage with relief or apprehension at having been offered a place. Far better simply to respond to their questions, to explain the nursery's settling-in policy, and otherwise concentrate on forming a warm, friendly relationship. Families who know that they have been referred to the nursery by social workers or health visitors because of doubts about their parenting capacity may be very defensive at first, feeling themselves to be under inspection, and it is most important for the visitor not to give the impression that this is why she is there.

On the whole parents are eager to talk about their children, and are more likely to talk freely on their own home ground than on what they may see as foreign territory. For some, the nursery may call up images of school, which their parents only visited when they were in trouble. It can take quite a time to overcome this association.

The visitor will want to discover some factual information – what the child likes or doesn't like to eat, important people in his life, whether he has a comfort object or sleeps during the day. What words does he know and/or use? Each family has its own vocabulary and it can be very distressing for a child not to be understood. Parents will also want information about how their child's day will be arranged and to get some idea what kind of person the nursery worker is herself.

It is preferable to ask open questions ('Tell me about. . .', 'How would you describe. . .?') whenever possible rather than questions which can be answered with a yes or no. Inexperienced interviewers often find this difficult, and it makes a good topic for a staff training session.

The initial visit also has another important function, that of demonstrating the non-sexist policy of the nursery. The key person can establish the principle that child care is equally the concern of both parents by making it clear that she wants to meet the father (or mother's partner) as well as the mother, emphasizing that she hopes to get to know them both. Even when the father is present, it is only too easy to slip back into addressing questions and comments to the mother, leaving the man as an onlooker. But if we are aware of this risk we can guard against it. It is not easy to act in a way that runs counter to deeply entrenched social attitudes, but if we hope for 'parent' to mean that and not just mother, this has to be understood right at the beginning. Brian Jackson's study of first-time fathers found that the assumptions of health visitors, social workers and other professionals were a powerful force in pushing men back into their traditional role (Jackson, 1984).

Visiting a child's home for the first time can seem a rather daunting task for a nursery worker, for which her training is unlikely to have prepared her, and she will need help and support from experienced staff. However, normally parents will welcome such a visit, provided it is made by appointment. Usually staff who have the opportunity to make such introductory visits have no doubt of their value, finding that it gives them a much more rounded picture of the child and the family.

Settling in

When the child first comes into the nursery, the key person will obviously take particular reponsibility for the settling-in period and make an effort to be present when mother and baby arrive in the morning. It is important for the key person to think carefully about what it means for the parent to observe someone else handling her child. It matters very much to the child to have the experience of seeing his mother (or father) and key person in friendly and confident relationship.

Almost inevitably, both mother and staff member will feel that each is observing and assessing the other in all sorts of subtle ways. This will be doubly true when the mother has, in any sense, been directed to bring her child to the nursery.

The early period can put heavy demands upon the staff member because of the significance of small details which she needs to think about in relation to the daily encounter with the parent. For example, is there always a comfortable chair for the parent to sit on in the group room? How does the nursery worker allay the mother's anxiety about whether her child will 'behave well'? Probably the child will not behave well because he knows that something very different is happening in his life, though he cannot identify, still less express, his anxiety about this. It helps for the nursery worker to show that she understands how different this may be from the child's normal behaviour and that she is in no way critical of the parent.

Separation

Thanks to the work of David and Appel in France, and in this country that of John Bowlby (1953), Mary Ainsworth (Ainsworth *et al.*, 1974) and the series of films made by James Robertson in the 1950s, we know a great deal about the experiences and reactions of small children parted from their loved adults. From around the age of 8 months most children show distress when a strange person takes the place of their mother or father. If the separation is prolonged, they pass through a series of recognizable phases, beginning with bewilderment, followed by violent protest; later, miserable crying alternates with periods of apathy. Unless there is a substitute for the parent with whom they can make a relationship, they may sink into a depression, not wanting to play or eat. Finally, they emerge from this into a state of apparent indifference which may look to the uninformed observer like a return to normal behaviour. This sequence is remarkably similar to the stages which have been recorded in research on bereavement in adults (Worden, [1983] 1991). Once our eyes have been opened, we can understand that for the child too young to have a concept of time, a separation short in adult terms may feel the same as losing a loved person for ever.

With this insight, we now try as far as possible to avoid inflicting such severe pain on little children. Practice in hospitals, schools, playgroups and nurseries has altered dramatically. We allow the child to become thoroughly familiar with new surroundings and the new caregiver before the mother attempts any separation at all. Then the mother leaves, at first for a very brief period, then gradually increasing the time she spends away, until the child is able to tolerate the whole session without her. Ideally we should be able to go at the child's pace and the separation should be accomplished without distress.

In the real world things are rather different. Some mothers may have an urgent need for relief from the constant care of the child and find it impossible to wait patiently for the moment when the child will separate without protest. Others may have little choice, with jobs that they will lose if they don't turn up for work. Nursery workers are sometimes critical of parents who appear to ignore a child's pain, but the mother may have made the quite legitimate calculation that, with jobs in short supply, the child might suffer more in the long term if she were to become unemployed, with the resulting drop in the family income. For this reason, stressful separations cannot be avoided entirely.

When the time comes for a mother actually to leave her child, it is well for the worker to discuss how this is to be managed and to give support and understanding. It is quite natural that the mother should want to reduce her own stress, but the nursery worker has to be confident that the separation is handled in the best possible way for the child, while not denying the pain.

One way of handling the moment of separation is for the mother and the worker to sit down together. The mother, with her child in her arms, can say something like 'Mummy is going now and she's coming back later'. Of course for a very young child the words 'coming back later' convey little, as he has no sense of what 'later' means. All he knows is that some change is imminent. When the mother has said this and given a kiss and cuddle, the worker helps her quite firmly to hand the child over and then leave. This can be a very trying moment for all concerned, but at least it is open and honest.

To appreciate more fully how a child must feel if the parent slips away when he is not looking, we can think back to some similar occasion in our own adult lives. For example, someone we love accompanies us to the station when we are going away. We get to the platform and settle ourselves in a carriage, while this person watches from outside the train. We then look away to get something from our luggage, and on returning to the window find that our close person has disappeared without a word or a wave. How do we feel? Probably abandoned, hurt and rather cross, almost as if we were not worth saying a proper goodbye to. No wonder children who start their day in this way express their feelings by being irritable and contrary.

Once the mother has left, the worker with the child on her lap may have to cope with a burst of crying which can be very upsetting for others in the group. The worker needs to find the confidence to listen to this quite appropriate crying and not try to hush it up or distract the child by waving a toy at him, making supposedly comforting noises or jiggling him up and down in her arms. Distress needs to be expressed in a context of quiet acceptance, in the same way that we would try to comfort an adult experiencing loss and grief.

It can be very difficult for a worker to allow a child to satisfy his need to scream if the other staff in the room do not understand the approach. This is a situation which needs to be discussed in a group room meeting, so that when it happens there is mutual support and understanding between colleagues.

One helpful thing to remember when we have a distraught infant in our arms crying 'Mummy, mummy!' is that we are not only experiencing his immediate distress but that his cries may well have touched off a resonance in our own past experience which makes the situation doubly upsetting.

Separation distress is not a problem which only occurs at the beginning of a child's time in the nursery. It can also happen when a child has been coming to the nursery for some time and is regarded as 'settled'. Suddenly, he expresses his feeling of loss with desperate crying. Once again the analogy with bereavement is illuminating. Adults who have lost someone they love often report unexpected bursts of misery long after they thought they had come to terms with their loss. Nursery workers need to realize that this is not a rejection of them and the care that they offer. The child may have been enjoying his play up to that moment and, once comforted, settle down to it happily again.

Quite often a child who has been attending the nursery cheerfully for some time falls ill with a minor physical upset and stays away for a while. When he comes back, the care and presence of his key person are of great importance in helping him to re-adjust and again cope with the separation from his parent. To understand this, we only have to think of how we feel even in quite ordinary social situations when we walk into a room full of strange people. How pleased we are to catch sight of someone we know, especially if they seem equally pleased to see us!

A closer relationship with a child needs to go alongside closer relations with his parent(s). The customary brief exchanges at the beginning and end of the day are no longer sufficient. Meetings of parents and key person arranged at intervals convenient to all provide an opportunity for proper discussion and need not take up a great deal of time. Careful planning is the crucial point, and when a worker's particular group is no more than four or five, it is not too difficult to organize. As one worker said:

> Knowing parents in this way seems to take such a lot of the strain out of the work, it helps to avoid our imagining things about each other. We're more real people to each other and can have much more trust.

The need to build in listening time for the children applies equally to a worker's relation with a family.

Change of key person

Aiming to give continuity of relationship to a child and his parent(s) can sometimes seem difficult to achieve with the inevitable staff changes and times when it is necessary for a child to change from one group to another. We have to remind ourselves of the difference between child and adult time scales. Six months, which may seem a short time to us, is a considerable slice of a young child's life, so a special relationship is always valuable even if it can only last for a relatively brief period in our terms.

After a close attachment has formed between a child and his key person, a change will involve pain for both of them and obviously should be avoided if possible. When it is unavoidable, the original worker needs support to acknowledge and work through her feelings, and so does the new key person, who may feel rejected when the child wants to go back and perhaps even cries for his previous worker. It can help everybody if the changeover is made gradually and if the child can still see the first worker from time to time. Flexibility and trust is needed between staff, with support from seniors, to overcome any strained feelings. It must not be forgotten that parents, too, may need help to make the transition.

As the key person system develops in a nursery, the interest and scope of the work will increase. Recognizing the nursery worker's intimate knowledge of her particular children means that she, and not only the head of the nursery, will come into contact with the variety of specialists who visit the nursery in the course of their work. In this way the speech therapist, health visitor, physiotherapist, social worker or community physician may well find that their relationships with the nursery become easier and more effective.

Apart from any special observations which she undertakes in collaboration with these outside specialists, the key person will take responsibility for assessment, monitoring and record-keeping in relation to children in her small group. This of course has particular significance when the child has special needs or difficulties or when there is a possibility of abuse or neglect. It will be the key person who speaks about a child who is the subject of a social services case conference and may even have to give evidence in court. Such occasions arouse anxiety even in experienced workers, but it may help if the worker quietly reminds herself that of all the people present, except for the parents, she is the one who knows most about a child with whom she spends so many hours of the day.

SOME EFFECTS OF INTRODUCING A KEY PERSON SYSTEM

As yet, there is no systematic research to show how the key person system compares with the more usual arrangements. However, it is our impression that in child care centres where a genuine key person system operates, nursery workers find much more satisfaction in their jobs. This was the experience of the head of a day nursery in north London, who wrote to us:

> Since we established a key worker system here closer relationships have been developed between staff and parents, especially in the baby room. Children seem to settle into life at the nursery more easily. Some who had been at the nursery for a while and were still

not happy, settled at once when they realised that one adult was their special person. Barry, who we had only seen tearful and withdrawn, became a smiling, outgoing, confident child almost overnight when he got his key person. For the first few days, he sat on her lap, then he took off and played with the other children happily, knowing that she was somewhere in the room.

Staff seem to have a special closeness with 'their' children and this has increased their understanding of them and their satisfaction in their work.

There are always the days when staff are ill or on holiday, and their children miss them for the day. On the other hand there are times when staff come into work even if they are not feeling too well because they care about what will happen to 'their' children.

Parents like to have one person to talk to rather than fifteen, and seem able to talk more freely knowing that that person takes special care of their child. The key worker appointments, a regular time set aside for a parent to talk in peace to their child's special person, have worked particularly well to establish a partnership between parents and staff in the best interests of their children.

SUMMARY

This chapter discusses the importance of intimate personal relationships for children's development and happiness. It suggests a form of organization which allows warm attachments to develop in a group care setting, taking full account of the impact on parents and nursery workers. Problems are acknowledged but can be overcome provided the principle is agreed.

Once the system is established, the key person takes on many important functions, such as managing the child's settling-in, easing separation, fostering language and cognitive development, home visiting, relating to parents, assessment and record-keeping and liaison with outside specialists and agencies. The job becomes more demanding but also offers far more interest and opportunities for learning, to the benefit of children, staff and parents alike.

4 Managing and working in a day care centre

That the birds of worry and care fly above your head, this you cannot change. But that they build nests in your hair, this you can prevent.

Chinese proverb

With few exceptions people choose to work with young children because they like them, enjoy their company and are interested in seeing them grow and develop. Children are a delight, and yet they make heavy demands on those who look after them. Amid the stresses of life in a nursery it is all too easy for the workers to lose sight of what brought them there in the first place. Unless they continue to find interest and pleasure in the job the quality of care will inevitably suffer.

Many problems arise from the unsatisfactory structure of day care and services for young children in Britain, discussed earlier. Recognizing these constraints, there is still much that can be done to provide greater job satisfaction to nursery workers, which will in turn be reflected in what they offer the children. This chapter discusses the key role of the head of the unit and her management of the staff team. How can she best enable the team to work well together, plan for staff development and support and create systems for effective communication and decision-making? We emphasize the need for staff to look after their own physical and emotional health and to find ways of coping with the stress inherent in the work. Finally, we show how staff resources can be extended by well-planned use of volunteers.

ESTABLISHING A COMMON PURPOSE

Much of the atmosphere in a nursery will depend on the way staff work together and the kind of leadership given by those in charge, especially whether there is a clearly expressed understanding of the aims of the service offered to the children and their parents.

Also lying behind the day-to-day operation of the nursery there is the broad policy of the responsible local authority or other administrative body to which the institution is accountable, whether this is a voluntary organization, private enterprise or workplace employer. The relevant trade union will also have its point of view to be taken into consideration. Unless an organization develops a coherent policy, problems tend to be resolved on an ad hoc basis and serious issues are never properly addressed. In the long run this becomes demoralizing for the staff. Where conflicts arise it is essential that they are discussed in terms of the policies involved rather than the personalities who carry them out.

THE ROLE OF THE ORGANIZER

The style of leadership prevailing in day care settings has been little discussed, though it is a crucial element in the way that they function. Many countries favour a collegiate model in which a group of equal professionals share leadership in rotation, and this has great advantages. However, in Britain we are only just emancipating ourselves from the strictly hierarchical structure inherited from the time when day nurseries were run like miniature hospitals. Local authority day nurseries are still headed by an 'Officer in Charge' with one or more deputies and sometimes a third level of senior nursery worker. Voluntary organizations often prefer a more neutral term, such as 'co-ordinator', and the value of teamwork and a democratic style of organization is increasingly accepted. Here we use the term 'organizer' to mean the person responsible for heading a child care unit, nursery or family centre, whatever his or her official title.

The position of a child minder or private day centre manager working on her own is rather different, but she, too, will certainly have to consider her relations with a number of other people in providing care for the children. A child minder is usually in practice part of a team, consisting of her husband or partner, her older children and perhaps her own parents, friends, neighbours, other child minders and the local authority social worker or pre-school worker. Despite the dissimilarity in the working situation, there are many parallels with organizing and caregiving in a group setting.

The manager of a nursery has a task which over recent years has become increasingly demanding. Expectations about the quality of the environment and care offered to children have risen but training and resources have not kept pace with them. In addition, the active presence of parents has brought a new dimension to her work, not only in the contact she has herself but in the skill she needs to enable other staff members to develop their work with families. All this puts a heavy load on the organizer, and she needs to enable her staff group to work as effectively as possible if she is not to sink under the strain.

Management style

In general, nurseries are staffed entirely by women and headed by a woman, which we may regret but are unlikely to be able to change in the near future. Traditionally women in factories, offices, shops and agriculture have worked in a rigid top-down management structure under the direction of a man. But a nursery setting gives the opportunity to women to exercise and demonstrate new and different ways of working together. There are useful models to be found in fields as diverse as publishing, the arts and wholefood distribution of management styles which make use of things that women are notably good at. These include willingness to negotiate, being able to listen to and empathize with another person and assess their state of mind, giving due attention to detail in work, and the capacity to do several things at once without getting flustered.

We need to think about how to use these assets in the most effective way. For example, understanding and listening to a staff member's point of view does not always mean accepting it. It may be necessary to negotiate a decision in line with the broad policy of the nursery which is not in harmony with the wishes of the individual. The organizer may then have to face complaint and hostility. This can mean a certain kind of loneliness which is experienced at times by anyone who takes on the responsibility of a leading role. It is important for the organizer to ensure adequate support for herself, which might be provided by a colleague from another nursery unit, a line manager, the chairperson of her management committee or by a personal friend who understands her work situation. Unless she has someone with whom she can safely share personal feelings, an organizer can become very isolated.

Delegation

Frequently, an organizer has to draw on the capacity to respond to demands from several different directions at once, but at the same time she needs to maintain an overview of the whole working of the nursery. A personal style which gives true value to negotiating, empathizing and attending to detail also requires built-in time for reflection. An organizer has to protect her own breathing space to enable her staff members to do the same. She has also to see that she is available to deal with the many unpredictable emergencies which may confront her. This means establishing a habit of delegation.

Delegation is not just a matter of convenience and reducing the workload on the organizer; it also promotes the professional growth of other nursery workers. The 'quicker to do it myself' style, just as in the education of young children, does not produce maturation in others. For example, we know that it takes more effort, especially if we are in a hurry, to encourage a child to fasten her own shoes. But the time and patience spent will pay off later because the child will have gained a skill. She is being empowered by us and this reduces her dependency and saves us time later.

The principle applies equally to adults. The organizer needs to consider each demand on its merits and to put the question to herself 'Who else can do this, or learn to do it?' Delegating in other words can be seen as transferring power and skill to another person. The organizer is still needed to take note of effort and achievement, to show appreciation and to help put things right if necessary while the other person is learning.

An example of the transfer of power is seen where an organizer, changing the practice of her predecessor, delegates to the cook the task of drawing up menus and ordering food and domestic cleaning materials. The organizer may need to arrange training opportunities and offer close supervision at first, probably helping the cook to work out menus for the first week or two until she feels confident about applying what she has learned. The cook in turn is encouraged to delegate to her kitchen assistant so that the work of the kitchen can go on smoothly if the cook is away. Similarly, the junior nursery worker who is given responsibility for day-to-day decisions will give appropriate responsibilities to the children, for example, involving them in clearing up and the maintenance of the group room. Thus, delegation is not only an effective management technique but a good model of practice.

Communication within the nursery

Alongside an ongoing programme of appropriate delegation, seen as part of staff development, the organizer has the task of ensuring that daily communication arrangements within the nursery work effectively. These communication networks need constant attention if they are to be maintained and developed, particularly when there are problems of staff changes and unpredictable absences.

Channels for day-to-day information need to be planned for and understood by everyone. Most nurseries have some form of office diary in which particular events like outings are noted or appointments booked with visitors such as the community physician or a college tutor. If there is a tendency for visitors to drop in without appointment, the organizer must insist that such arrangements are agreed in advance, otherwise it becomes impossible for her to plan her own time effectively.

Much of the contact with outside people will be done by telephone and efficient ways must be found to ensure that messages, often from parents, are noted correctly and passed to the staff members concerned. The organizer needs to give special attention to this, otherwise conflicts and anxieties can easily arise. If the organizer finds that she is constantly interrupted to take on the role of messenger, some other way will have to be devised for information to be passed on. For instance, small self-adhesive message slips put up on a clearly designated noticeboard can relay a message accurately to staff in a group room. It is very difficult for a staff member fully occupied with the children to break off to take a verbal message and it is often preferable for her not to be disturbed.

The whole problem of internal communication is one which can be usefully introduced at a staff meeting so that everyone grasps the problem and becomes part of the solution. The organizer has a more difficult task in keeping communication flowing between staff when the nursery building is inconvenient, for instance when a converted house is used and there are stairs and passages to be negotiated. Nursery workers in this kind of building can come to feel very isolated in their group rooms, and the organizer should be aware of this and give thought to how she can minimize the problem, for example, by regular visiting of all the group rooms and by showing her interest in what is going on.

Managing staff absence

The arrangement of shifts, holidays, attendance at in-service courses or case conferences all call for detailed planning by the organizer. Absences through staff illness, which are largely unpredictable, create a major planning problem, particularly when the responsible administrative authority fails to provide staff replacements and flexible temporary support. In many centres problems are exacerbated by the lack of adequate clerical help or basic office equipment, such as a word processor and photocopier. The amount of paperwork required by the local authority is often considerable and it is a shortsighted policy not to provide help which would enable the organizer to devote her time to the human aspects of the work.

When a key person system is functioning, children will feel keenly the lack of established continuity if a staff member is absent. Here, the organizer has responsibility to ensure that the alternative arrangement (described in the last chapter) operates effectively. The staff's own self-care and attitudes to their own health are discussed later, but it has been found that in a number of nurseries the sickness rate in staff is noticeably reduced when they have greater personal satisfaction in their working relationships, both with children and with other staff.

Staff absence inevitably produces a disruption of nursery arrangements and agreed desirable routines. The organizer needs to make sure that the previous system is re-established when the staff member returns. An example is when children have to be temporarily regrouped into larger numbers at mealtimes. Attention is needed to see that the original small groups are set up again as soon as possible.

Although everything should be done to keep unplanned staff absence to a minimum, it does sometimes have the advantage, if the organizer steps in, of giving her an opportunity to observe how daily arrangements and agreed practices are being carried out.

Ongoing guidance and explanation from senior staff, relating working practices to policy, are very necessary. It is often best to avoid immediate intervention, simply observing and taking note at the time, in order to raise points of educational and social importance later in the context of staff meetings and individual supervision. The role of the organizer as observer and educator at every level of the day-to-day work means that the staff's understanding of the underlying aims of the nursery can be developed and a general consensus established and maintained.

BUILDING THE STAFF TEAM

Not many centres are in a position to recruit a handpicked group of workers. Most staff groups consist of a mixture of experienced and new staff, older and younger, some who have chosen the work and others who have just fallen into it. In local authorities staffing provision depends to a large extent on the political complexion of the administration and whether day care is given low or higher priority in funding. There will be wide differences in the extent to which the organizer and existing staff are involved or consulted about new appointments.

Three important issues that arise are the ratio of staff to children, the professional qualifications considered appropriate for the work and the balance of the staff team. If the organizer and staff are clear about the direction and quality they want for the service, they may be able to exert influence even if they have no formal role in the selection process. First, on staff numbers the essential point is that effective work with families cannot be done on a no-cost basis. Staffing ratios that might have been adequate when all that was expected of nursery workers was, to quote one organizer, 'to care for children during the day and smile pleasantly at mothers when they arrived to collect them', need to be substantially improved to reflect the new scope of the work.

Second, a team composed entirely of workers with the basic child care qualification awarded by the National Nursery Examination Board (NNEB) is seriously lacking in professional expertise and opportunities for cross-fertilization of ideas. Until a proper educational and training base for early years work has been established, day care teams need people from teaching and social work backgrounds as well as child care workers. Third, it is important that the team includes people with a range of different interests and skills and preferably men as well as women.

Another point which still needs emphasis is that the staff group should reflect the ethnic composition of the neighbourhood and the families who use the centre. We have often been in nurseries where most of the children were black and all the staff were white. Energetic and imaginative efforts have to be made in such a case to recruit black staff, and if no qualified applicants are available, to take on suitable people as trainees with a well-worked out staff development plan for them. It is obviously important for black children to have role models from their own culture, but it is equally important for white children and families to see black people in positions of responsibility if old stereotypes are to be dispelled.

Gathering a well-balanced yet diversified staff group is only a first step towards creating an effective working team. Some nursery staff groups operate only as individuals, each relating separately to the head. Although they may do good work, Phyllida Parsloe has pointed out in the social work context that such 'individualist' teams have serious drawbacks and that 'collective' teams are likely to generate a wider range of approaches and provide better support for their members (Parsloe, 1981). An important characteristic of collective teams is that they have mechanisms for meeting and sharing ideas and decision-making.

STAFF MEETINGS

The feeling that some meetings just take up time which would be better used getting on with the work is often quite justified. If meetings are not felt to be getting anywhere, a mood of cynicism and impatience is likely to develop, especially if they involve staff giving up precious personal time. However, staff meetings are absolutely vital to the effective running of a nursery, like any other collaborative enterprise, and they need to form a regular part of the centre's routine.

Some centres, particularly those where the majority of parents are not in full-time work, recognize the importance of meetings by closing one afternoon or even a whole day a week, and using the time for purposes which require freedom from responsibility for child care. Others have to add staff meetings on to the end of a tiring working day, which has serious drawbacks. An intermediate solution is early closure on, say, one day every two weeks. Even this is likely to exclude the ancillary staff, whose involvement can be very valuable.

The organizer should be clear about the purpose and conduct of staff meetings so that she can argue the case with her management to enable them to happen more easily, either by adjusting opening hours or by provision of relief staff. The staff meeting has to be given priority by, for instance, switching on the answering machine and ignoring the ringing telephone.

The purpose of the meeting needs to be understood and shared with all who come to it. If support staff, outside people or volunteers are included, which may be appropriate from time to time, special care needs to be taken to see that they are fully integrated into the matters under discussion. The staff meeting can be a very important element in communication within the nursery and also a way of enhancing the skill and understanding of staff members in their daily work with children. If an organizer feels dissatisfied with the quality and outcome of staff meetings, she will need to seek information and advice from her own management, from colleagues in charge of other units, or ask her organization to set up a training day on the topic.

Planning and organization of meetings

To be worthwhile a meeting needs to have a focus of interest planned beforehand. When this concerns an important policy issue (examples might be a proposal for a major fund-raising effort, setting up a volunteer scheme, opening records to parents, remodelling the outdoor area), the topic may need to feature on the agenda of several meetings, starting with a general discussion to explore the idea, a 'brainstorming' session at a later meeting and eventually the formulation of an agreed plan. Even matters to do with the day-to-day running of the nursery need to be clearly presented by a staff member who takes responsibility for setting out the problem or proposal and suggesting possible ways forward. It is often more effective for the organizer to work with one of her staff to do this rather than always taking the lead herself.

In deciding on the format for the meeting, the question is how to achieve efficiency without bureaucracy. Discussion at nursery meetings is often informal and rather unfocused, which can produce a feeling of frustration at the end that nothing has been achieved. The key to effective meetings is careful preparation and follow-up, which does require a certain degree of formality and a greater willingness to put things on paper than may have been the custom in the past. On the other hand the conventional style of agenda and minutes can also become boring and unproductive.

Our experience of staff meetings is that they work best when considerable trouble is taken with both practical and organizational arrangements. The following guidelines may be helpful:

- The agenda for the meeting should be known at least a day in advance and either posted on the staff noticeboard or, ideally, distributed to each member of staff.
- The time of the start and the end of the meeting should be agreed and carefully respected.
- The room should have seats ready for all those who will attend, placed in such a way that everyone can have direct eye contact with everyone else.
- Vacant seats near the door should be left ready for latecomers (in an after-work meeting some staff may have to wait until the last parents have collected their children).
- When part of the staff meeting has to be used for giving out information this should be as clear and concise as possible, if necessary reinforced by a written note.
- Staff members other than the organizer should be asked, in rotation, to note any decisions made by the meeting, particularly who has agreed to do what. These notes should be posted or circulated as soon as possible after the meeting, preferably the

following day, with the initials of the relevant staff member attached to each action point. In addition those attending the meeting, including students, should be expected to make notes for themselves of any significant matters that come up during the meeting.

- Every meeting should start with a check on action arising from the previous one (*not* a review of minutes, which can be time-consuming and invite a re-run of previous discussions).

It is easy for staff to become preoccupied with questions relating to their own working conditions. One way of keeping the children and families in view is to set aside part of each or alternate meetings for a staff member to 'present' a child for whom she is key person and invite discussion. It is important that this should not always have a problem focus. It can be interesting and encouraging to hear how a colleague has enabled a child to make significant progress or has helped to change a parent's way of looking at things.

When individual children or their parents are discussed, there must always be a careful reminder about confidentiality; it is a fine line which divides information from gossip and prejudiced comments.

Handling difficulties

Some problems which may confront the organizer in staff meetings are how to deal with staff members who never speak, what to say to the person who is always criticizing and what to do when the staff group comes to a collective decision which is contrary to her own view.

Silent members can sometimes be persuaded to contribute by an encouraging word during the meeting, but an indirect approach may be better. The organizer might find some point of friction in the working day which affects this worker. It can be suggested that she, together with a colleague, prepares a contribution based on her view of the problem and ideas for improving things and bring this to the next meeting. In her supervision session the worker can be helped to find the best way to articulate her point of view, so that her intervention is clear and persuasive to the rest of the staff.

It is essential to give the critical staff member special attention and a full hearing. In making her complaint she may well be voicing the negative feelings which others share but are unwilling to express openly. Sometimes a difficulty seems to become focused on a particular staff member, and it is very important to keep attention on the problem and not on the person.

The third situation, when the collective view differs from her own, can be hard for an organizer committed to a democratic style of decision-making. Sometimes she may have to accept that the time is not right for some change she wants to introduce and, at least temporarily, accept the majority decision. At other times this is impossible because of the policy of the local authority, financial constraints or the requirements of the law. For example, in one nursery, staff felt exploited by the behaviour of a few parents who persisted in arriving late to collect their children and wanted to retaliate by withdrawing the children's nursery places. Having explained why this was not an acceptable solution, since several of the children were thought to be at risk of abuse and nursery attendance was part of the plan for their protection, the organizer exerted her authority to insist that some other way should be found to deal with the situation.

Room meetings

In addition to full staff meetings, it is worth establishing a practice of regular group room meetings, even when these only involve two people (though they are also a sensible level at which to include volunteers). Sometimes staff say, 'But we are talking to each other all the time, there's no point in anything as formal as a fixed meeting'. However even 20 minutes of discussion about the more general issues of running the room can be a useful habit to develop. Senior staff can stand in for a short while to make this possible. Such meetings provide an opportunity for nursery workers to plan new activities which require preparation or to examine together in detail which are the moments of the day when they experience most stress and fatigue and how this can be reduced.

STAFF DEVELOPMENT

The continual care over years of successive groups of very young children does not conform to the normal life cycle of adults. If nursery workers are to retain their motivation and responsiveness to changing needs and social conditions, they need a sense of going somewhere, a view of themselves and their future which allows for professional growth and increasing responsibility. Staff development thus has three aspects: learning to do the job better, continuing personal and professional education, and career planning.

One form of staff development that occurs naturally within the nursery is the example of competence demonstrated by experienced staff. Their voice, actions and general manner in relating to children and colleagues are a significant model. This needs to be supplemented by a formal supervision system, as described in the next section.

A small but important point is that the budget should allow for the building of a staff library, regularly added to, and preferably accessible to parents as well as staff. It is also important to allow for subscriptions to relevant periodicals and a daily (quality) newspaper to be kept in the staff room.

Occasional days when the staff group comes together to work on organizational issues, perhaps with an outside adviser, or to learn about some new development or approach, can be very valuable. These should be built into the annual calendar as they are in schools, and if this is not current practice, the organizer needs to be assertive in requesting a change. The inconvenience to parents can be minimized by plenty of advance notice and help with alternative arrangements if necessary.

A whole day for all the staff together, including the support workers, can be very profitable, providing time for reflection in the nursery environment on common aims, pinpointing causes of difficulty and together planning changes in the working day. After identifying the problems these can be studied in three ways: how to eliminate them, how to modify them or how to agree to put up with them and stop complaining! By this process much of the energy expended in irritation and conflict (often unexpressed) can be freed for use in more constructive and enjoyable ways.

Outside the nursery there are courses, conferences and workshops run by social services training departments, educational institutions and voluntary organizations. It will depend on the policy of the administration responsible for the nursery or day care facility what opportunities staff can expect, but the organizer needs to press strongly for staff to have time off and funding for professional development, which is as important for the staff group as a whole as for the individuals concerned. The larger voluntary organizations usually build this element into their budgets, but community nurseries are likely to have more difficulty. Private centres should be required to make provision for ongoing staff training as a condition of registration.

A course outside the nursery has the great advantage of enabling staff to get to know other early years workers and have contact with developments elsewhere. When a staff member is released to attend a course, the organizer has a considerable task in enabling the remaining staff to carry the undoubted extra burden and convincing them that there will be benefits to all in the longer term. It is vital that the organizer interests herself actively in the content of the course and helps the nursery worker involved to find ways of applying what she has learned and sharing her experience with the rest of the staff.

The value of continuing personal education should not be overlooked. Many nursery workers have suffered from discrimination against women in the education system and in their families, as a result of which their formal education has been cut short. Encouragement to attend evening classes to extend their knowledge of literature, art, music, languages, sociology or psychology, or to study through the Open University, will not only extend their own horizons but feed back into their work in the nursery.

Career opportunities for early childhood workers are at last beginning to open up, with the expansion of multi-purpose family centres, modularization of courses, the development of the National Vocational Qualifications structure and the move towards recognition of previous experience. Although few women are free agents in career terms, they can still be helped to formulate plans of which their work in the nursery and learning within and outside it form part, so that they take some control of their working lives instead of being blown in the wind.

SUPERVISION AND CONSULTATION

The provision of regular supervision for all staff in the nursery is a relatively recent development, imported from social work. It has the dual function of ensuring accountability for the quality of the work and offering a basis for staff development (Parsloe, 1981). The value of supervision needs to be understood and agreed by the whole staff group and the time set aside for it strongly protected so that, for example, it is not interrupted by telephone calls or given lower priority than other claims on senior staff. The principle which lies behind supervision is similar to that which underpins the key person system for children; adults, too, need the assurance of some special individual attention.

Sometimes an organizer finds it hard to imagine finding time for regular supervision slots. This is often because she operates an open-door policy, and is constantly interrupted by requests for a 'quick word'. There has to be a balance between reasonable availability and a style of 'feeding on demand' which can make it impossible for the organizer to do her job properly and is ultimately unhelpful to the staff.

Emergency 'drop everything' happenings are sometimes inevitable, but when the difficulty is a minor one, it may be more appropriate for the staff member to manage by herself and if necessary discuss the incident at a subsequent supervision session rather than seek immediate guidance from the organizer. When a regular supervision system has been established, it is noticeable how time-consuming consultations about trivial matters are reduced. This can mean real progress for staff who develop confidence in their own judgement and ability to make decisions.

When a key person system is working effectively, senior staff can keep closely in touch, through supervision sessions, with the progress of each child and their parents' relations with the nursery. With the framework which this provides, the 6-monthly reviews, which have become common practice in local authority nurseries, are based on consistent observation and the children will be indirectly aware of a quality of concern for them as individuals.

Often nursery workers may confide to a senior staff member in a supervision session, that they are experiencing stress in their personal lives. As well as listening to their troubles there is a need to discuss how the demands of the day's work can be faced all the same, so that private difficulties do not invade relationships within the nursery.

The supervision structure should include the cook and other ancillary staff, whose essential part in the effective running of a nursery is sometimes only recognized when one of them is absent. The domestic staff are often more permanent than the nursery workers, more deeply rooted in the local community and can develop valuable relationships with individual children and families. The strength of the staff group is enormously enhanced when the personalities and contribution of the support staff are fully and explicitly integrated. This mutual respect and consideration should be expressed in a practical form, so that any change of arrangements which affect them is fully discussed with them. Examples would be play with paint, sand and water which may involve extra cleaning, or the arrangements for mealtimes suggested in Chapter 10. Nursery workers can also help the children to understand what adequate cleaning up requires, and ensure that they show consideration for support staff.

Where changes are introduced it is important for the domestic staff to understand their educational significance, and for them to have an opportunity to raise their concerns in their own supervision sessions (perhaps in a group). Attention to detail and its human implications have been mentioned as one of our strengths as women, and this is an example of the kind of situation in which it can be put to use.

EMOTIONAL AND PHYSICAL WELLBEING

The wellbeing of the carers is much discussed in social work circles but far more is required in specific practical ways to reduce what can be called the occupational hazards, both physical and emotional, for nursery workers. Research in the United States and Australia has shown that they suffer disproportionately from back trouble, respiratory illnesses, gastrointestinal disorders and depression (Ryan, 1988). Unacknowledged stress can lead to conflict within the centre and with parents, and to frequent absences due to sickness, increasing the load on other staff and creating instability.

There is also a direct effect on the children. Bain and Barnett (1980) found that staff experiencing severe stress developed defensive techniques similar to those observed among hospital nurses (Menzies, 1960). They denied their own feelings and distanced themselves from those they were caring for, treating children as a group rather than as individuals and devaluing the importance of attachment and personal relationships. This often leads to a condition, sometimes called burnout, where the worker derives so little satisfaction from the job that she leaves and perhaps switches to another type of work (Clyde, 1988). Although this may be the right decision for the individual, equally it can mean the loss to the profession of a thoughtful and sensitive person.

Physical health

Health awareness is an essential component of staff development, and, at least in family centres, is increasingly seen as an important aspect of work with parents. One of the best ways for staff to become better informed about health is to organize a health club for the families using the centre, at the same time learning themselves about issues such as smoking, alcohol, diet, exercise and ways of coping with mental and physical stress.

Child care is physically demanding and workers need to be fit if they are not to become exhausted. They may need help to plan their diet rather than relying on quick energy-boosting snacks, and to build in time outside work to get involved in some sport or active recreation.

Back trouble is a particular danger in child care work. An important point here is to plan to do away with any unnecessary lifting. We have already emphasized in Chapter 2 the importance of organizing rooms so as to minimize the need to move furniture. Substituting small mattresses and sleeping bags for rest beds avoids the lifting and stacking of metal frame camp beds, frees storage space and allows the bigger children to give useful help to staff.

Carrying children who could quite well walk or crawl on their own is another common source of back trouble; the practice of carrying a child on one hip, if done consistently through an adult's working life, can create great strain on the alignment of the body. We often pick up a child because we want her to be in another place without the trouble of negotiating with her, even though we know that it would be better for our backs and for the child's independence to do so. If there is a feeling of rush, it is tempting to try to speed things up by carrying a child to the bathroom or dinner table. Staff can develop each other's awareness of this pattern and agree to try and change it.

Lifting heavy children on to changing tables can be avoided by providing a small set of kitchen steps so that a child can, under supervision, climb up herself. This has a double purpose – to save the adult backstrain and to encourage the child's collaboration in the care of her own body.

The old myth which stems from the hospital tradition that staff are not working unless they are standing should be firmly dismissed. Chairs of the right type and height should always be available. As far as possible the caregiver should sit down on an adult-sized chair to cuddle or comfort a child. When seated the knees and feet take the strain and not the lower back. Upright chairs are essential in the group room for occasions when sitting on a low settee or on the floor is not the most comfortable or appropriate position for the adult.

People who work with young children are vulnerable to infection, especially before they have been in the job long enough to develop some immunity, and this accounts for a high proportion of sick leave. Some precautionary measures are possible – for example, the exercise of strict personal hygiene, insistence on washing hands after changing nappies however inconvenient it may be at that moment, never moving from physical care of one child to another without washing in between, attention to the disposal of paper tissues (see Chapter 7) and not using communal towels. With the increasing risk of HIV infection, in some areas nursery staff are required to wear gloves. This is a difficult matter to judge; it may be unavoidable, but it would be sad to see an impersonal, hospital-like atmosphere creeping back into nurseries.

Caring and loss

One form of emotional strain associated with the work which is not sufficiently acknowledged arises from the constant making and breaking of affectional bonds as children move into new groups or leave the nursery. This is where the role of the supervisor is vital in helping the worker to come to terms with the reality that she has only a temporary role in the child's life, but that the experience of loss, though painful, does not diminish the value of the relationship either for herself or for the child.

COPING WITH STRESS

Nursery workers often comment on the stress they experience in their daily work in a number of different situations: in their direct contact with children during the day; when difficult incidents occur with parents; when they come into overt or unexpressed conflict with other staff members; and when visiting specialists or other outside people make unplanned demands on their attention.

Stress in day-to-day work

Group room meetings are a good occasion for staff to examine in detail which are the moments during the day when they experience most stress. When periods of tension have been identified the questions to be asked are: Is this stress inevitable? Can it be modified by better planning? Can it be eliminated? For example, in the early morning a number of children and their parents arrive in a cluster and the worker, on her own, feels torn between giving attention to parents and supervising the activities of a growing number of children in the room. In the group meeting the problem faced by the staff on the early shift needs to be discussed so that where possible the pressure of numbers can be spread out by negotiating with parents about their time of arrival. When the staff member cannot give full supervision to the children because of the need to listen to parents, one possibility is to provide specific play material to occupy the children which is not offered at other times of the day.

In the period from about 11 a.m. to 1 p.m. an effective key person system can reduce confusion and create greater calm in more intimate contact with each small group of children. Instead of being a time of rush and noise, this part of the day can bring greater satisfaction for both adult and children. Generally, the smaller the group of children for whom a staff member is responsible, the less the strain. For example, storytelling sessions can be split up so that instead of one staff member reading to a large group while the others patrol the boundary, each adult tells a separate story in a different place to her own small group.

Relations with parents

Stress arising from relations with parents partly derives from the fact that many people with children in local authority day care face serious anxieties and difficulties in their home lives, for instance, living on inadequate welfare benefits in substandard accommodation. Sometimes nursery workers to whom they pour out their troubles empathize to such an extent that they experience acute distress themselves. The supervisor needs to help them channel what may be quite justified anger about social injustice in productive directions, such as becoming politically active or supporting relevant pressure groups, rather than taking on the parents' despair and depression.

A related problem is that parents under stress may react unreasonably or aggressively to seemingly small irritations such as a child getting paint in her hair, or respond defensively if the worker wants to discuss their child's behaviour. Sometimes the worker may even be subjected to direct physical or verbal attack. Inevitably such events place a heavy strain on nursery workers in which the support and guidance of the organizer is essential. If nursery workers can gain confidence in dealing with potentially aggressive encounters calmly and effectively, on the lines suggested in Chapter 14, they will demonstrate to any children who may be present that there are ways of responding to conflict other than by counter-aggression.

Tension between staff members

Nothing is more exhausting than an atmosphere of misunderstanding and conflict between fellow workers. Sometimes people working together are afraid to raise an issue because of what they fear might happen if they were really to speak their minds.

Silent disapproval and unspoken resentments are very corroding to personal relationships, and they can and do exist in any group. However, one of the differences between a personal or family group and a professional group is that the underlying aims of the work are explicitly agreed and accepted, so that differing personalities can find respect if not liking for each other. With a proper structure of communication and consultation through staff meetings and regular supervision, disagreements can be brought out into the open and dealt with before they undermine the working of the group. All staff have a responsibility to play their part in creating a good atmosphere, understanding that if they fail to do this they are certainly harming themselves. Senior staff, of course, play a crucial role in keeping their ear to the ground, defusing potential conflict and conciliating between opposing views when necessary.

Managing visitors

The responsibility for managing the wide range of potential visitors to a nursery centre lies with the organizer. She sometimes needs to be firm, not only in limiting the number of visits by people who want to observe the work, but in indicating the best way to be present in a group without causing distraction.

Outside specialists can provide support and valuable expertise, but they can also be a source of stress unless their visits are carefully co-ordinated and the central role of the key person is fully recognized. Arrangements should never be left to chance – 'I'll pop in during the morning' is the death knell to any effective collaboration. Precise appointments should be made so that the nursery worker is not put in the difficult situation of dividing her attention between the children and a visitor with whom she needs a period of calm and concentration to discuss a basis for their collaboration. The practical difficulties of time and space are very real. If by good planning these can be overcome, there is still much to be done in enabling nursery workers and visiting specialists to work out how they can complement each other's particular skills.

In recent years specialists such as physiotherapists and speech therapists have increasingly involved parents of children whom they are treating. The worker who spends many hours with the child in the nursery needs to be involved in the same way so that she, too, can complement the therapist's work.

For example, a community physiotherapist was able to engage both nursery staff and children in her work with Sarah, a little girl whose disability affected her walking. She wanted Sarah to practise particular movements and devised a game which encouraged her to do this involving the whole group of children. In this way the child being treated did not feel isolated, the nursery worker could learn by participating, and the problem of finding space and time for individual treatment was solved. This kind of imaginative approach offers many possibilities which can be developed between nursery staff and visiting specialists, provided an initial basis of trust has been created.

EXTENDING STAFF RESOURCES

How often we have heard at the end of a training course the despondent reaction, 'Oh, we'd love to do that but we just haven't enough staff.' On closer enquiry what is really meant is that there are not enough adults in proportion to children. There are two ways of tackling this problem (apart from recruiting more staff): one is by employing people for specific purposes on a sessional basis, the other is by using volunteers.

Although many nurseries and family centres invite individuals to help on a casual basis, by far the best results are achieved by setting up a properly planned volunteer scheme. There are many useful models available, for instance, the now widespread home-visiting programmes for young families under stress known as Home Start (Van der Eyken, 1982), but this section draws principally on the experience of a nursery head, Chris Leaves, who was able, by using volunteers, to expand substantially the scope of her work, based on a small day nursery in Peterborough (Leaves, 1985).

Setting up a volunteer scheme can be seen as falling into three phases: recruitment and selection, preparation and training, and ongoing support.

Recruitment and selection

The first aim is to publicize the scheme and attract a large number of enquiries, knowing that these will dwindle rapidly once an expression of interest has to turn into a commitment. A good start is to invite a local journalist to visit and write an article about the work of the nursery. Local radio and free papers are also useful sources of publicity. Posters and leaflets have less impact. In the Peterborough scheme thirty of the original fifty enquirers accepted an invitation to visit the nursery; twenty returned application forms, of whom four were screened out by the essential police and health checks, and eleven eventually became regular volunteers. It is clear from this that a good deal of work is involved in processing enquiries and application forms, but help may be available from a volunteer co-ordinator, either employed by the local authority or by a voluntary body.

Preparation and training

Some schemes run extended training courses lasting several weeks, but having taken the plunge volunteers are usually eager to get started, and training on the job is more likely to sustain their motivation. A compromise which worked well in Peterborough was two days of intensive preparation followed by regular follow-up sessions. The two days included warming-up exercises, games, activities and case studies designed to introduce the volunteers to the work with children and to the problems faced by families using the centre. One of the key objectives was to help the volunteers to develop non-judgemental attitudes towards parents. It also covered practical subjects, such as nursery routines, bus times and how to claim expenses. The importance of commitment and reliability was stressed, and each volunteer filled in a form to say what time they were prepared to give.

Volunteers in action

Following the preparation days each volunteer was matched with a staff member who agreed to offer 10 minutes' supervision and consultation at the end of each session. In addition, a monthly support meeting led by the organizer was built into the scheme, centred on a particular activity but also providing an opportunity for the volunteers to share experiences and get to know each other. This social contact proved very rewarding for them and was probably a major factor in their continued participation.

Although setting up a volunteer scheme is time-consuming, the benefits to the nursery can be very substantial. Volunteers bring new interests, experiences and skills, adding an extra dimension to what goes on. They can release staff to work with individual children, or do it themselves, enable staff to take children on outings, and act as ambassadors for the nursery in the community. They become interested in the children and their parents and form friendships with them.

At the start of the Peterborough scheme nursery staff had divided tasks into ones they thought volunteers could do and those that should be reserved for professionals. In practice it was found that, given support, volunteers were capable of doing almost anything. This is an important point, since volunteers frequently drop out because they are confined to menial and boring tasks, when what they really want is to work with people (Parsloe and Williams, 1993).

PROVIDING A HIGH-QUALITY SERVICE

The presence of volunteers, however well-prepared and helpful, is yet another factor adding to the complexity of the organizer's task. Management of child care centres is a seriously neglected area. Research, coming mostly at present from the United States, suggests that many of the general principles of management in human services settings apply, but there are also special factors involved in caring for young children (Phillips *et al.*, 1991). Certainly, the task of the organizer is a demanding one, and people in this position need to be active in seeking appropriate training and support for themselves as managers, as well as for their staff. The evidence is very clear that good-quality care for children depends on the staff group working effectively as a team in an atmosphere which offers stability, job satisfaction and openness to planned change and flexibility.

SUMMARY

The task of a manager in a nursery or family centre is to enhance the enjoyable aspects of caring for young children and help to minimize the inevitable stresses. Effective organization is essential if the staff team is to work harmoniously together. Thought needs to be given to communication systems, staff meetings, in-service training and career development. The physical and emotional wellbeing of nursery workers should be a high priority. Outside specialists can provide valuable help in working with individual children if collaboration is carefully planned. A model for extending the staffing resources of the unit by using community volunteers is described.

5 Babies in day care

The baby new to earth and sky
What time his tender palm is prest
Against the circle of the breast
Has never thought that 'this is I'.

Tennyson

About 20,000 children under a year have a mother in full-time employment, and many more go back to work part time before their child's first birthday. In other countries, such as Sweden, which have legislation protecting the income level and position in the workforce of mothers, there is a downward trend, with fewer babies in out-of-home care (Moss and Melhuish, 1991), but in Britain the trend is the other way.

Economic pressure and the shortage of jobs are making women with congenial employment increasingly anxious about giving up work when they have a baby. If they do, they may have great difficulty later in finding employment that matches their qualifications, and they will certainly have lost seniority and probably reduced their career prospects (Joshi, 1987). Single mothers are in a particularly vulnerable position. They can look forward to an extremely grey and limited existence if they rely for their income on welfare benefits (Millar, 1989; Bradshaw, 1990).

This needs to be borne in mind by nursery workers and child minders, who are sometimes critical of parents who seek day care for very young children (Moss, 1986; Ferri, 1992). A further point to remember is that, though shortage of time is always a problem for working parents, a baby is likely to receive a higher level of care and attention from a mother with a satisfying job and an adequate income than one who is struggling with all the problems which poverty brings. There is very little evidence that day care for children under one year is harmful in itself, though poor quality care, either by a parent or anybody else, certainly is (Clarke-Stewart, 1991). All the same, few mothers leave their babies without misgivings, however much they want to return to work, and many find the early weeks of separation extremely painful (Brannen and Moss, 1988).

NURSERIES AND CHILD MINDERS

Is it possible to provide high quality care for babies in a group setting? There is not enough evidence to give a firm answer either way (Moss, 1991), but clearly there are many problems about ensuring responsive, individualized care for very young children in a nursery. For a start, it is extremely expensive because of the high adult–child ratio required. A further difficulty is that babies' needs are unpredictable, fluctuating, but intense and immediate. There may be periods when there is nothing much for the caregiver to do, alternating with times when all the babies in the room are demanding attention at the same time. Their daily rhythms change as they grow in ways that bear no relation to nursery routine.

In practice, the majority of mothers seeking to maintain continuity of employment have little choice about child care arrangements. Unless they have a relative willing to look after the baby or can afford to employ a nanny they will have to use a child minder. Very few social services day nurseries and almost no workplace nurseries take children under one. Private nurseries, responding to market forces, often start by offering care for babies but later find it does not make economic sense.

Child minders offer an invaluable service, and much of the criticism they have suffered should be directed at the government or local authorities who have failed to provide adequate recognition, training and support for their work in the way that, for instance, has been done in France (Jackson and Jackson, 1979; Moss, 1992). Ideally, child minders should be linked to nursery or family centres so as to provide continuity of care from babyhood through to school age, but that looks a long way off.

On balance we think home-based care is better adapted to the needs of babies than a group setting, provided the child minder understands that her role goes far beyond physical caring. Good care by one person is almost certain to be more loving and sensitive than care by a number of different people, however competent. The key person system is only a partial attempt to compensate for this inherent disadvantage of group care.

We simply do not accept the argument that babies are undiscriminating about the adults who look after them; they may *tolerate* a number of caregivers, but show clear preferences from an early age. It is only by knowing a baby very well indeed that we are able to understand his subtle communications and to interpret pre-verbal sounds.

We do not intend to duplicate the vast mass of advice and information on the care and upbringing of babies which is available today. Here we highlight a number of aspects of a baby's life which are of particular importance to those entrusted with their care outside their own homes.

CRYING: A BABY'S LANGUAGE

There is great natural variation in the amount of time babies spend crying, and it also differs from month to month. Babies who hardly ever cried in the first few weeks will suddenly go through a period of what seems to their parents to be continuous screaming. On the whole though, babies cry for a reason, and a persistent background of crying in a nursery always indicates something lacking in the care that is being offered.

Living close to a baby we become able to distinguish between, and so to interpret, the messages which lie behind the differing kinds of cry. He may be experiencing hunger, pain, physical discomfort, loneliness or maybe just a general feeling of malaise.

When a baby's screams persist and he seems unable to accept our comfort, we sometimes feel an impulse to hand him to someone else because we cannot stand the strain. When that person hands him back still crying, our understandable frustration may be communicated to the baby through the growing tension of our hands and bodies, causing him to accentuate his cries.

This is the moment to study how we are breathing and to take responsibility for our own feelings. By deliberately focusing our attention on breathing with our diaphragm, and not with the upper chest, stress can be immediately reduced enabling us to regain composure and feel in control of ourselves. As soon as we can do this we are in a state to listen intently, perhaps telling the baby so in our quietest, gentlest voice, 'I'm really listening to you. I don't yet understand what you are trying to tell me, but be sure I will not leave you'. This prevents us from raising our own voice and allows us to give soft massage rather than the agitated pats, jiggling up and down and anxious chatter with which adults often express their own distress when a baby will not stop crying.

When under pressure in a group of other babies who also need attention, this kind of personal tranquility can be very hard to reach, but it is a way in which we can transmit the messages of reassurance that we want to give while staying alert and receptive to what the baby is experiencing.

It is worth remembering that many nursery staff, as infants, may have gone through the now-discredited child-rearing practices of another generation, when it was commonly advised to 'let baby cry it out'. We would not leave a deeply distraught friend in solitude if we could possibly help it, so why do this to babies who cannot even speak in words? Connections of this kind may help to guide us in our handling of the babies for whom we care.

Feeding

Crying in young babies is more often than not due to hunger. Although we no longer expect the sensations of a baby's stomach to correspond to the movement of hands on a clock, we still irrationally feel that it is unreasonable of a baby to demand a feed only an hour or so after the last one. We forget that he may then sleep for five or six hours without stirring.

Feeding for a baby is *the* basic experience. It not only means ingestion of nourishment but sustained interaction with a close adult, an opportunity for communication which contributes to all aspects of his development.

When there is more than one baby to be bottle fed, a real problem may face the nursery worker who has to harmonize as best she can the differing bodily rhythms which each infant in the group will have. As the baby grows, his feeding rhythm will change just as his sleep pattern does. It requires good observation and flexibility to ensure that it is the baby's individual needs and not nursery routine that sets the timetable, and that it is always the baby's key person who feeds him when she is there.

In a busy room, with other staff and children present, there is a risk that the baby's key person will be distracted from giving total quiet attention to him alone, which is as important as the milk he sucks. She needs to create an undisturbed corner to ensure that the experience is quite unhurried and comfortable for the baby as well as for herself. The old fashioned 'nursing chair' if one can still be found, was ideal for bottle feeding. The height was designed to allow the feet to rest firmly on the floor and the back was straight and supportive.

Looking at a baby at his mother's breast, or feeding from his bottle, we observe that of the nursing couple it is the baby who is active, deciding the speed and the intensity with which he sucks and his mother who responds to his movements, adapting the position of her arms and body to enable him to feed comfortably. The quality of their relationship is expressed in 'the primal gaze', the baby seeking intense eye contact as he feeds (Goldschmied, 1974).

When weaning starts, with new tastes and textures, their roles will be reversed. The caring adult is the active partner, but she must be delicately responsive in her timing, offering the spoon just when he gives the signal, by opening his lips, that he is now ready for some more. If she herself is overactive or anxious, then a tiny battle of wills may begin. A baby can then become aware of tension and resist her pressure; this can be the start of 'feeding difficulties'.

The important question at this time is to see how his active role, so evident at the breast or bottle, can be fostered so that as soon as practicable he has direct contact with the food and can gain skill in manipulating it with fingers. Later, this energy centres on the complex task of carrying the food successfully upon a spoon from plate to mouth. Before this skill is gained, it will help, as we offer a loaded spoon, to give him a spoon to hold and brandish also. This is our message to him, that we acknowledge that later on he will handle the spoon for himself.

In allowing a fair degree of freedom there is no need for excessive mess on face or hair or floor. Putting only a small amount of food at a time in the bowl or plate being used can limit small disasters and the disarray which many adults find it difficult to tolerate – especially it seems when the baby is a girl. This demanding phase is easier to manage if we can find satisfaction enabling an infant to enjoy his food at a time when his autonomy is gradually emerging. He would say 'thank you' if he could – in fact he does so by his replete smiles and obvious pleasure in our attentive company.

The direct handling of food, kept within reasonable limits, is a foretaste of play with messy things like sand and water, clay and paint, which he encounters later on. The baby's growing skill in handling a spoon, parallels his mastery of eye–hand–object–mouth co-ordination which he exercises in his play at a well-stocked Treasure Basket.

MOBILITY

In addition to the five senses of touch, smell, taste, hearing and sight, the sense of movement of our body (the kinaesthetic sense) is a vital element in the growth of our own self image. Movement, in a restricted space, is already very much a part of the experience of the infant in the womb (how often do we hear the laughing complaint that 'baby seems to have football boots on'!).

In infancy this sense grows fast when freedom of movement allows the baby to take tiny risks, which create confidence as to what he can attempt and achieve. A baby lying upon his back on a firm but comfortable surface – a blanket on the floor is safest – will use the opportunity to the full to stretch and squirm and roll and heave. In this way he can make contact freely with his feet and hands as understanding grows that they are his own extremities. Bare feet are essential for this so that toes can be grasped and sucked with all the notable stimulus that this provides. Bare feet also allow the baby to use a big toe with which to lever himself in rolling on to his stomach and back again, to his evident delight and satisfaction.

Babies need very early to be put on their stomachs for short intervals, always with their elbows bent beneath their chin, so that the head is free to turn about. Soon, if inviting objects are put close in front of him, a baby will learn to transfer his weight to one shoulder, leaning on that bent arm to free the other to stretch out and grasp the object which attracts him. In his efforts to reach out the baby starts to make humping 'seal-like' movements, inching forward as the idea of crawling seems to grow. At one moment he draws his knees under his body and soon will make alternating movements of hands and knees enabling both sides of his body to develop in balanced co-ordination.

When a baby has mastered crawling and is enjoying this newfound freedom to explore, it is wise to teach him how to manage stairs in safety. We show the child how to sit on the top step and turn himself around with hands on one step and bended knees upon the step below. If shown a few times how to go down on hands and knees facing backwards he will soon become most proficient, protected from the risk of falling. It is all too easy for someone to leave a stairgate open, and teaching toddlers to manage stairs themselves as soon as possible is an important safeguard.

Young children seem to know when they want to pull themselves to an upright position but need secure points on which to do this, which in a nursery should of course be provided. Some adults have the tendency to pull children on to their feet too soon, for even the most efficient crawling seems to make them feel uneasy. It is worthwhile to pause and consider how much safer it is for the infant to remain crawling until he is physically more mature and there will be a shorter period when he will need to make frantic grabs on lamps or tablecloths to sustain his wobbling steps.

TECHNICAL AIDS TO BABY CARE

There are an increasing number of aids to the care of babies, some of them very useful, but others which should be looked at with a critical eye. They may be designed to make the adult's task easier, but not necessarily to the benefit of the child.

Playpens

At one time wooden playpens were found in every nursery, and at home if there was the space. One great drawback of the playpen is that it is a too convenient way of ignoring a baby or of restricting a crawling child. Added to this, the height of the surrounding rail means severe back strain when the adult leans over to lift a baby out. Because of the upright bars the adult cannot bend her knees to lift so that all the weight is taken on the arms and upper back. This is a serious health hazard.

The other type of playpen, more often used at home because it occupies a smaller space, is usually called a 'lobster pot'. A baby confined there sees the world through a rather dense white netting, which is something none of us would want to do for more than a few moments. Remember how when we want to see outside we always lift back a net curtain from a window? A playpen has its use as a secure place for a crawling baby if the adult must leave him unattended for a short time, such as when another child needs urgent help. But secure places can so easily become prisons, and even if a seated baby is supplied with a well-stocked Treasure Basket, he is still cut off from adult contact.

Transporting babies

The folding pushchair or buggy has virtually replaced the pram and revolutionized mobility for parents with young children. However, a serious drawback is that they are mostly designed so that the baby faces forward. This means that the baby cannot keep eye contact with his adult and conversation is inhibited.

The baby finds himself in a kind of moving plastic limbo, carving a way between oncoming legs and feet. Any adult who has been pushed in a wheelchair through a hurrying crowd will tell you that the experience of meeting this human flood can be quite disturbing. A baby can only hope to hear the occasional disembodied adult voice to reassure him that he is not alone in space. Nurseries and child minders should try to obtain pushchairs that enable a baby to face the person pushing him and be sure of his adult's continuing presence.

For carrying small babies a variety of slings are now available. They tend to be used by parents much more than in nurseries, but they have two advantages: first safety, in leaving the adult's arms and hands free to fend off an obstacle or break a fall, and second, avoiding physical strain by disposing the baby's weight more evenly at the centre of the body rather than on one arm and hip. From the baby's point of view, provided he does not feel squeezed up, he has the advantage of closeness to his adult's body and the rhythm which her movements bring.

The backpack style of carrier is suited to a young child who can sit up well, though care needs to be taken that there is no chafing. Nursery workers not accustomed to using one of these must be most vigilant in passing through doorways or entrances, not forgetting the extra space needed at the back of the head and shoulders.

Baby bouncers and swings

Swings can be freestanding or hang from a door lintel. The second type is safer, because it is only too easy to forget that the baby is getting stronger all the time until he swings so vigorously that he tips over the whole assembly.

Baby bouncers, where the baby sits with his extended toes touching the floor, can be amusing for a short while provided the adult participates in the fun, but do nothing to aid natural muscle development and should not be overused.

Baby walkers

A common type is a circular frame on small wheels. The child leans on the frame and propels himself with his toes. This activity may give an illusion to the adults that a child is learning to walk. In fact it may delay walking as the child is not learning the essential ingredient of balance, and the feet are not well placed on the ground. In addition, this type of walker can be extremely dangerous because of the great speed with which an otherwise relatively immobile infant can move around. The risk is less in a nursery environment, but at home the child may be across the room and out of the door in the time it takes a caregiver to turn round.

A much better form of baby walker is a strong low wooden truck, heavy enough not to tip up, with a handle at shoulder level which gives support and confidence and which will not go fast when pushed by a child who is practising first steps. The truck can also be used for loading wooden bricks or other objects and is sometimes used instead of a doll's pram. It is worth investing in the very best quality that can be afforded as this is a piece of equipment with really long-term value.

Reclining baby seats

These are light and portable and very useful in the transition from a baby lying prone and being able to sit up securely. They have certainly made the lives of babies in this phase much more interesting, enabling them to look at all the interesting things going on around them instead of gazing at a blank ceiling. A baby can sit in his reclining seat on the kitchen table while his child minder prepares a meal so that as she works a little sociable interlude is possible. However, babies should never be left on a table unattended even for a second as they can easily work themselves to the edge and fall over.

It is important not to use a reclining seat in weaning unless it can be adjusted to be upright. The leaning back position is not a good one for taking solid food, and can present a difficulty if food goes down the wrong way (think about trying to eat when lying ill in bed).

Clothing

This has of course improved immeasurably, and attractive clothes which involve the minimum disturbance in dressing or undressing the baby and the least possible work for caregivers are readily available. Knitted matinee coats with pearl buttons are a thing of the past (somewhat to the regret of grandmothers). Disposables have removed the enormous burden of washing, disinfecting and drying towelling nappies, though at some expense to the environment. The question of disposal of soiled nappies needs attention; in one nursery we were appalled to see the bottom shelf of the food trolley used to transport the nappy wastebag through the kitchen to the dustbins!

Babies would probably much rather not wear nappies at all, and they show their appreciation of brief moments of freedom while being changed by waving their legs about (or when they can, rolling over and crawling rapidly away). Some adults seem to have a compulsion to package them up neatly again, and in doing so may strap up the adhesive flaps too tightly, which can cause chafing on the inner thigh.

The towelling stretchsuit which can be thrown in the washing machine is the next best invention after the disposable nappy. It means the whole body can be kept covered and the feet warm when sitting on the floor or sleeping in a cot. However, because babies grow so fast, there is a need to remain vigilant – lengthening legs can mean that toes which need the maximum freedom of movement can become squeezed up and constricted. Until the suit can be replaced with a larger one, the legs should be cut off at the ankles and the baby's freed feet covered with socks or bootees. Baby suits without integral feet have the advantage that a baby's toes can be easily uncovered and allow him a firmer grip and better propulsion on a carpet surface in his early efforts to begin crawling.

BABY TOYS IN THE NURSERY

An abundance of toys in the form of animals of all kinds, some attractive and others grotesque, find their way into nurseries. These animals are frequently of plastic, which by no stretch of the imagination could be called 'cuddly', or of synthetic materials with an unpleasant texture. A clear distinction needs to be made between a favourite and personal soft toy, animal, traditional teddy or doll, and the indiscriminate collection of such items which frequently clutter up a nursery.

The special object, which may also be a piece of woolly blanket or other material, has for a long time been understood by most adults to have a real significance for a child. Many parents will have had the experience of hearing a frantic wail fifty miles down the motorway as realization dawns that Teddy has been left behind. There is nothing for it but to turn round and go back for him. Such a toy or item generally has a special name by which the family will laughingly refer to it – 'Ellen's tee-tee'. Attachments to familiar and well-used objects persist into our adult lives – we heard a rumour that 'tee-tee' is now attending Edinburgh University. These personal objects should be treated with proper respect by caregivers and always kept where the children can have easy access to them.

However, places where young children are looked after often accumulate large numbers of soft toys and plastic animals with no personal meaning for the children. Staff would do well to have a rigorous and regular sorting out and casting away of a good proportion of these items which use up valuable storage space.

PLAY EQUIPMENT FOR BABIES

In providing play material for this age group it is essential to ensure that there is a great variety and richness of experience offered, giving the infants the opportunity to explore with mouths and hands a wide range of textures and shapes. A particular way of doing this, the Treasure Basket, is described in the next chapter.

However limited the budget, an investment in strong, wooden equipment is well worthwhile. Some items will need to be obtained from specialist firms which produce equipment designed to stand up to use in groups of children, others can be made by a woodworker, not necessarily professional, or by nursery workers, parents and volunteers. The following items engage the sitting baby's developing manipulative skill and produce an immediate result, encouraging repetition and practice. They also have the chararacteristic of being solid and will not be knocked over as the child uses them.

Cylinder block

A solid block of wood measuring 8 × 5 × 2in. (203 × 127 × 51mm.). The block has six holes into which fit six wooden cylinders. A seated baby will enjoy taking out the cylinders, one by one, for mouthing, banging and waving. Only later will the baby be able to put them back into their holes, so the adult must do this, and the baby will get much satisfaction from the repetition of this simple process.

One-hole posting tin

This toy offers a baby the experience of 'there' and 'not there', and a repeated sense of discovery.

Take a fairly large tin with a press-on lid, not more than 5in. (127mm.) high, for easy access to the hand of a seated baby. Choose a number of balls – wooden if they can be found, but table-tennis balls are more easily obtainable. Provide a small, strong basket or wicker tray in which the balls are always kept for use in conjunction with the tin. Cut a hole the size of the balls in the tin lid, then cover it with adhesive shelf-paper, turning the paper inwards to cover the sharp edge of the hole.

The child will discover for himself that the balls will slip through the hole making a satisfying sound as they hit the bottom of the tin. Eventually he will try to retrieve the ball by putting his hand through the hole, and will find that this is impossible. He will probably put his eye to the hole and try to locate the ball which he realizes is there, but of course his own face blocks out the light. He will rattle the tin, but will need the adult to take off the lid so that he can retrieve the balls and, with the lid replaced, repeat the process. A plastic container is less satisfactory because the ball falling through the lid does not make such an interesting noise.

Post and rings

Commercial versions of this toy are available in plastic, but are too unstable to be satisfactory.

Take a wooden block, 7 × 4.5 × 1.5in. (177 × 114 × 38mm.), and screw or glue into it a wooden cylinder or piece of thick dowling 8in. (203mm.) long. Provide 14 curtain rings of unpolished wood, supplemented with brass ones to add variety and opportunity for discrimination. The adult can co-operate with the child to their mutual amusement. Of course the babies will use the rings to put on toes, slip on to hands and look through as well as slotting them on to the cylinder but that does not matter as long as the rings have a secure container for storage purposes which is kept with the block.

'What's inside?' toys

For initiating this kind of play the adult needs various containers, and objects to put inside them. Some possible receptacles are strong egg boxes, small baskets or boxes with lids, and cardboard cylinders. Suitable items to put in them are ping-pong balls, golfballs, shells, short lengths of chain, walnuts, big chestnuts and avocado pear stones. The child greatly enjoys opening the container and discovering what is inside, first simply emptying out and later beginning to replace items or sliding them through the cylinders. These are very good toys for interactive play between babies and caregivers. The adult has an essential role in keeping such collections in good order in containers ready for use and not scattered about. By the end of his first year the baby becomes increasingly fascinated by the activity of putting objects into containers and emptying them out.

SUMMARY

Caring well for babies in a group setting is difficult and costly. To be truly responsive to their fluctuating needs, ever-changing rhythms and subtly varied communications requires an individualized system of care so that the nursery worker can get to know her special children intimately. Babies need interest and variety in their lives as much as older children, and careful thought should be given to the surroundings in which they spend their days and the playthings offered to them.

Caregivers need to be aware of the reasons why parents choose to use day care in order to avoid judgemental attitudes, but also so that they can appreciate and be sensitive to the mixed feelings which many mothers experience in leaving their young babies.

6   The Treasure Basket

When an Aboriginal mother notices the first stirrings of speech in her child, she lets it handle the 'things' of that particular country: leaves, fruit, insects and so forth. The child, at its mother's breast, will toy with the 'thing', talk to it, test its teeth on it, learn its name, repeat its name.

Bruce Chatwin, *The Songlines*

This chapter considers one of the important ways in which the play and learning of babies can be encouraged as soon as they can sit up comfortably and before they begin to crawl. By now the baby will be awake for much longer periods of the day. Of course much of the time will still be taken up with feeding, washing and changing, and we would emphasize the importance of building in time for the interplay that goes on during these activities and which is such a vital element in the baby's waking life.

A baby's first toy is the body of her caring adult. A baby grasps her parent's fingers, handles her mother's breast, entwining her fingers in her mother's hair or her father's beard, grabs at earrings, necklaces or spectacles. The baby's focus is on the close caring person, experiencing the familiar warmth, the smell, the surface tension of the skin, the vibrations of voice and laughter and all that goes to make up daily handling and interchange. But the baby also needs opportunities for play and learning when she is not receiving individual attention from her close adult.

Awareness of her own body grows as a baby crams her small fist into her mouth and, lying on her back, identifies her feet and toes, getting to know these extremities by sucking them as well. From an early age, a baby will grasp an offered rattle and it is no accident that favourite rattles are usually those with short handles. This makes easy the spasmodic waving and banging which seems to be so much enjoyed even when it means that baby, much to her own surprise, accidentally taps her own face, seemingly unable to figure out how this has happened. Eye, hand, mouth co-ordination marks a big step forward, but like all skills, if it is to develop, the baby needs opportunities to practise.

As a baby's waking time extends and she begins to sit upright, first propped up by cushions or in a reclining chair, then independently, a whole new horizon opens up. It may be that she can now see the underneath of the table, our shoes and ankles, the moving hem of a trouser leg, in addition to the other interesting items in the room. She has a kind of worm's eye view of the world, but none the less intriguing for that.

VARIETY AND QUALITY IN INFANT PLAY

This period of being able to sit up comfortably brings a new small piece of autonomy to a baby, but it also brings new vexations. We have all noticed a baby of this age alert and aware of what is going on around her and yet 'grizzling'. The usual explanation is teething, which may sometimes be true, but it can also be that she is simply bored. Her close adults can't attend to her every moment and yet she is ready and waiting, it seems, for the next thing to happen. She is right to complain, and it was in response to the dissatisfaction which babies of this age clearly show with the often limited and not very interesting playthings offered to them that the 'Treasure Basket' described in this chapter was devised.

We know that babies' brains are growing fast, and that the brain develops as it responds to streams of input coming from the baby's surroundings, through the senses of touch, smell, taste, hearing, sight and bodily movement. The Treasure Basket gathers together and provides a focus for a rich variety of everyday objects chosen to offer stimulus to these different senses. The use of the Treasure Basket is one way that we can ensure a richness in the baby's experience when the brain is ready to receive, to make connections and so to make use of this information.

None of the objects in the Basket is a 'bought toy', and many can be found in the home environment of young children. Parents, asked about their children's favourite playthings, nearly always remark on their fascination for diving into the kitchen cupboards to get at the saucepans, their interest in shoeboxes and delight in playing with the car keys. Once they achieve mobility these are the things children choose to play with, not always to the convenience of their parents, and the contents of the Treasure Basket are selected partly on the basis of this observation.

But here we are considering what can be made available to the child who is sitting up but is still rooted to the spot, which can be a time of great frustration. Things can be seen and heard but are not within the grasp of an outstretched hand. It is here that a well-stocked Treasure Basket, provided by a thoughtful adult, can offer experience of absorbing interest, enabling a baby to pursue vital learning for which she is ready and eager. When planning a baby's diet we give great attention to her menu, offering the range and quality essential for her daily nutrition and rapid growth. But what about her 'mental' diet, which nurtures her developing capacity to use eyes, hands and mouth in concentrated activity?

DISCOVERY AND CONCENTRATION

As we closely observe a baby with the objects in the Treasure Basket, we can note how many different things she does with them, looking, touching, grasping, mouthing, licking, waving, banging, picking up, dropping, selecting and discarding what does or does not attract her. She also uses an object in her hands and mouth as a laughing communication with the close-by adult or with another infant seated at the Basket. It is striking to observe how the whole body is involved – if feet and toes are uncovered they respond in a lively way to the stimulus and excitement which activity with the chosen object induces. All-in-one stretch baby suits, while useful for keeping toes warm at times, can be constricting and limit awareness and communication with these extremities. We often complain that babies seem to want to pull their socks off all the time. Perhaps they are trying to tell us something!

By sucking, mouthing and handling, babies are finding out about weight, size, shapes, texture, sound and smell, and as they choose an object we can imagine that they are saying 'What is this?' Later on when they can move about they will seem to say, 'What can I do with it?' (Hutt, 1979). Then, further exciting horizons will open up for them if we provide the tools they need.

The concentration of a baby on the contents of a Treasure Basket is one thing that astonishes observers seeing it for the first time. Attention may last up to an hour or more. There are two factors which lie behind this and it is difficult to say which comes first, in fact they operate together. There is the infant's lively curiosity which the varied objects arouse, and her will to practise her growing skill in taking possession, under her own steam, of what is new, attractive and close at hand. Alongside this is the confidence which the attentive, but not active, presence of the grown up provides.

The fact that the adult is not active does not mean that we put down the Basket beside the baby and let her 'get on with it'. She needs the safety which our interested presence gives when she is faced with the challenge of objects, which she may be handling for the first time.

In any new experience we, as adults, have two kinds of feeling. We are curious and excited by a situation which is new and strange, but this also arouses doubt and anxiety. Before we embark on a new initiative or follow up an opportunity for change, we seek information and reassurance from others who we feel already know the ropes. Some people seem temperamentally more willing to undertake something which might hold risks. Others are more cautious. But if we have a friend to encourage us whom we trust, then we take on some of their confidence and find that diving off the side of the pool or scrambling up a rocky hill is not so frightening after all.

It is not that we need to encourage babies to handle the play material – given a chance they will do so. But in the unknown there is always some element of threat, and it is the adult's attitude of calm interest that allays a baby's anxiety and so frees her energy for concentrated enjoyment.

FIRST STEPS IN DECISION-MAKING

Watching a baby as she explores the items in the Treasure Basket, it is fascinating to see the zest with which she chooses the objects which attract her, the precision she shows in bringing them to her mouth or passing them from one hand to another, and the quality of concentration as she makes contact with the play material. We see her intent observation, her ability to choose and return to a favoured item which attracts her, sometimes sharing her pleasure with the responsive adult. She is in no doubt about her ability to select and experiment. The idea of two things which are alike appears to be present in her mind as she continues to handle, compare and discard while her active learning proceeds apace.

We all know of people who, faced with a wide variety of styles in a shoe shop, are quite unable to decide which they want. It might not be too fanciful to say that if they had started off with experience of the Treasure Basket, it could have stood them in good stead in later life (see Figures 6.1 and 6.2). The ability to choose wisely, whether in relation to simple things like food and clothes or complex ones like

Figure 6.1 Choice.
Photo: Anita Hughes

friends and jobs, is something which children need appropriate opportunities for doing from very early days – appropriate in the way choices relate to the stage they are at and the amount of information they possess at the time. Once the Treasure Basket has been assembled it offers infinite opportunities for infant decision-making with little effort required from the caregiver other than ensuring that the items in the Basket are clean and regularly replenished with new objects.

The importance of this last point perhaps needs underlining. Unlike a bought toy that remains the same until it is outgrown or broken, a Treasure Basket should be constantly changing and evolving. Perhaps the closest parallel for adults might be the staff noticeboard at work. If it is actively used to convey information, with items frequently added and outdated notices removed, we are inclined to scan it eagerly every morning, hoping to find something new and interesting. If it is nobody's job to keep the board in order so that the current notices are lost among a jumble of old ones and each day we see the same things, we soon lose interest and eventually stop looking at it at all. A baby who always finds the same old objects in her Basket probably has quite similar feelings.

Babies, like adults, need comfortable working positions. Those who

Figure 6.2 Concentration.
Photo: Anita Hughes

are not quite steady in sitting up may keel over and need settling down again. They will need a cushion behind them if they are still inclined to topple over backwards. The best position, and this is why not more than three babies can be accommodated, is for each to be seated at an angle to the basket so that an elbow can rest upon its edge and an extended hand can reach easily into it.

THE ADULT'S ROLE

Perhaps one of the things which an adult may find it difficult to do at first is not to intervene, but to stay quiet and atttentive. If we think for a moment how we feel when concentrating on some enjoyable but demanding activity, we do not want or need someone constantly to suggest, advise and praise our efforts, we just want to get on with it, though we may be glad to have their friendly company. In this respect babies are not so different from grownups.

Sometimes adults, especially staff in nurseries, feel that unless they are active at the Treasure Basket, offering objects to the baby, helping her to hold the 'right' end and so on, they have no role to play, failing to realize the importance of the emotional anchorage which they offer, creating by their presence the confidence which enables the babies to play and learn.

When a baby is at home or with a child minder and playing with her Basket there is no need for the adult to devote all her time and attention to the child, provided that she is sufficiently within earshot and can exchange looks and words which maintain their contact. A group care setting is very different, and when two or at most three babies are seated round the Basket they need close adult supervision. Babies also need protection from mobile children who come to investigate. If older children continually want to join the infants and use the Treasure Basket, this means that there is no appropriate play material to interest them elsewhere in the room, and steps must be taken to remedy this. The right of babies to be undisturbed, as well as the educational value of their play, needs to be properly recognized.

It is also necessary to take account of the possible danger to a baby seated at a Treasure Basket when there are mobile children about. An older child has the strength to lift objects which are too heavy for a baby, and in their hands a heavy pebble or a metal spoon, perfectly safe for a baby to play with, can do serious damage in an instant. This is no reason to deprive the baby of the interesting experiences which such objects can offer, but it does underline the importance of close supervision when children of mixed ages are present.

INTERPLAY BETWEEN INFANTS

The Treasure Basket provides an opportunity to observe social interaction between babies at an age when it used to be said that infants are not interested in each other. Observing two or three babies seated at the Treasure Basket it can be seen immediately that this is not true (Elinor Goldschmied's video, *Infants at Work* (1989), see p. 241). Babies, though intent upon handling their own chosen objects, are very clearly not only aware of each other, but for much of the time are engaged in active interchanges. It is the availability of the objects that stimulates these exchanges, which sometimes develop into little tussles for possession. These interchanges with other babies are different from those which they have with adults and must indeed be something of a shock when encountered for the first time. At these moments it is the other baby and the object of common interest which holds their energy within the context of the attentive adult's presence.

Mothers sometimes find this hard to accept; for them it is the small beginning of the separation, the move towards later independence which is a central part of the infant's growth. The view that babies are not interested in each other may have its origins in our own difficulty in recognizing that even at this early age babies can create for themselves, for short spells, a little social scene with each other in which we as adults only play a marginal part.

However, the interchange of intense looking, of glances, smiles, pre-verbal noises of great variety, touching each other and sharing objects, all spring directly from the experiences babies have with their close adults. Institution-reared infants who have had multiple caretakers or those whose homes have not provided enough loving care and stimulation do not respond in this way. The 'abandoned and illegitimate' infants with whom Elinor worked in post-war Italy did not interact with each other at all, even though they spent all their waking hours lying or sitting together in a playpen. They remained silent, unsmiling, noiseless, only rocking to comfort themselves in their deep isolation. These infants, well-cared for in physical terms, had no personal relationships or stimulus through play. Their contact with their natural mothers had been so shortlived that, having received so little, neither could they give. They had had no opportunity to learn the beginnings of social behaviour.

MOVING ON TO THE NEXT STAGE

Babies differ greatly in the speed with which they attain independent movement, and by eight or nine months some will already be making first attempts at crawling and beginning to move about, while others are still at the rolling and squirming stage. Mobility opens the way to every kind of exploration, and it is at this stage that transferring things in and out of receptacles becomes an absorbing occupation. This interest appears early in some infants, and a good-sized tin placed beside a baby seated at the Treasure Basket will offer her the opportunity to take the first steps towards that kind of play, moving objects from the Basket to the tin and emptying them out again.

QUESTIONS AND ANSWERS ABOUT THE USE OF THE TREASURE BASKET

We have found that babies offered the chance to play with a well-stocked Basket are almost universally appreciative, provided they are given time and the support of an attentive adult to overcome initial feelings of strangeness. The same cannot be said of caregivers, and we have often been surprised at the vehemence of the hostility expressed, especially by young nursery staff and students. We can only speculate on the reasons for this, though the feeling that objects that cost so little (if anything) cannot have much value, is certainly a factor. Some questions and anxieties come up so often that they seemed worth dealing with here:

Q: *Why doesn't the adult take an active part and talk to the babies as they play, so as to encourage language development?*
A: Observation of babies at the Treasure Basket suggests that their minds are very actively engaged and that the pre-verbal noises which they make in the course of their play are a significant part of the process of language development. Talk by the adult at this time is merely distracting. The session at the Treasure Basket is only for a relatively short part of the day; close adult contact and conversation with the infant will take place continuously at other times, particularly during changing, washing and feeding.

Q: *What if the baby just sits and looks at the Basket? Shouldn't the adult do something to start her off?*
A: It is not necessary for the caregiver to take the initiative to 'encourage' the infants, because they are well able to initiate their own learning and exploration by and for themselves. It is important to allow them to go at their own pace and spend as long as they like getting used to the appearance of the basket before they start to handle and explore the objects. They also need freedom to make their own choices. Sometimes a baby will spend 40 minutes alternately sucking and waving a bottle brush, ignoring all the other items painstakingly assembled in the Basket. That is her decision.

Of course sometimes a baby will indicate clearly by her behaviour that she is not in the mood for this kind of play at the moment, and this, too, should be respected.

Q: *Surely some of this material is very unhygienic and could cause cross-infection?*
A: Like any other playthings, the material in the Treasure Basket requires regular care and maintenance. All the objects suggested in the list below are washable, wipeable or disposable. Some (for example, the apple) will need to be changed after each session. Anything that cannot be satisfactorily cleaned should be discarded. With proper care there is no reason why Treasure Basket items should carry greater risk of infection than conventional toys.

We need also to remember that the group care of infants in itself must present increased risk of cross-infection. Bored babies without stimulating play material are unhappy and grizzly. There is evidence that when adults are in the equivalent state, that is depressed and dissatisfied, their level of immunity to infection is lowered (The *Lancet*, 20 July 1985). The same is true of babies.

Q: *Aren't some of these objects dangerous – they could be thrown, or swallowed or used to poke another baby's eyes?*
A: Items for the Treasure Basket must always be very carefully selected with safety in mind. Obviously objects with sharp edges or points or small enough to be swallowed are to be excluded. The main protective factor is the limited capacities of babies of this age. They can wave an object or pick it up and drop it but they cannot throw or poke. Parents may need reassurance about this.

The great variety of potential items for a Treasure Basket (the list given in this book contains ninety-three, and certainly does not exhaust the possibilities) means that there is no need for anybody to include an object which causes them anxiety about its safety – if in doubt, throw it out! But it is worth saying that on the whole people tend to be over-cautious. If you think an item might be swallowed, put it in your mouth and see if you could swallow it yourself. You will probably find it quite impossible.

As we have already mentioned, the situation is different when older children are present, and the items for each session need to be selected with this in mind. Babies seated at the Basket must always be supervised and not crowded up together. If too close, one baby might tap another with an object which has a handle, but they would not have the co-ordination to poke. Observation of trios of babies shows that they are very circumspect in the way they use an object with a handle, manipulating it with skill and judgement.

Q: *Isn't it likely that a baby faced with such a pile of objects might feel confused?*
A: The babies show us quite clearly that they know how to select and discard, often returning to a favoured item in the course of play.

Q: *Doesn't it take a lot more trouble to collect all these items than to buy toys from catalogues or shops that are specially designed for babies by experts?*
A: Bought toys have their uses but good quality ones are extremely expensive, difficult for parents to obtain outside large cities, and because babies develop so rapidly are likely to be used only for a short period. Some people find it much easier than others to collect items for the Treasure Basket. It seems to depend upon developing one's 'imaginative eye' for what will interest and stimulate the senses. Once

that happens people involved in the care of young babies can become very excited by the search. It is a good way of engaging parents – fathers as much as mothers – in the educational work of a child care centre.

Q: *Why are you so insistent on excluding plastic objects from the Basket? Isn't plastic an inescapable fact of modern life?*
A: That is an important part of the reason. If we look at the playthings that are commonly provided for young children, both in their own homes and group care settings, they are almost entirely made of plastic or synthetic materials. We have to ask what quality of sensory experience these objects can offer, remembering that at this age touch and exploration by mouth are as important as sight.

An exercise which we have used with parents and nursery workers illustrates this point. The participants, seated in a close circle on chairs or on the floor, are asked to close their eyes. We then distribute a number of plastic toys which each person is invited to explore for a moment and then pass on to their neighbour, so that everybody has a chance to handle each object. We ask them, with their eyes still shut, to share their impressions, which are usually sparse and hesitant: 'smooth', 'knobbly', 'hard', 'doesn't smell very nice'. Some people can't think of anything to say.

The exercise is then repeated with objects from the Treasure Basket. The passing of objects from one person to another does not proceed so smoothly; they are reluctant to give them up, wanting to rub them over their faces, tap, shake, sniff, even lick them. At the end the words pour out, with animated discussion of the different objects and guessing at what they could be. Finally the objects are set in two heaps on the floor and the participants told to open their eyes. Following this experience they have no difficulty in recognizing the *sameness* of plastic toys from a baby's point of view as opposed to natural materials which can offer such an enormous variety of sensations through the mouth, ears, nose, skin and muscles as well as the eyes.

GUIDELINES FOR THE USE OF THE TREASURE BASKET

1 The Basket should be not less than 14in. (351mm.) in diameter and 4–5in. (101–125mm.) high. It is essential that it is flat bottomed, with no handle and strong enough for the infant to lean on it without tipping up. It should have straight sides and be made of some natural material, *not* plastic.

2 Fill the basket to the brim with objects to allow the baby plenty of scope to sort through and to select what appeals to her.
3 See that the baby is seated comfortably (with a supporting cushion if necessary). If placed sideways, see that the rim of the basket is near enough for an elbow to rest upon it.
4 The adult should sit nearby, not talking or intervening unless the infant clearly needs attention.
5 The Treasure Basket should be continually changing and evolving with the introduction of new objects. One way of introducing variety is to have a number of Baskets stocked with different items.
6 The objects in the basket need care and maintenance – regular washing or wiping and elimination or replacement of damaged items.
7 If there are older children around, create a 'safe space' in a corner of the room with a piece of carpet for the babies seated round the Basket. The adult should protect the infants from intervention by mobile children.

SUMMARY

Babies who can sit independently but not yet move need a wide variety of different objects to engage their interest and stimulate their developing senses and understanding. The Treasure Basket is a practical way to assemble collections of such objects and make them available to sitting infants. Two key points are emphasized: (1) the objects should be made of natural materials, not plastic; (2) the adult's role is to provide security by her attentive, but not active, presence.

SUGGESTED ITEMS FOR THE TREASURE BASKET

None of these objects is plastic, none is a 'bought toy', and most are in common everyday use by adults. The purpose of this collection is to offer maximum interest through:

- Touch: texture, shape, weight
- Smell: variety of scents
- Taste: more limited scope, but possible
- Sound: ringing, tinkling, banging, scrunching
- Sight: colour, form, length, shininess

Natural objects
    Fir cones, differing sizes
    Large pebbles

Shells
Dried gourds
Large chestnuts
Big feathers
Pumice stone
Corks, large sizes
Avocado pear stones
Walnuts – large
Piece of loofah
Small natural sponge
A lemon
An apple

Objects of natural materials
Woollen ball
Little baskets
Bone ring
Bone shoe horn
Small raffia mat
Wooden nail brush
Toothbrush
Shaving brush
Small shoe brush
House painting brush
Cane bag handles
Cosmetic brush

Wooden objects
Small boxes, velvet-lined
Small drum on wooden frame
Rattles – various types
Bamboo whistle
Castanets
Clothes peg – two types
Coloured beads on string
Cubes – short lengths of wood
Cylinders: bobbin, cottonreel
Curtain ring
Napkin ring
Spoon or spatula
Egg cup
Small turned bowl

Metal objects
  Spoons – various sizes
  Small egg whisk
  Bunch of keys
  Small tins – edges smoothed
  Small ash tray
  Toy trumpet
  Pattipans
  Lemon squeezer
  Typewriter spool
  Small funnel
  Brass curtain rings
  Small harmonica
  Garlic squeezer
  Scout whistle
  Bottle brush
  Small metal frame mirror
  Bulldog paper clip
  Keyrings linked together
  Bunch of bells
  Triangle
  Metal egg cup
  Closed tins containing rice, beans, gravel, etc.
  Tea strainer
  Tin lids – all types
  Metal beaker
  Lengths of chain of differing types
  Bicycle bell
  Large scent-bottle top
  Tea infuser
  Costume jewellery

Objects in leather, textile, rubber, fur
  Puppy 'bone'
  Puppy ring
  Leather purse
  Small leather bag with zip
  Coloured marble 'eggs'
  High bouncer ball
  Velvet powder puff
  Fur ball
  Length of rubber tubing

Small rag doll
Tennis ball
Golf ball
Leather spectacle case
Bead-embroidered purse
Bath plug with chain
Small teddy bear
Bean bag
Small cloth bags containing lavender, rosemary, thyme, cloves

Paper, cardboard

Little notebook with spiral rings
Greaseproof paper
Tinfoil
Small cardboard boxes
Insides of kitchen-paper rolls

7 The second year of life

I've forgotten the word I wanted to say and my thought, unexpressed, returns to the world of shadows.

O. Mandelstam

Studies of day nurseries and child minders suggest that children between one and two get the least planned attention and are considered to be the most difficult age group by caregivers. In mixed-age family groups they are often seen as disruptive, having lost interest in baby toys but still too young to be involved in the more structured activities provided for older children. As they develop the capacity to move around rapidly, they have to be watched all the time. This second year is one of extraordinarily rapid growth and development, but unless careful thought is given to how their particular needs can be provided for, the experience for children, especially in group care, can easily be negative and limiting.

INDEPENDENCE AND NEGOTIATION

A child in his second year wants above all to practise his new-found skills of mobility, manipulation and speech. This may often be most inconvenient for adults. Consider, for example, what is involved for both adult and child when we take a toddler for a walk. To him, the immediate experience is that of moving under his own steam and responding to the myriad exciting things, such as the row of empty milk bottles outside the door, which he encounters. We, on the other hand, may have our own objective, which is to get to the Post Office before it closes. He sees a little low wall by the path on to which he clamours to be lifted so that, with our supporting hand, he can practise walking and balancing. This we know will cause a delay which we definitely do not want.

Faced with this situation there are a number of choices open to us. If we remember early enough the attraction of the wall, we can avoid his demand by taking another route. Alternatively, we use our superior physical strength to pick him up and carry him, protesting, past the wall, ignoring his screams.

A third option is to say, 'Just once because I'm in a hurry', promising a longer exploration on the way back. Of course 'on the way back' means nothing to him at that moment, but at least we have tried to find an honest compromise, to model an attempt to reconcile divergent interests.

What makes dealing with an energetic toddler so demanding of our patience is that little incidents of this kind are happening all the time. The adult has a choice: whether to enforce her own wishes or to negotiate a solution which also takes into account the child's perspective.

A young child's time scale is quite different from ours. As adults we have learned to switch quickly from one situation to another and we develop an ability to do this, however unwillingly. Children cannot 'change gear' in this way and we must concede them time to adjust and to grasp what it is we want them to do. Many an upset and tantrum can be avoided if we remember this. Every tiny interchange where adult and child interests differ has significance in creating for the child a confidence in our respect for him and our understanding of his world. In moments such as these we might remind ourselves that the peoples of the world are also seriously engaged (not yet very successfully) with just this problem of how to resolve their conflicting interests. The urgent need for doing so may give our efforts with young children a wider significance than we may have thought hitherto.

This attitude certainly does not mean letting a child do just what he wants, for that can create anxieties and confusion for a child just as much as excessive prohibition and control. It is aiming at a viable balance that takes so much of our energy.

When a child is able to get about on his own and evidently enjoys his new-found power to separate at will from his adult, parents sometimes find it puzzling that at the very moment of moving away, their child also becomes more demanding of their closeness, even to the extent of 'clinging'. We have to remember that independence, though exciting and desired, can also be rather frightening. We need a secure base in order to have the confidence to venture out from it. Erik Erikson, in his classic book *Childhood and Society* (1955), identifies acquiring 'basic trust' as the first developmental task, which gives the child freedom to explore and learn. As adults we hope to find this security within ourselves; children need to experience it from their relationships with close adults so that gradually they make their own the kind of confidence which can enable them to tolerate doubt or stress and to take risks.

There is an interesting similarity here with adolescents who, while they may test, sometimes aggressively, the limits of their parents' tolerance, still desperately need the secure base that the family provides and suffer if they do not have it (Parker *et al.*, 1991; Stein, 1992).

DEVELOPMENTAL LINES

In the second year of life there are so many notable changes and so many new demands that we make upon a child, that it is useful to set them out, to remind ourselves how much is achieved during the period between 10 and 20 months. We have become used to the idea of seeing early development in terms of 'ages and stages' which can be a rather static and fragmentary way of looking at the many facets of a young child's life.

Anna Freud (1965) formulated an approach to assessing child development which she called 'developmental lines'. This approach allows us to think how different aspects of development flow together to make up the total of the child's personality at any one moment. In the first two years he is moving from almost total dependence to a relative independence in broadly four ways: through movement and manipulative skill, in self-feeding, in early pre-verbal language developing into speech, and in bodily care leading to bowel and bladder control. The pace at which a child moves forward along these lines has clear connections with how his close adults see his progress and the quality of his relation to them.

MOVEMENT AND MANIPULATIVE SKILL

Once crawling has been established, at last an infant can attempt his objective of reaching the door through which his close adult has momentarily disappeared (see Figure 7.1). He can move into the excitement of the descending stairs or open door leading to the garden. A quite new sense of 'I can do it for myself' can grow, but as yet with no sense of danger or of caution, and that is what makes this period so exhausting for the caring adult.

Figure 7.1 Movement and manipulative skill.
Photo: Dominic Abrams

In the nursery these dangers are, of course, avoided, but unfortunately sometimes at the cost of creating an environment which is lacking in variety or which has little to excite the child's capacity for curiosity. We make suggestions in Chapter 2 about equipment and group room arrangement for this age, and in Chapter 11 about how the outdoor learning area can be made both safe and stimulating.

Play material to satisfy these children's ceaseless interest in handling and experimenting with any objects close at hand, is described in the next chapter.

FEEDING

During his second year, the child moves from almost complete dependence on adults towards the ability to feed himself. The adult's anxiety for the infant to accept new tastes and textures may create tensions and refusal if the child's tempo is not fully sensed.

In this second year when autonomy is being gained in so many ways, a growing child's natural hunger is the spur to appetite. He needs to satisfy this urge to eat as directly and enjoyably as possible. We give great importance to eating and drinking as a creative part, from earliest days, of a child's feeling about himself. This is closely linked to the person who accompanies him through this experience, which is why, particularly for these very young children, the key person system has a special significance in relation to mealtimes.

The emphasis in our culture on children learning to use a spoon as early as possible can be a cause of stress. When young children are allowed to be active in feeding themselves with their fingers, this has two advantages: (1) they are not obliged to wait entirely on the adult's help and control; and (2) handling food directly provides varied tactile experiences. When spoon-feeding is going on, the child, as suggested in Chapter 5, can be given his own spoon to 'help' in the process, even if not much food finds its way into his mouth at first.

Nursery workers should be aware that in some minority ethnic cultures it is normal for both children and adults to eat with their hands. It is obviously important not to imply that this is 'wrong' (as in a distressing incident recounted by Iram Siraj-Blatchford (1992)). In this case teaching the child to use implements in the nursery requires sensitivity on the part of the key person and discussion with parents. It needs to happen in a natural, unforced way and not be rushed.

One further important point for this age group is the need to ensure that children as yet without language can let the adult know that they are thirsty. There should be a jug of water and mugs at some place in the room where they can see and point to it – otherwise the child is powerless to alter the discomfort of thirst which he may feel in his endlessly active play.

COMMUNICATION AND LANGUAGE

The precise way in which language develops is still a matter of considerable controversy among psycholinguists, but it seems clear that there is a very strong predisposition to develop speech. Most children, except those who are profoundly deaf, eventually do so, even in adverse circumstances. In normal conditions it is during their second year that children make the great leap from babbling, which may contain one or two recognizable words, to a vocabulary of up to three hundred words (Bee, 1985). Early vocabulary growth is very slow, but once past ten or so words, the child begins to add a new one every few days. By the end of the second year many children are putting together three- or four- word sentences and grammatical forms are beginning to appear.

The rate at which children learn to talk, as with other developmental lines, varies widely, although it tends to follow a consistent sequence. Gordon Wells, who carried out one of the most detailed longitudinal studies of young children's speech ever undertaken, concluded that the most important factor was the extent to which close adults *communicated* with the child. Children who learned to speak early were those whose parents listened to them and responded to the meaning expressed by the sounds the child made. Parents who tried too hard to teach the child new words or corrected pronunciation or grammar were more likely to inhibit speech than encourage it (Wells, 1985).

Talking and listening to children

Speech development is one of the few areas where there remains a question mark over the effects of day care in the earliest years. Some studies have found that children attending nurseries full time are slower to develop language.

One of the drawbacks of a well-run nursery can be that a child in his second year who has not yet acquired speech can pass through the nursery day without much need to talk, and so lose out on the essential practising which a mastery of language demands. We need to be vigilant about how much *listening* we do. This is particularly urgent in working with children at this stage in their development. Unless we keep a steady awareness of a young child's need to practise speech, there is a risk that his capacity to think and reason may also be held back.

Background noise

There are some children who when they talk can only shout, as they have not yet learned to modulate their voices. This can cause the surrounding adults to raise their voices too, adding to the clamour. In some nurseries young children have to struggle to make themselves heard and understood above the noise of pop music on the radio, sometimes justified on the grounds that this is what the children hear at home. We think this is a good reason for not providing it in the nursery. It certainly inhibits conversation, even between adults who are fully in command of language.

We can probably all remember occasions in a noisy café or pub when we shake our heads in exasperation and exclaim 'There's such a racket I can't hear a word you're saying', and we give up trying to carry on a reasonable conversation. Even more so, children who are unsure of their own speech will tend to retire into silence, feeling that they just cannot compete.

In addition to being very important for the development of children's language, keeping the noise level down helps to create a calm, unflustered atmosphere. No calling across the room needs to be one of the ground rules of nursery life, applying to children, staff and parents alike.

Just as gaining the ability to move independently is a great personal liberation, so also for a young child having words to make himself understood is a vital part of dealing positively with the many frustrating experiences which he must face in growing up. We often say 'I was speechless with anger' when we find ourselves unable to collect our thoughts into coherent words when something enrages us. At such a moment we are experiencing a state which is very near to that of the child who has just had his treasured toy snatched from him. A child in his second year has a huge task not only to understand all that we say, but to summon appropriate words from his limited vocabulary to make us understand what he is feeling.

Words and objects

One important aspect of language development is the attachment of words to objects, acquiring a vocabulary. This is something we find very difficult when learning a foreign language at school or in an evening class, but it becomes much easier if we spend time abroad and have, for example, to go shopping and ask the name of the object we are seeing and handling. In the same way the child's innate drive to learn about the nature and behaviour of objects around him is a key element in his acquisition of language.

As he gains in mobility he has the opportunity to handle and manipulate an increasing variety of objects. Observation of children during heuristic play sessions (see Chapter 8) shows clearly how direct sensory experience enables them to gain precise knowledge of objects.

A child will, for example, choose a length of chain, put it into a tin, slide it out again, and repeat the action over and over again with undiminished concentration and enjoyment. The self-directed action, with the feelings and bodily sensations that go along with it, mean that the words 'tin' and 'chain' eventually become embued with the meaning that this experience brings to it. First, the child needs to have direct contact with objects during his play, and only then will the word attached to the object become meaningful. This process enables him to build his rapidly increasing vocabulary into the tool of language in the context of his general learning and relationships.

Music and rhyme

Children react to music from a very early age, in fact the famous Japanese violin teacher, Shinichi Suzuki, advocates playing Bach and Vivaldi to them when they are still in the womb. Babies in their first year respond to music by chuckling and crowing and by musical babbling, which is quite distinct from speech babbling. Moog (1976), researching children's musical preferences, found that when they are very small they seem to like simple instrumental music best, but by the second year most children prefer songs with words.

At this age what children enjoy most is hearing familiar nursery rhymes or songs sung over and over again. They can often be heard attempting to join in, and they love to fill in a missing word. Although they like repetition it is good to introduce them to new rhymes and verses from time to time. One tends to hear only a very restricted range of nursery rhymes in day nurseries, mostly the ones reprinted in mass-produced illustrated books. There are many hundreds of other songs, rhymes and finger-plays traditionally sung to young children (see, for example, Iona and Peter Opie's *Oxford Nursery Rhyme Book*). Nurseries could play a part in reviving some of these and teaching them to parents.

Nursery workers do not need 'good' voices to give children pleasure by singing to them. If tapes are used, these need to be selected very carefully, preferably with advice from the county music adviser or a local musician. Many commercial recordings designed for children are of poor quality, with inappropriate accompaniments. They also tend to use unsuitable adult voices.

Really it is far better to show children that singing can be spontaneous and informal. Children love made-up songs about themselves and the things that they do every day. This is something the key person can do regularly in her small group, or while giving bodily care to a child, either using a formula ('David wears a blue shirt'; 'This is the way we – wash our hands') or completely freely.

In the group she can also help children to listen to different small, quiet sounds, building on the experience of sound they will already have had with some items of the Treasure Basket and in heuristic play. If she can play a guitar or recorder they will enjoy short pieces and, carefully supervised, pluck the strings or blow the recorder themselves to see how the sound is made.

Some children in their second year will sit and listen intently to a piece of music for quite a long time, and often want to hear it over and over again. Others have an attention span of only a few seconds, but may still enjoy moving and 'dancing' to music, though usually without much reference to the rhythm. If there is a staff member with a special interest in music, she might start building a collection on tape of different pieces for nursery use. There is an enormous variety of recorded music to choose from, including the whole range of non-western music as well as European medieval, renaissance, classical and contemporary music.

Books and stories

Children love to hear stories long before they can grasp their full meaning. By the age of two they will gaze at books for quite long periods. Until they grasp the idea of turning pages without tearing the paper, they will need indestructible books, board, not rag, or specially made for them as explained below.

During this year children are making the leap from identifying a common object, say an orange, to pointing to the picture of an orange and learning from the adult what it is called. This making of connections between the tangible reality and the abstraction of a colour photograph is a complex cognitive process. To be of use, the illustrations of picture books must be quite realistic, not falsified in colour or in shape.

To make indestructible picture books

Take an album with a strong cover and plastic envelopes (a representative's display book is ideal). Cut pieces of stiff paper in different colours to the size of the envelope and mount on them pictures of identifiable objects within the child's daily surroundings – fruit, flowers, domestic animals, mugs, plates. The pictures can be cut from catalogues or magazines, carefully relating the predominant colour of the picture to the mount. Two sheets, back to back, go in each plastic envelope and the pictures can easily be changed or grouped in categories for older children. Children will continue to enjoy these books right through their third year, and with reasonable care the albums will last for many years.

Harry, aged 16 months, was observed turning the pages of one such book and looking intently at a colour photograph of a plate of chocolate-covered biscuits. After looking for a moment he bent down his head and licked the page. He said one word – 'bikit'.

There is a tendency to put the subject of language development in a separate box, which seems to suggest that it can go on independently from all the other things which happen in a child's life. This misses the essential point that language is a tool of relationship. When we get on well with somebody the conversation flows, while with other people we can think of nothing to say. Young children are no different from us in this. If we try to speak to someone who is looking over our shoulder all the time, obviously only half listening, we become very cross and frustrated. Giving full attention to a child as he tries haltingly to express himself can be difficult for a nursery worker amidst the distractions and demands of a group, but is essential if we aim to help a child gain command of language.

BODILY CARE

For a child in his second year quite large parts of the day will still be taken up with caring for his physical needs. Too often this is regarded as a matter of routine, to be casually shared among whichever nursery workers are available. It can lead to the kind of insensitive, depersonalized treatment of children described by Trudy Marshall in the study referred to earlier (1982).

Physical tending may in fact offer some of the best opportunities during the busy day for one-to-one communication and spontaneous play between the child and adult. It is especially important for language development that as far as possible it should be his key person who provides bodily care for the child so that she can learn to respond to his signals and preferences in the way that sensitive parents do. All staff need to understand the reason for this policy if it is to be made to work.

Bowel and bladder control

There was a time when it was thought that the proper way for babies to learn bowel and bladder control was to hold them out on a potty from a few weeks old. A great deal of time and anxious energy was spent on this ritual, and many mothers felt proud and gratified that their baby was 'clean' by 6 months. Indeed, temporary success might be achieved but tended to break down later on to everyone's dismay. The consequent feelings of distress, and indeed anger, on the part of parents at this failure of early toilet training was clearly seen in referrals to Child Guidance Clinics.

Until more recent times this kind of practice was pursued energetically in nurseries, and children, as soon as they could sit up, were put on potties in the bathroom and kept there, sometimes for quite long periods until they had 'done something'. When left in this way, they would sometimes relieve their bored puzzlement by initiating a game of humping their potties about on the floor, to the entertainment of each other and the exasperation of the staff.

Our present view is based on a better understanding of the development of the nervous system, the growth of a child's ability to control and release his muscles, and of the way our bodily functions are connected with our emotional states. (The change in attitudes may also have something to do with the invention and mass production of the disposable nappy!)

In approaching toilet training, probably towards the end of the second year of life, the significant factor is the relationship which a child has with the person who asks him to co-operate. Otherwise why should he change his previous satisfactory experience of passing a motion when he wanted in his nappy? He responds on trust, though it may seem most perplexing when the adult, seeing the faeces he has produced for her in his potty, says 'good boy' but promptly flushes it away as something to be disposed of as soon as possible.

When toilet training is started at home, it is most important that family practice and nursery approach are fully harmonized. If this is not done, then the child, already having to gain mastery of a complex process, will be placed in a state of confusion. The key person has the responsibility of seeing, through her contact with the parents, that no strain is created for the child. This underlines further the importance of the key person being responsible for her small group in the bathroom before the midday meal.

Independence in the transition period

While a child is learning to ask for and to use his potty, there will still be times of the day when he will be wearing a nappy, for example, when preparing for a sleep. Often his nursery worker needs to have him on the changing table, especially when he needs washing and drying before a clean nappy is put on. Children, asserting their legitimate independence, may try the adult's patience by opposing this.

A positive way to deal with this daily occurrence, as suggested earlier, is to provide a pair of small, steady household steps and encourage the child, with help, to climb up on to the level of the changing table by himself. Thus, both conflict and back strain are avoided. We show the child that we respect his responsibility for his own body and that we do not intend to force him to submit to our superior physical power.

There are times when a child will refuse to sit on his pot and the adult can experience this as an act of hostility. However, when it comes to a matter over which a child has his own bodily control, there is no way that the adult can 'win' and it is wise to accept this gracefully. A child who persistently refuses the pot may be responding to over-severe toilet training at home, and if the problem persists it calls for discussion with the parents.

On reflection we can see connections with the attitudes we want children to develop towards their own bodies if they should in later years need to defend themselves against risks of sexual abuse from known adults.

Washing and grooming

Washing faces, drying hands and first attempts at brushing teeth, all form part of that basic bodily care which adds up to feeling good about oneself. As adults, we hardly need to remind ourselves how different we feel after a tiring day when we can have a bath or shower. The unmistakeable pleasure on a child's face during an unhurried bathroom time as his key person gently combs or brushes his hair, helps him to wash, and tells him how nice he looks underlines the value of this detailed care.

A key worker can do this for her small group in a way that is impossible for a large number of children in an 'assembly line' atmosphere. We know ourselves how we resent and feel demeaned by the cry of 'next please' if we find ourselves waiting our turn in a hospital outpatient department. Recalling our own experiences of depersonalized handling in matters of bodily care can give us greater sensitivity in how we conduct bathroom time for young children. Our body image is something precious and entirely personal to each one of us and our attitude towards ourselves is deeply bound up with our early experiences at the hands of adults.

Attitudes towards cleanliness

Just as the predominant view of toilet training has shifted, so have ideas about the age at which it is reasonable to offer children 'messy' materials. It is important to understand the thinking which lies behind this shift in practice. In the process of toilet training we ask the child to relinquish his pleasure in handling his own bodily product but provide him with alternatives. The energy which goes into one immediate and primitive interest transfers into creative activity with materials such as clay, water, dough, sand and finger paint.

A child who has experienced severe toilet training or comes from a home where great emphasis is laid on keeping hands and clothes clean at all times, may show doubt or anxiety about playing with materials which might be considered dirty or messy. This feeling must be totally respected, but it is the responsibility of his key person to discuss the matter with his parents and to gain for him their support and agreement that (with proper supervision and protective clothing) he may play with these things.

In later life there are people who find it most distasteful, if not impossible, to carry out a task such as gutting a fish, planting seedlings in mud, cleaning out a rabbit hutch, or working with clay or papier-mâché. Maybe this strong aversion has its roots in a too severe denial in early life that such things can be, not only legitimate but, in their way, pleasurable and creative.

Wiping noses

A detail of bodily care, rarely mentioned but well worth considering, is how we deal with the endless task of cleaning children's noses when they cannot yet do this for themselves. Particularly in areas where many families live in damp and inadequately heated houses or flats, some children suffer from almost continuous nasal catarrh in winter, which may cause them considerable discomfort in breathing and can also affect their hearing. One of the drawbacks of grouping young children together is the high incidence of cross-infection from respiratory problems and we should make every effort to reduce this.

We can probably recall, in childhood, having our noses wiped roughly by adults, who often did not pause to notice that the delicate skin around the nostrils was sore. In the nursery, where the problem is multiplied by numbers, the gentleness and respect needed for this aspect of care can all too easily be overlooked. Of all the forms of bodily care that we offer to a young child, it is probably the most difficult to do sensitively and the one some nursery workers positively dislike.

One step towards self-care is for children to learn how to blow their own noses. This is quite a complex skill to master because it means that a young child has to get the idea of snorting, which is the opposite of sniffing, and then to grasp the connection between the handkerchief or tissue and the control of the small muscles of his nose so that he can respond to our telling him to 'blow'. He will need to see us actually doing this ourselves to understand and then put into practice the process involved. It is the child's key person who needs to find the time to help him to learn this skill.

A second practical measure is to give some thought to the disposal of used tissues. When we are, for instance, sitting in a corner with a small group engrossed in some activity or at mealtimes settled round a table, generally there is a box of tissues on a shelf nearby. But what happens to the dirty tissues? One possibility is to ask the child whose nose you have wiped to go and put the tissue in the bin, or you may get up yourself to make less disturbance to the group. More often we have observed the worker put the dirty tissue in her pocket or stuff it into the inside of the roll of soft toilet paper which is commonly used for reasons of economy.

There are two separate points to make here. First, we should note that there is a body of opinion, partly but not exclusively associated with psychoanalytic theory, which holds that using toilet paper to wipe noses creates a confusion in the mind of a young child who is at the stage of developing understanding of different bodily processes. Toilet paper should be kept in bathrooms and used for wiping bottoms, not noses. The other point has to do with reducing the risk of cross-infection. The principle of avoiding disturbance to the group which would be caused by constantly getting up and down to dispose of soiled tissues is obviously a good one, but not by putting them in a pocket, where body warmth will favour the multiplication of bacilli. We suggest a practical solution to this problem.

Take two fairly large tins (e.g. the kind peeled tomatoes come in). Make sure there are no rough edges and wash and dry them thoroughly. Fix them together with a clothes peg. In one tin put the clean tissues and line the other with a small plastic bag. The soiled tissues are put into the second tin, from which the plastic bag, when full, can easily be removed intact and thrown away. This tin will not even need washing out as there has been no contact with the soiled tissues. Each room should have a sufficient number, say five or six, of these portable bins set about on window sills or shelves, under the table at mealtimes, or beside the adult if she is seated with a group for storytelling. The bin can easily be carried into the garden during outdoor activities.

The key person with her small group can initiate a little game of learning how to snort and explain exactly to the children what the tins are for. They will have no difficulty at all in understanding what she is proposing. Wiping noses thus can become, instead of a tedious repetition, a truly educational exercise in self-care.

PLAYTHINGS FOR CHILDREN IN THEIR SECOND YEAR

The second year spans a period of very rapid development. At the beginning of the year the mobile infant will still find satisfaction in exploration of textures and shapes by mouth and hand and in the simple toys described in Chapter 5. By the age of two some children will already be engaging in most of the kinds of play described in Chapter 2 and beginning to use more structured materials. Here follow some suggestions for play equipment for children in their second year designed to help them practise both physical and manipulative skills.

1 *Slide*
  A simple solid wooden structure with three low steps leading to a small platform with a slide on the other side. Low rail supports both sides.
2 *Playbox*
  A solid, 2ft square box with a large round hole in one side for crawling in and out of. A curtain can be fixed to cover the hole, allowing 'hiding and finding' games.
3 *Stacking boxes*
  A strong, wooden box with two smaller boxes inside. The measurements of the largest box should be 11 × 17 × 11in. (280 × 430 × 280mm.) – not too high for a child to climb in by himself. The smallest box can be filled with wooden building blocks. This is

probably the most versatile piece of play equipment of all and will certainly be used well into the third year. It is worth having two or three sets if at all possible.

The uses of these boxes include: getting in, sitting in, getting out, being pushed, using for support in first steps (which means that the boxes must be heavy enough not to tip up when leant on by the child). A cord can be fixed on the largest box to allow an adult to pull it along to give the child a ride.

Put end to end, the boxes make a train and turned sideways can be a 'hidey hole'. Turned upside down they can be sat on, climbed on and (with adult help) jumped off. Set in a row they can be stepping stones for practising balance and tiny experiments in risk taking.

The boxes should be fitted with small felt pads underneath each corner so that they can be pushed along, but no wheels, as the box can be difficult for the child to control in a group.

4 *Hollow bricks*

These are best made of plywood in two sizes, 7 × 4 × 3in. (177 × 102 × 76mm.) and 9 × 7 × 3in. (228 × 177 × 76mm.), and can be varnished or painted with non-toxic paint. As they are relatively light the child can build a tower which will do no harm if it falls.

5 *Baby walker*

This should be of the trolley type, described in Chapter 5: a low wooden box with a metal handle at shoulder height for easy pushing. It must be sturdily built so that it will not tip up when a child leans on the handle and the wheels should be slow-moving to avoid children bumping into each other. More than one is needed when there are several children in the group just taking first steps.

6 *Large, simple posting box*

Shop-bought posting-boxes, often made of light plastic in garish colours, are too complex for very young children to use satisfactorily. It is worth having a well-designed one made in polished wood. Measurements should be 7 × 7 × 11in. (177 × 177 × 280mm.), with only three apertures in the top side: a round hole, a square hole and a slot. There can also be a round hole, 4in. (102mm.) in diameter, in the lower part of one side of the box. Wooden cubes, cylinders and rectangles, at least six of each, are needed for posting, and these should be kept in their own basket or tin so that the children can always find a ready supply when they want to use the posting box. As we observe in the conduct of a heuristic play session, even young children quickly learn and enjoy this kind of order. Of course they will experiment with trying to post other shapes as well and should be allowed to find out for themselves what will and won't go through the holes.

SUMMARY

During the second year of life the child's growth proceeds along a number of developmental lines. He moves towards independence in mobility, manipulative skill, feeding and bodily care, and acquires the ability to communicate in words. The key person plays a crucial role in enabling this process to occur smoothly, in close consultation with the child's family. Careful management of the environment can reduce conflict and enable workers to offer a model of compromise and negotiation which demonstrates respect for the child's individuality.

This period sees the transition from bodily care carried out by others, which is such an important part of a baby's daily experience, to self-care, which is beginning to become possible in the second year. It is a time of rapid growth towards independence in every aspect of life, yet the child's physical ability to move away from his caring adults at the same time holds for him the duality of his need for them. He experiences a change in his relationships as more of his own life comes under his control. The growing sense of self finds clear expression when the words 'me' and 'mine' emerge into daily use. Along with this goes an intense urge to explore and experiment with any object that comes to hand.

8 Heuristic play with objects

> There can be no effective and satisfactory work without play; there
> can be no sound and wholesome thought without play.
>
> Charles Dickens, 1854

In this chapter we describe a new approach to the learning of children
in their second year of life which has been developed and put into
practice by Elinor Goldschmied in collaboration with child care
workers in England, Scotland, Italy and Spain. This approach is not
just part of a generally rich environment that we would want to
provide for children of this age group, but a special component of the
day's activities which needs to be organized in a particular way for
maximum effectiveness. For this reason it is called here by an
unfamiliar term, 'heuristic play with objects'. Put simply, it consists of
offering a group of children, for a defined period of time in a
controlled environment, a large number of different kinds of objects
and receptacles with which they play freely without adult intervention.
We consider first the underlying principles, then practical arrangements and end the chapter with a list of suggestions for objects and
materials.

LEARNING BY EXPLORATION AND DISCOVERY

Heuristic learning is defined in the *Oxford Dictionary* as 'a system of
education under which the pupil is trained to find out things for
himself'. It has been a dominant strand in English primary education
for many years (though at the time of writing under political attack).
Up till now not much thought has been given to how the principle
might be extended into educational provision for very young children.
By using the specific term 'heuristic play' we want to draw attention to

the great importance of this kind of spontaneous exploratory activity, giving it the significance and dignity which it merits.

Increasing mobility is the central factor in the child's developing abilities in the second year of life. The newly acquired skill in moving is practised ceaselessly throughout the waking day, and it is often this passion for moving about which creates anxieties for the responsible adults and causes them to restrict the child and limit her opportunities for learning. If the family is in poor accommodation, the mobile child may spend much of her day strapped into a pushchair or confined to a playpen. Even when housing is good very few people are prepared to redesign their living space entirely to suit the needs of a small child. How many times a day do we have to say 'No, don't touch' when they want to grab and handle our most precious or dangerous (for them) objects. The urge to use their increasingly precise eye–hand–object co-ordination combined with lively curiosity becomes a source of conflict.

It is often said that the concentration we observe in infants seated at the Treasure Basket is lost once they can move about. Typically caregivers comment that children between one and two 'flit from one thing to another', that the play material available does not hold their attention for more than a few minutes. They are not interested in puzzles or putting pegs in their 'proper' holes, and would usually rather throw them on the floor. In fact the child is saying to us 'there are other things I want to do first'. Their level of competence cannot be satisfied by play material where there is a 'right' answer, determined by adults.

Children in their second year feel a great urge to explore and discover for themselves the way objects behave in space as they manipulate them. They need a wide variety of objects with which to do this kind of experimentation, objects which are constantly new and interesting, and which certainly cannot be bought from a toy catalogue.

Watching children of this age brings to mind the ancient story of Archimedes in his bath. When he discovered the law of the displacement of water due to the volume of his body, he is said to have leapt out of the bath crying exultantly 'Eureka – I have found it!' The Greek word 'eurisko' from which our word heuristic is derived means 'serves to discover or reach understanding of'. This is exactly what young children do of their own accord, without any direction from adults, provided they have the materials with which to pursue their explorations. Far from losing the ability to concentrate, it becomes clear that, given the right conditions and materials, the child in her second year can develop concentration in a new way.

HEURISTIC PLAY IN ACTION

Heuristic play is an approach and not a prescription. There is no one right way to do it and people in different settings will have their own ideas and collect their own materials. Indeed, one of the great merits of the approach is that it releases creativity in adults and makes the task of child care more stimulating. However, the practical advice in this chapter is based on many years' experience in different countries and on detailed observations of a large number of children, many of whom have been filmed on video and subjected to close analysis.

There follow some brief descriptions of children engaged in heuristic play in groups of about eight. The children are of four nationalities but there are no obvious differences in the way they use the material.

Susan (13 months), seated by a large tin. She picked up a length of fine chain, waved it about, watching the movement, held it until nearly still, put the chain with precise finger movements into the tin. Then she tipped over the tin and poured the chain out. She repeated the sequence of actions three times with complete concentration.

Antonio (14 months), crouched between two smallish buckets, one filled with bottle corks, the other empty. With quick, neat hand movements, he transferred the corks one by one into the empty bucket. Among the ordinary corks there were two champagne corks, larger and with a shiny covering, and a sauce bottle cork with a red plastic top. Finding a champagne cork, he looked at it intently, threw it aside, and continued transferring the ordinary corks. When he came across the second champagne cork and later the red-topped one, he discarded them without hesitation, showing his developing ability to discriminate and categorize. Once the second bucket was full he tipped it up, emptying out the corks on the floor.

Miguel (15 months), holding a small shallow tin, picked up a pingpong ball, placed it in the tin and made a circular swishing movement, observing intently how the ball twirled around. He increased the speed of the circular movement and the ball jumped out. He retrieved the ball and repeated the process.

Noel (16 months), standing holding a large red hair roller, picked up a smaller, yellow curler from the floor and slotted it through the red one. He repeated this action with evident pleasure, his eyes fixed on the objects in his hands. Then he looked about and chose another red roller of the same diameter as the one he was holding. He tried to pass the second red roller through the first. He paused and squeezed the two rollers together, trying to put one inside the other. Unable to do this, he dropped the second red roller and looked about, picked up a smaller, yellow roller and passed it through the original red one. He repeated this action three times, then, with a satisfied air, dropped both and moved elsewhere.

Jacqueline (17 months), seated with her legs together in front of her near a collection of ribbons of different colours and textures (satin, velvet, lace). She chose a length of red ribbon, laid it across her ankles, then took a length of fine chain and laid it parallel about two inches above the ribbon on her leg. She took a yellow ribbon and laid it parallel to the chain, repeating the process until the arrangement of alternating ribbon and chain reached to just above her knees. She looked intently at what she had done and smiled to herself.

Clemente (17 months), sitting on the floor with his legs apart, took a broad-based tin, turned it upside down, placing a slightly smaller tin, also upside down, on top of it. On this 'tower' he placed a yellow hair roller. Turning to look at another child nearby, he accidentally touched the lower tin and the roller fell off. Clemente picked up the roller and replaced it on the tower. He looked at it carefully and with his right hand gave a very gentle tap to the upper tin. The roller wobbled but did not fall off. He gave a slightly harder tap with the same result, then a harder one still, causing the roller to fall. He replaced the roller and repeated the process.

Janet (19 months) sat on the floor close to a nursery worker, holding a shallow box with a lid. She picked up four corks, one after the other, and placed them in a row to fill one part of the box. She took another cork and tried to made a second row below the first. There was no space to do this so she placed two corks sideways, leaving an unfilled space in the box. She looked about, took a short length of chain, held it up until it stopped its dangling movement, and let it gently down to fill the space. Then she closed the lid of the box and turned to the adult with a smile. The adult smiled back without comment.

Some important points are illustrated by these observations:

1 The children made their spontaneous selection from a wide range of materials (described below). They worked with purpose and concentration. Their physical energy and developing manipulative skill were an essential part of the satisfying and pleasurable activity. This led to constant practising and gaining in competence.

2 In the process of exploration of the material the question of right and wrong ways to use it does not arise. The children observe directly as they handle the object what it will and will not do.

Everything they undertake is successful; the only failure to carry out an intended action is when the nature of the material itself obstructs the child's efforts – as in the example of Noel who discovered that two hair rollers of the same diameter will not slot into one another.

3 This element of guaranteed success creates a very different experience for the child from much of the 'educational' play material often given to children of this age, which has a result predetermined by the design devised by an adult maker. This is not to say that materials of this kind have no value, but they have a different function, appropriate to a later stage of development than the one we are discussing here.

4 Children engrossed in their own discoveries do not come into conflict with others in the group, largely because there is so much material available that they are not required to do any sharing, which it is premature to expect at this age. This is in sharp contrast to the normal experience of nursery workers who have to intervene frequently in the course of the day to keep the peace amongst children too young to have language or negotiating skills.

Moreover it has been observed during heuristic play sessions that children, as they approach the age of two, begin to engage in co-operative exchanges with others which arise from the exploration of the material, initiated originally for themselves.

The descriptions of the children's activities given above illustrate how they will move items in and out of spaces, fill and empty receptacles. From the mass of objects available, they select, discriminate and compare, place in series, slot and pile, roll and balance, with concentration, growing manipulative skill and evident satisfaction.

Of course all this also occurs spontaneously in the process of play with anything that happens to be available, but usually in spite of adults and not because of them. These patterns emerge from children's naturally developing bodily activity provided that they are facilitated by the environment. What is different is the recognition that we should create space and time to cater for this type of play, acknowledging that children in their second year have specific educational needs just as much as 4-year-olds.

Apart from the obvious pleasure that children find in the materials, heuristic play may have a major role in developing the ability to concentrate. This is strongly associated with cognitive development and educational progress, as research by psychologists such as Jerome Bruner and Kathy Sylva has demonstrated (e.g. Bruner, 1980). Very young children engaged in heuristic play have been observed playing

Figure 8.1 Heuristic play with objects: exploration and experiment.

intensely with a group of objects for thirty minutes or more. Superficially this activity may appear to be random or pointlessly repetitive, which is probably why adults are often tempted to intervene. In fact close observation shows that the play has its own internal logic. The repetition is very like the activity of scientists who develop their knowledge by carrying out the same experiment over and over again with tiny variations. Sometimes great advances result from accidental observations, as in the case of Fleming's discovery of penicillin. The same is true for children. For them one thing leads to another in a pleasurable process of discovery, which in turn leads to practice and the growth of skill (see Figure 8.1).

INTRODUCING HEURISTIC PLAY IN A GROUP SETTING

It is important that staff understand the purpose and thinking behind this type of play, that it is intended to enrich and not to replace the work that they are already doing. In order for it to succeed the staff as a group need to be committed to the idea. This is much easier if they can see it in action, ideally by visiting a nursery where it is already happening, or failing that by watching heuristic play on video and meeting people who are using it in their work with young children.

Because time and space have to be created to make an effective heuristic play session possible, even those not directly involved may have to make concessions and adaptations. That makes it essential that anyone thinking of introducing heuristic play into their establishment should carry the whole staff group with them.

There are some basic organizational points which should be observed if there is to be maximum satisfaction for the children.

1 Play materials: at least fifteen varieties should be provided, with a separate draw-string bag for each kind. This may sound a lot, but there are so many possibilities: a child care centre in Barcelona where heuristic play has been in operation for some years has accumulated 36 different types of object. A row of hooks, labelled with the type of object, is needed to hang up the bags when not in use.

There must be plenty of items, 50 or 60 in each bag, and at least 20 receptacles for a group of eight children. Suggestions for materials to be provided are given later.

2 A clearly defined space is needed for the session, large enough to allow the children to move about freely. Carpet helps to reduce the noise level; quietness is an important feature of the session.

3 All other play material should be put away during the period chosen for this activity.

4 A limited period of the day should be selected and reserved for heuristic play with objects. A good length of time is one hour, allowing for getting materials out and putting them away. It is important to select a time when the maximum of staff are present so that one member of staff can devote her full attention to a small group (eight children at most). If a child should need changing during this period it is best done by another staff member.

5 To avoid the children crowding together, the whole of the space available should be used. To this end the adult preparing the session distributes around the room or play area tins of varying sizes. How many tins are needed depends on the number of children in the group, but there should never be less than three per child. We have found tins much better than baskets or boxes for this purpose. The worker then selects a number of bags of objects (say five) to make a good combination, for example, chains, cardboard tubes, pompoms, tin lids and curtain rings. These items are placed in separate or mixed heaps from which the children will make their own choice without needing direction or encouragement.

Children need time to consider how they will play with the material.

As we explain below, the role of the adult is to give unobtrusive attention, and the concentration which the children show makes talking superfluous.

6 As the children become absorbed in exploring, the objects will be spread over the floor. They need to be quietly reorganized from time to time so that the material always looks inviting.

7 The worker keeps the empty bags beside her chair until she decides it is time for the items to be collected up by the children at the end of the session. Sufficient time, say about fifteen minutes, should always be allowed for tidying up without rush so that this is as enjoyable as the activity of playing.

THE ROLE OF THE ADULT IN HEURISTIC PLAY WITH OBJECTS

Much of the adult's work is done outside the heuristic play session. She will be collecting objects, caring for them, ensuring that damaged ones are repaired and washed as necessary or thrown away, thinking up new types of interesting items. At the beginning of each session she selects and sets out the objects and receptacles as described above. During the session she will be doing some inconspicuous re-ordering, and finally she will initiate the collecting up of objects by the children, putting them away in the bags and hanging each bag back on its peg.

Beyond this she is essentially a facilitator. She remains quietly seated on a chair, attentive and observant, perhaps studying a particular child and noting down what he or she does with the material. The adult does not encourage or suggest, praise or direct what the children should do. The only exception to this is if a child begins to throw things about and disturb the others. In that case the best plan is to offer a receptacle and encourage her to place the things in it.

Involving children in clearing up

Another task for the adult is to keep an eye on the clock, to allow time for an unhurried end to the session. The children should collect the items from the floor, bring them to the adult and put them into the individual bags which she holds open for them. As each article is put in, the adult can check it to see that it is in good order, eliminating any which need replacing. In this way she shows that she cares for the playthings even if they consist of common household objects or scrap materials.

When the adult decides that it is time to start clearing up, it is a good

Figure 8.2 Heuristic play with objects: clearing up.

plan first to tidy away the receptacles. If one child is still busily engaged, she should be left undisturbed for as long as possible and those children who have already finished should be involved with the tidying away. Ideally the receptacles should be placed on a highish shelf above the bag pegs, and the children can hand them to the adult.

It is inadvisable to make a general appeal such as 'Who is going to help me?' as there is always a risk that the answer will be 'not me'. A better tactic is to give an object to a nearby child, say a hair curler, and indicate by a gesture that she should put it into the open bag. The adult can then use simple comments ('there's one under there', 'behind the chair', 'one by your foot') to show that all the objects of the same kind are to be put into this bag. Each phrase is linked directly to an action, so that even very small children have no difficulty in accomplishing the task (see Figure 8.2). If there are several adults in the session each one will be holding a different bag, so that if the child picks up an object other than the one being asked for, she can be directed to the other person.

In this way the whole floor is cleared and there is a general feeling of satisfaction in having done the job together. Even the youngest children of 12 or 13 months will understand very quickly that the adult wants the items collected. Only later will they grasp that the adult is asking for specific objects. Enabling the children to select and see differences and similarities is part of the adult's task as she directs the collecting up of the items.

There are three reasons for emphasizing that the adult should remain seated while the children collect up the items. First, and perhaps most important, it protects the adult's back from the strain of picking up large numbers of objects from the floor. Second, it reinforces the policy of 'tidy up as you go' which is a most useful habit for children, or anyone, to learn. Third, it provides a natural way of expanding the children's developing vocabulary as they identify by name each item which they bring to put in the bag. Moreover, the children are practising selection and discrimination between different categories of objects, the first stage in sorting, leading eventually to the mathematical concept of sets.

Child care workers meeting heuristic play for the first time occasionally find it difficult to accept the apparently passive role of the adult, and especially the fact that there is no unnecessary talk. But what would an adult say to a child absorbed in heuristic play? Inevitably she is tempted to comment and make suggestions, inhibiting the discovery process and interfering with the child's concentration. There will be other times of the day when the adult will sit on the floor close to the children for cuddles and conversation.

Of course there are also times when speech is necessary during heuristic play sessions, most usefully during the clearing-up stage. We would emphasize, too, that none of these guidelines are absolute and should never be taken to the point of causing the adult to behave in an unnatural or rejecting way towards a child. We have, for example, seen a young nursery worker, anxious to follow the rules, ignore an obviously distressed child who was holding up her arms and crying for attention. Clearly a child who is upset for any reason cannot play and must be comforted. If the upset is temporary, the child may return to play after a brief cuddle, but if one child in the group is unhappy or unwell and unable to settle it is best for another adult, if available, to take her away, as otherwise the whole group may be disturbed.

More usually staff who have experienced conducting this kind of play session have noted that an atmosphere of quiet concentration develops. Children become absorbed in pursuing their own exploration of the material for periods of half an hour and more, without direct reference to the adult. As noted above, conflicts between the children rarely happen because there is abundant material, but many friendly interchanges are observed, both verbal and non-verbal.

The activity is very enjoyable both for children and adults. For the adults it can be a interlude of calm in a busy day which gives them a chance to observe the children in a way not easy at other times. However, the inactivity of the adult is largely deceptive since it is her quiet but attentive presence which makes the whole thing work. She needs to be on the alert to see that the material is well spread out and that the children are not bunching together in a way that invites conflict. Children will also have physical needs to be attended to during the session, though nose-wiping and nappy-changing can be done so as to cause as little fuss and interruption as possible.

HEURISTIC PLAY IN DIFFERENT SETTINGS

It is not suggested that a heuristic play session should be offered to children every day, and the staff should use their discretion about this. There are advantages in giving it the feeling of a special treat, which will remind adults of the need to create a clear time and space, when they are not to be interrupted by ringing telephones or other distractions. Similarly, it underlines the need to treat the material with care and respect, to keep it in good condition and pack it up carefully at the end of each session, not leave it lying around underfoot.

In day nurseries this can provide a special activity for an age group which is otherwise often overlooked. It is the equivalent of the common practice of withdrawing the older children for more structured activities outside their group rooms. In 'family' groups where the under twos often have to compete for attention with the older ones, it can enable a staff member to give special attention to a small number of children. A selection of the bags can be easily transported to any clear, quiet space.

For larger groups it is best if a particular room or area of the nursery can be set aside for heuristic play (even if it is also used for other purposes) and equipped with carpet, hooks on which to hang the bags and chairs for adults. In other settings this will rarely be possible, but with ingenuity conditions can be created in which a heuristic play session can take place. For example, for child minders a bedroom, provided the bed does not take up too much space, is very suitable since it will probably be carpeted and not regularly used during the day.

Playgroups could run heuristic play sessions for 1- to 2-year-olds, either alongside the regular playgroup session if there is enough space, or at some other time. The growing number of parent-and-toddler groups could make use of the fact that there are always plenty of adults available, to offer heuristic play with objects to the 1- to 2- year-olds in some sessions. Conditions may not be ideal, but even in church halls it is usually possible to create a quiet corner and find someone to donate a suitable piece of carpet.

In family centres and day nurseries caring for children whose home conditions are poor, and whose parents may need help in building a better relationship with them, heuristic play has an invaluable contribution to make. These children are especially likely to have been denied the freedom to explore and experiment in their home environment. For the parents a heuristic play session provides a unique occasion when they can sit quietly and observe their child without feeling any obligation to control her behaviour. During this period they need not feel under scrutiny themselves or worry about whether they are doing what is expected of them. The chance to take part regularly in heuristic play sessions may be particularly important for parents who have been referred to the nursery or family centre because child abuse is suspected or admitted. Heuristic play can also be helpful to older children with learning difficulties, who can play with the material at their own level, or to those with mobility problems. Nursery workers often feel defeated by the problem of how to offer adequate and appropriate activity to children in their care who have special needs: heuristic play may offer some answers.

MATERIALS REQUIRED

One part of the adults' role is to collect, buy or make a good quantity of the items listed below. Many of the objects can be collected by parents, staff and friends, for example, empty tins, metal jar caps, pinecones. Others, such as woollen pom-poms, can be easily made. Bought items, from hardware stores, shops selling kitchen equipment or haberdashery departments can be quite inexpensive – wooden laundry pegs, haircurlers, table tennis balls.

Also needed are draw-string bags in which these different items are kept when they are not in use. The bags must be large enough to take the number of objects required for the group (16 × 20in./406 × 508mm. is a good size) and made of a material which is tough enough to stand up to heavy use but not too stiff. They must open wide at the top to allow children to drop in the objects at the end of the play session.

The adults need to search continually, with an imaginative eye, for different objects suitable to add to the bag collection. This is a good way to involve parents and volunteers, and can become a strong interest for them. Many of the items are similar to those included singly in the Treasure Basket, providing the widest possible variety of size, weight, colour and texture.

One of the attractive and creative aspects of these varied materials lies in the infinity of possible combinations which go far beyond the imagination of any one person. It has been calculated that four bags with 60 items in each allow for the possibility of 13,871,842 combinations!

SUGGESTED ITEMS FOR HEURISTIC PLAY

To collect or make
    Woollen pom-poms, not too big, in primary colours
    Small bags and boxes
    Cardboard cylinders of all kinds (such as insides of kitchen paper,
        clingfilm and computer rolls)
    Ribbons of velvet, silk and lace
    Wood off-cuts from a carpenter
    Old keys, tied together in small bunches
    Metal jar tops
    Cockle or snail shells
    Large chestnuts
    Bottle corks
    Pine cones
    Tins and containers of all sizes

To buy
    Curtain rings, wooden and metal
    Wooden laundry pegs
    Hair rollers of differing diameter
    Ping-pong balls
    Large and small corks
    Rubber door stops
    Varied lengths of chain, fine- to medium-sized links
    Large bone buttons

SUMMARY

As they acquire mobility children have an increasing need to explore and experiment which is often frustrated, and can lead to a negative view of this age group. This chapter explains the theory behind heuristic play with objects, a particular way of offering a planned learning experience to children in their second year. Providing heuristic play in group settings requires careful working out of practical details: time, space, materials and management. The adult's role is that of organizer and facilitator, not initiator. Given generous supplies of well-chosen objects, children in their second year will play with concentration and without conflict for extended periods.

Note: E.G. wishes to acknowledge the work of Katrine Stroh and Thelma Robinson, based on that of Dr Geoffrey Waldon, in connection with this chapter.

9 Children in their third year

All mothers should keep a book wherein to write the sayings of their children – when a child speaks of honey as bee-jam, it reveals the creation of language.

William Barnes, *Dorsetshire dialect poet*

'An explosion of self-awareness' is one of the ways in which the experience of a child in the third year of life can be described. In a nursery group, often with limited space and the bustle of activity of the older ones, the nursery worker has the demanding task of adapting herself to the tempo of children at a variety of stages of their growth. Special thought needs to be given to the children aged between two and three who are only just becoming aware of the explanations and the negotiating which are so much part of being in a group. They need to feel safe and to understand what the adults expect of them.

It is useful to take a general overview of what the year from two to three will hold. Following the theme of developmental lines (Freud, 1965), we can look at mobility and manipulative skill, feeding, bowel and bladder control, language and the great range of play and learning which underpins and integrates all the aspects of a child's sense of self.

In his third year the child moves with a certain degree of autonomy into a period of consolidation while seeking a vast amount of information about his immediate world. He tries to interpret how this relates directly to himself, and strives to respond to the complexity of the often inexplicable demands which both his adults and his peers make upon him.

Because a child often does not have sufficient information to make sense of what is happening, he has to deal with anxieties and frustrations which need imaginative understanding from his adults. Happenings which cannot be explained take on a mysterious and magical quality. Children are not alone in this for we, as adults, often have similar feelings when, for instance, we hear of sending a photograph by Fax to America, or of astronauts taking walks in space. We always need to respect and not laugh at the child's attempts at understanding.

DEVELOPMENT IN THE THIRD YEAR

Bodily mastery and manipulative skill

By the age of two a child will run safely in a straight line, and later round corners. As he nears the age of three he will be able to negotiate obstacles. As he practises climbing up and getting down from furniture and apparatus, his ability and judgement rapidly increase. At two years he walks upstairs, two feet to a step, but by three he can do so with alternating feet, though going down he will still use both feet on each step.

At three years he has command of a wide variety of movements, walks and gallops with enjoyment and control. There is often a cry to the adult to 'watch me' with pleasure and pride in skill achieved.

Feeding

At two years a child can spoon-feed himself quite competently without spills and can lift and drink from a cup. By three years he will pour from a small jug and be using a fork and knife. He chews well and, if given the opportunity, is well able to serve himself, taking his time in doing so. His growing command of language enables him to ask for food and drink and to indicate his preferences. By three years he enjoys the social aspects of meal times and talks animatedly with chosen companions.

Bladder and bowel control

At two years a child can indicate his need and will probably be dry during the day. During the coming year he will need help in pulling down his pants, gradually learning to replace them, though at three years he will still need help with any straps or buttons.

There is great variation in the speed at which children achieve bladder control, and, as is well known, this area of development is extremely sensitive to any kind of stress or anxiety. An upset in the family or an illness can easily cause a temporary regression, and it is very important for nursery workers to accept this without reproach or impatience. For a child who has been dry for some time, wet pants are uncomfortable and sometimes embarrassing. Treating the incident in a matter-of-fact way without any implication that the child has been 'naughty' is most likely to avoid a setback becoming a long-term problem.

Some children are simply slower than others, which can create problems for parents if the child's move to a playgroup or nursery school is dependent on his being reliably dry during the day. Nursery staff and child minders should resist pressure to give too much importance to the matter, for instance by constantly interrupting the child's play to suggest a visit to the bathroom. It is worth checking that clothes are easy for the child to manage independently, getting rid of buttons, buckles, straps and zips as far as possible.

In his general bodily care the child gains skill in handwashing and brushing his teeth. He is interested in his own appearance and observant of others.

Language

One of the commonest reasons why children are offered places in day care centres is that their language development is delayed. Yet studies of day nurseries and nursery schools often remark on the poor quality of speech in such settings and the low level of communication between children and adults (Mayall and Petrie, 1983; Moss and Melhuish, 1991). Sometimes the staff are criticized for not talking sufficiently to the children, which is certainly important, but the other side of the question, as we said in Chapter 7, lies in the quality of personal relationships and the interesting, active experience which is offered to each child.

How far do the adults organize the day so that they can listen attentively to children? This needs to be a subject of constant staff discussion, with a special focus on the needs of children whose family language is not English. Once again it is helpful to think of ourselves learning a foreign language, say in preparation for a holiday. We aim to master simple phrases so that we can get information about travel or buying food. We may feel quite confident, listening to our language tape, asking and replying to familiar questions. The difficulty arises once we are abroad when, in reply to our question, we get an avalanche of words which are beyond our grasp. We can latch on to key words but still risk misinterpreting the sense. Often we urge people to speak more slowly, meaning that we need time to interpret what they are actually saying. Where children are becoming bilingual, nursery workers need to be especially alert to this aspect of equal opportunities.

At this age, even children with a wide vocabulary and a good command of language cannot be expected to appreciate the subtler aspects of adult speech. This can lead to misunderstandings. For example, Jan, a child minder, had been visiting a friend with Sally, a usually amenable 2-year-old whom she had been looking after for several months. As they were leaving she said to Sally 'If we have time on our way home perhaps we'll go to the zoo'.

Sally, who had much enjoyed their previous trip to the zoo, picked up the last few words of the sentence, not grasping the significance of 'if' and 'perhaps'. When it turned out that there was not after all time for the zoo, she was understandably disappointed and frustrated, and promptly had a tantrum.

FACILITATING LANGUAGE DEVELOPMENT

Recognizing that the subject of a young child's development of language is a large and complex one, we try to indicate ways in which workers can organize the day to enable this process of thinking and imaginative power to take place. The emphasis laid here on the need for activities to be carried out, whenever possible, with small groups of four or five children, is based on the knowledge that communication takes place in an atmosphere of trust and tranquillity, with nursery workers playing their vital role as facilitators or enablers.

Another point to re-emphasize is the need to keep a low noise level in any group care setting. Background music can seriously inhibit language development and cassette players and television should only be used for specific purposes, if at all.

Practising speech

In earlier chapters we have shown how meaning becomes attached to words through a child's direct sensory experience and play. If the key person system is running effectively, the pre-dinner 'Island of Intimacy' provides a significant time when the small group of children are sure of their nursery worker's full attention. This is a point when the key person can make a note of how each child's language is progressing.

It is particularly important that occasions of this kind are built into the structure of the day for children in their third year. When feelings and ideas come faster than words, a child will often stutter in eagerness. It helps if the worker gently holds the child's hand, and if the others are clamouring, asks for a bit of quiet, showing her genuine consideration for what the child is struggling to say. As Barbara Tizard showed in her comparison of children's talk in nursery school and at home (Tizard, 1984), the quality of conversation depends very much on how much the adult knows about the context (which of course is taken for granted by the child). This underlines the importance of the key person getting to know the other significant people in a child's life and visiting the family at home from time to time.

By two years a child will know anything from fifty to three hundred words and be making up two- to three-word sentences. Subsequently his vocabulary increases rapidly; by two-and-a-half most children will use well over a hundred words, including what, where, I, me and you. He may constantly ask 'What's that?' as he moves about handling objects, trying out his skill in endless explorations and demanding a response. The overstretched adult may exclaim 'Oh do be quiet' or, as we have all done, 'For heaven's sake keep still for a minute'. If the child could only explain the urge which drives him to move and to talk he might say 'Can't you see I have to practise this difficult new thing I can do if I'm to get better at it?'

Our quite frequent incomprehension of what is central for children could be taken by them as a message that moving and speaking are undesirable activities in themselves. In fact we often see in day centres children from very disadvantaged families who have, sadly, internalized that message. Luckily children are resilient and their inbuilt desire to grow and learn is hard to repress. But to cope with the seemingly tireless demands of 2-year-olds we need to negotiate with them so that our different interests can be as far as possible satisfied, rather than falling into conflict.

In practising speech children in their third year often talk to themselves continuously as they play, even when they are not addressing anyone in particular. If we listen carefully to children talking to themselves, we hear them rehearse or play back conversations about events or situations which are significant to them, just as we adults do in moments of silent reflection. It is part of the process of understanding and digesting experiences which touch our feelings and absorb our interest.

It is noticeable that a child's command of language will often take a leap forward in response to a new stimulus or a fresh enjoyable experience such as a holiday. Seen in this light, the value of outings organized by nursery workers takes on an added significance (see Chapter 11).

Understanding children's thinking

The daily care of young children in this age group, with all the testing out and challenge to adults which growing awareness of self and others rightly involves, can be very demanding. One of the compensations is that it can also be very interesting. Satisfaction in the job can be enhanced immensely for the key person who gives close attention to the language of her small group of children and what it reveals about their thinking.

Marco, on a beach for the first time, gazed at the sea and commented, 'It's too full up'. Rebecca, also a month or two past her second birthday, asked, 'Can I go in the big bath?' Matthew, waking after a night of heavy snow exclaimed, 'There's an all white outside'.

Emma, at nearly three years, was standing beside her grandmother watching an aeroplane crawl across the sky at a great height. The adult commented 'Perhaps that's the plane I shall go to Italy in tomorrow'. Emma gazed at the plane, tiny in the clouds, and said 'But how will you get in?'. The adult's simple, but serious, explanation enabled her to begin to understand the connection between size and distance.

Anna at three years announced in the nursery bathroom 'I'm going to eat lots and lots and lots, and then I'll get fat like Mummy and have a baby'. Anna was using the information she had about eating and weight, applying what she knew to a situation of which she was ignorant. At that moment it was important that no one laughed, which might easily have happened. Adults often respond with ridicule or even anger to children's 'difficult' comments about sex and reproduction for which they are unprepared. Nursery workers need to discuss these matters in supervision or with colleagues so that they can answer children's questions without embarrassment and recognize their curiosity as legitimate.

As they use their newly acquired language, children are constantly giving us vital clues about what is important to them and what they need to understand. It is part of the nursery worker's task to be aware of these pointers and not to brush them aside.

Children are extremely logical within the limits of the information they possess, but because this is necessarily restricted they are liable to misinterpret things they hear. For example, Daniel, just four, was asked, 'What did you do at nursery today?' To this he replied, 'Oh, we heard about Jesus, and he was nailed to a crossing by his hands, but it was long ago and there were no cars, so he wasn't hurt. Then there was Moses, and he wasn't well, so he went up the mountain to talk to God and God gave him some tablets and he got better'.

We can see how the child has tried to modify the appalling vision of the first story, and to make sense of the second by relating the 'tablets' to those he had seen his mother take during an illness. But the incident illustrates some of the perplexities we can create for children by an ill-considered choice of subjects and of words.

Sometimes children self-talking give us very important information about their situation. Alessio, two-and-a-half years, aggressive and turbulent in his chaotic home and constantly reproved at the nursery, sat alone on a small swing in the garden murmuring in a sad rhythm 'Alessio is a bad boy, Alessio is a bad boy', painfully internalizing the negative image he was constantly receiving from the world. If such a cry for help falls on deaf ears, the adults are failing in their job.

STORIES AND RHYMES

Through this third year a child has a growing pleasure in listening to repetitive jingles and nursery rhymes and in hearing favourite stories over and over again. Storyreading can make a useful contribution to language development but only if it is carefully handled with attention to the individual experience of each child.

Many nurseries (and playgroups) make a practice of reading stories to a large-mixed age group, perhaps numbering up to fifteen children. This is usually done with the object of releasing staff to do other things, but rarely works like that since extra adults are needed to keep order, hush the child who wants to ask questions or start a conversation with his neighbour, or bring back the little ones who would rather wander off and play. Inevitably in a large group some won't understand what it is all about, some would prefer a different story and others just don't feel like sitting still at that particular moment.

Children are likely to get far more out of storyreading (or storytelling) if the large group is split up among the available staff, who each use a separate space and judge their choice of story by the age range and interest of their small group. In this way, rather than 'keep quiet and listen' the children can have a chance to express their own thoughts and reactions to the story. The story becomes a trigger for interesting conversation which can be related to other experiences, and the reader has the chance to find out what the children have understood. Stories do not necessarily have to come out of books; a nursery worker who makes up and tells her own stories can have a special kind of direct communication with her small group.

Good children's books are not cheap, but hardbacks covered with library film will last a long time, and in a group setting paperbacks are usually a false economy. An adequate budget needs to be allocated for additions and replacements. Books need selecting with the same care as toys, and unwanted gifts should be eliminated with equal determination. There is a wonderful range of books available for this age group, and no excuse for tolerating the feeble stories and crude or confusing illustrations often to be seen. The local children's librarian is usually very willing to advise, and it may be possible to arrange to have a rotating collection on loan. Nurseries still need their permanent stock, though, as children like to return to their favourites again and again.

As well as choosing books for their literary and artistic qualities, nursery workers also need to be alert to the messages they convey, and we say more about this later in the chapter.

MUSIC

By the age of three, children who have had a rich experience of music with their close adults will be able to sing a recognizable tune and will often have an extensive repertoire of nursery rhymes. They love dancing to music and are very interested in making music themselves and in seeing adults play instruments. A staff member who plays the guitar is a great asset (piano is less good because the player cannot face the children). Perhaps a parent who plays can be invited to visit and demonstrate by playing a short piece, and allowing the children to examine and touch the instrument. Musicians are usually delighted to be asked to play and talk to young children but not many nurseries think of inviting them.

Most nurseries have a collection of musical instruments but, unless there is a staff member with a special interest, these are not often well-chosen or effectively used. Any instrument which does not make a pleasant sound should be discarded – which means throwing out the cheap plastic whistles and tin xylophones which sometimes seem to accumulate. Musical possibilities for young children have been enormously extended by the availability of instruments from other cultures. It is worth going to a considerable effort to obtain these from specialist shops because they are often ideally suited to this age group, enabling children to make and hear a great variety of different sounds. The only drawback is that they have to be chosen with considerable care because some of them are rather fragile.

Musical instruments should always be kept in a safe place and used in a planned way, like the objects for heuristic play. Given a reasonably soundproof room and an attentive adult, a small group of children approaching their third year can learn to play different rhythms, choose instruments and, with help from an adult, create a satisfying musical sound. They can also learn to listen to each other and to different kinds of short pieces of music and talk about what they hear. However, what matters, as with all kinds of play, is the child's experience, not any kind of end product or performance. Music at this age should be a natural extension of playing with sound as described in Chapters 5 and 7.

Making music is an activity in which it is easy and enjoyable to include parents if it is made clear that no previous musical knowledge is required. Fiona Stuart provides a useful model for setting up a weekly session for parents and children together (Stuart, 1992). There are also many suggestions in David Evans's invaluable book, *Sharing Sounds* (Evans, 1978).

PLAY IN THE THIRD YEAR

Imaginative and sociable play

A 2-year-old at home or with a childminder can learn so much by observing and participating in the 'real' work of running a home. The child in a day centre can easily miss out on this experience. It is tiring for the adults constantly to involve children in the care and maintenance of the group room, as we suggested earlier, and it is tempting in a mixed group to turn to the older children or speed things up by doing it yourself. However, if the worker can focus on maintaining a really well-stocked and attractive home corner and dressing-up area as a permanent feature of the group room, much of the 2-to-3-year olds' imaginative and sociable play will reward her care. The 2-year-olds will play with pots and pans, filling and emptying receptacles in a way which echoes their previous absorption with the activities of their heuristic play with objects, talking and interrelating busily as their imaginative play develops apace.

If one worker, as suggested in Chapter 2, takes a special responsibility for this kind of activity she does not need to 'play at' tea parties or with the dolls, but is present as a point of reference. In this role she can see that the practice of 'tidy up as you go' is followed, using simple indicators such as 'Let's put the clothes on this dolly' or 'Which bed will you put this teddy in?'. By her unobtrusive intervention and consistently maintaining a quiet contact with these youngest ones she enables the play to go on smoothly. Where children in their third year are part of a mixed-age group, staff need to give particular attention to providing opportunity for this kind of imaginative play, so closely related to the growth of language.

Imaginative play throws up issues which staff need to think about on their own and with parents. With dressing-up clothes and the Home Corner available to all the children, what do they feel about boys dressing up in skirts and necklaces or playing with dolls, or girls showing a preference for cars and hammer and nails? Although most nurseries now exclude guns and overtly military toys, how does the nursery worker react to the child who turns every available object into a weapon or a bombing plane? Is it enough for nursery workers to accept children's preferences, conditioned as they already are by so many other influences, or should they be directly challenging stereotypes of male and female roles, encouraging boys to come into the Home Corner and girls to play with bricks and trains? Do the materials available for imaginative play reflect the different ethnic groups that make up our society, whether or not families from these groups currently use the nursery?

If the nursery has the advantage of staff members of different ethnic origins, this responsibility should not be left to them, but full use should be made of all that they can contribute to deepening understanding of their own cultural traditions.

Painting and drawing

In using paint the 2-year-old experiments with colour, passing the brush from one hand to another, scrubbing the paint on to the paper. Later his painting strokes become more varied. By three years he is beginning to paint pictures, matches primary colours and may 'name' what he paints. With crayons he will begin with circular scribbles, going on at a later stage to drawing a person with a head and gradually adding in other physical features.

The progression in children's drawings is a fascinating subject which has been much studied by psychologists (Freeman and Cox, 1985). At one time it was thought possible to measure children's intelligence by asking them to draw men and women and constructing standardized scores based on the number of features they include – arms, legs, ear, etc. Although such drawings do give some indication of a child's developmental stage the approach has been much criticized for its inbuilt cultural bias and the test has largely fallen out of use. However, it can be very interesting to collect samples of a child's drawing and painting over a period of, say, 6 months and this could also be a good focus for a discussion between parent and key person.

Parents who have never had the opportunity to use paint themselves may find it difficult to appreciate the pleasure and effort that children experience in their first attempts. One of the more distressing experiences for a nursery worker is to see a child's treasured painting stuffed into the dustbin on the way home. Staff need to spend time and thought on the best way to help parents give recognition to their children's achievement and not to judge a child's work by inappropriate standards. Nursery workers can show their own appreciation by careful mounting and display of selected items. It may sometimes be best to give parents the option of keeping the child's work in a folder at the nursery, which provides a later opportunity for discussion as parent and key person together look at how the paintings change over time.

Sand and water play

It is good practice to have a member of the group-room staff who takes special care of the various types of play material available. As well as ensuring that the equipment for play with malleable materials is well maintained, it is also useful for her to make some careful observations of the progression in children's use of sand, clay, mud, dough and water, birdseed and lentils. Unless there is some specific observation of this kind undertaken by staff, much of the play with these materials can be very desultory and unproductive.

The 2-year-old has fun discovering the behaviour of the various substances by pouring, slapping, kneading, poking and manipulating them directly with his hands (often trying eating too!). He does this before going on to use the variety of tools available. He needs scope to do this freely within the limits of mess which the environment and the adult can permit. He may go on to making castles or puddings, mixing dry materials with water, shaping and moulding things to which he may or may not give a name.

At a later stage, boards, rolling pins and metal shapes can be provided, dough becomes biscuits which can be cooked and eaten and there is a recognizable end product. The staff member observing will note how important it is to allow the first exploratory play to take place, not falling into the trap of making objects herself or imposing adult perceptions on the child, but waiting for him to make his own imaginative leap as his skill increases.

Water play also progresses and in the later stages can encompass such useful activities as washing items of play material such as Lego, or dolls' clothes and cot sheets, wiping down tables, and washing and drying one's own face and hands.

As they approach their fourth year, children develop the ability to use simple tools and learn different techniques. A group of three children with staff supervision can make a fruit salad, cutting up the fruit with knives and squeezing juice, activities around which a great deal of lively conversation will take place. Using scissors, pasting, making collages, selecting and threading beads increase manipulative skill while providing a sense of achievement in a task completed.

As with a heuristic play session, the principle of tidy up when finished gives a sense of pleasure in order and also lightens the nursery worker's task. She, of course, offers a model of someone who cares for the materials themselves and encourages others to do so. Puzzles, building blocks and construction sets need to have the same treatment.

CHILDREN'S ATTITUDES AND SENSE OF IDENTITY

We have already referred several times to the importance of earliest childhood experiences in forming children's view of themselves and of other people and preparing them to live in a multi-cultural society. There seems to be some evidence that the third year of life is particularly crucial in the formation of racial and gender identity and in the acceptance of diversity. Certainly by the age of three, children are found to have taken on many of the cultural and gender stereotypes presented to them on television, in newspaper and magazine advertisements and by the adults around them (Jackson, 1980; Milner, 1983).

If a day care setting is to have any hope of countering these largely negative influences, the organizer and staff need to have a clear idea why it matters and an agreed policy on how to tackle the task. Small improvements are always possible, but there is a great risk of tokenism and merely cosmetic changes unless the policy is underpinned by a carefully planned staff training programme and reinforced by discussion in staff meetings and supervision (see Chapter 4).

We have probably reached the point where most professional early childhood workers would not themselves use racist terms or make openly racist remarks and would discourage any child who did so. The difficulty is to move beyond this stage to recognize the extent to which discrimination is embedded in British history and institutions and manifests itself in every aspect of our daily lives.

When the issue is first raised, nursery workers and teachers often claim to treat all children the same or to provide a neutral environment. This frequently means one in which diversity is not acknowledged or discussed, still less valued. It creates a framework of conformity in which white, often middle-class, life styles, dress, food, homes, music, art and religions are 'normal' and all others deviations, and therefore likely to be ignored or seen as inferior.

Adopting a passive approach to discrimination on grounds of colour and race is as bad for white children as for Afro-Caribbean or Asian ones. This can be difficult for nursery workers to recognize if they have not thought much about these issues before. If all the children in the nursery are white, staff may feel the whole issue is irrelevant to them. Yet if it is not addressed, racist attitudes absorbed from home or the media will go unchallenged. It is worth noting that black and mixed-parentage young people who took part in a recent study told their interviewers, rather surprisingly, that their most painful experiences of racial abuse were in primary, not secondary school (Tizard and Phoenix, 1993).

It is important to distinguish between race, as manifested in skin colour and facial features, and culture. The emphasis on culture sometimes leads to what has been called the 'tourist curriculum', with wall pictures of people in exotic costumes, celebration of festivals and special meals featuring 'ethnic' styles of cooking (though usually eaten in a western manner). These events can be enjoyable and interesting social occasions, but they do tend to stress the *foreignness* of non-white people, when most parents of black children in nurseries are, and feel, British, and have a life style which is influenced more by social class and the neighbourhood they live in than by the country of origin of their parents or grandparents.

Children in their third year are very interested in their own appearance and love to inspect themselves closely if there are floor-length mirrors available. They will also compare their skin colour and hair texture with those of other children and ask questions about differences. Nursery workers sometimes react with embarrassment to such questions, almost as if race had replaced sex as an unmentionable subject.

In fact, good use can be made of the opportunity to reinforce children's positive images of themselves, pointing out that people come in all kinds of beautiful colours. However, children will not believe this unless they see it reflected in the images around them, their jigsaws, picture books, dolls, puppets and, most importantly, in the people who look after them.

A rather wider range of playthings is now available from specialist suppliers, but a survey of high street shops by members of the Working Group Against Racism in Children's Resources (WGARCR, 1991) revealed a grim picture. They found very few black dolls or puzzles with black children, hardly any books or cards representing black children or adults, and some toys which represented black people in a negative and stereotyped way. The story was the same in all areas, whether multi-racial or largely white. The survey concludes that 'there is very little in the high street toy shops to indicate that black children and communities are part of this society'.

In order to compensate for this discrimination, the day care setting needs to tilt the balance the other way, which may arouse opposition both from staff and parents if they do not fully understand the reasons. It can be especially hard when a negative reaction comes from black parents, but it has to be remembered that one survival strategy for oppressed people is to deny the existence of the oppression, and above all not to be noticed. Changing or developing nursery practice in this way has to go along with an active programme of staff development and parent involvement.

Some nurseries have children from a wide range of national backgrounds, an asset which the Children Act, 1989, calls on day care centres to recognize and affirm. One elementary, but significant, point is that every adult in the centre, including ancillary workers, should know how to pronounce the child's name correctly, and not, as we have too often heard, make up some anglicized equivalent which sounds roughly similar.

For some workers it will be a new idea that as much value should be given to children's learning of their home languages as to English. This is a fundamental reversal, which puts the onus on nursery staff to learn as well as the child. With a key person system the worker can ask parents of children in her small group to teach her some words and phrases in their own language. Can she greet the child and say goodbye, express tenderness, offer comfort, approval and sympathy, understand a few of the child's special words, perhaps sing a favourite song? In turn, she can reassure the parents that the child will learn English without their making special efforts to speak it at home – a second language is learned best when the first language is well-established.

It is a great help to have bilingual staff members, even though not all the children's languages can be represented. Perhaps parents can fill some of the gaps and also provide a bridge for new families speaking the same language.

The nursery environment can be immensely enriched by actively taking on elements of different cultures. Using Turkish, Icelandic and Bangladeshi hammocks for sleeping babies instead of beds or mattresses is one example given by Pam Schurch in a vivid description of the Lady Gowrie Child Centre in Sydney (in Stonehouse, 1988), which consciously builds on the ethnic diversity of the families that use the Centre.

Gender

Girls and boys are treated differently both by fathers and mothers from the moment of birth (Jackson, 1987). By the time they reach their third year gender identity is usually well established and their play preferences are clearly influenced by perceptions of what is appropriate for boys or girls (Derman-Sparks, 1989).

The question, already raised in Chapter 1, is whether nurseries should accept or challenge conventional images of masculinity and femininity. We have made our own views clear, but just as we cannot necessarily expect our readers to share them, so it is pointless to try and impose non-sexist practice in a nursery unless staff understand and share the values that underpin it and are able to carry parents along with them. This may be difficult if they themselves come from families where traditional gender roles prevailed and trained at a time when the issue was seldom considered. Raising awareness among staff is the first essential step. The National Children's Bureau training pack (Drummond *et al.*, 1989) offers some unthreatening ways to do this, as does an excellent discussion paper for student nursery nurses (Aspinwall, 1984).

The next step, once again, is to look critically at the images of girls and boys, women and men, presented to the children in the nursery environment. Publishers of popular children's books, having been severely criticized, are now much more conscious that they should present girls in active, energetic roles, and show boys, for example, washing up or caring for babies, but older books for children nearly always depict women and men in their conventional roles. Most toys available in high street shops are strongly differentiated, those designed for girls being predominantly domestic and those for boys either mechanical or connected with war and fighting (Dixon, 1989). The greetings cards sold in newsagents shops illustrate the stereotypes in their crudest form.

Nursery workers, then, are to some extent rowing against the tide (though with help from the wind of equal opportunities), so to make any headway they have to look for, or make, books and pictures showing women and men engaged in non-typical activities. They need to become conscious of their own unthinking behaviour, such as dividing children by sex or making comments about their play related to their gender rather than the activity. How often do we make a point of encouraging girls to play with construction toys or be physically adventurous? Are boys offered as much chance as girls to bath the dolls? In conversation with children do we assume that they are mainly cared for by their mothers?

The shortage of men in child care settings is a major obstacle because it conveys the message that only women know how to look after and teach young children, and that only women can be gentle and caring. It can be very hard for a man to work in, or even to enter, the female-dominated atmosphere of a day care or family centre. Trevor Chandler has described some of the problems, but also the opportunities it opens up (Chandler, 1990). Once there are men on the staff, the chances of drawing in fathers are greatly increased. Phil Lyons, who ran a men's group in Wexford, found that men greatly welcomed the chance to talk about more intimate feelings and express their sadness at what they experienced as exclusion from the lives of their children.

Disability

How children can be enabled to understand and respond positively to differences of appearance, behaviour, mobility, sensory and learning capacity, has been much less discussed than racism and sexism. Awareness of disabilities tends to come later than awareness of gender and race, but by the middle of the third year, children notice and ask questions about physical differences, and may show signs of discomfort which should not be ignored. It is very important for the adults to answer questions clearly and briefly, at the child's level, and not to evade or suppress them.

Children with disabilities are even less likely than black children to see themselves reflected in the world around them, in books, pictures, toys or role models. It will take some ingenuity and inventiveness for nursery workers to tackle this form of discrimination. One possibility is to make use in the nursery of toys and equipment made by people with disabilities and tell the children about them (see list of organizations). Another is to have at least one picture painted by a foot or mouth artist, along with a photograph of the painter at work.

Some centres have taken on the idea of 'persona' dolls, each with its life story, particular family situation and individual characteristics, including in some cases various types of disability. The approach is described in by far the best book we have come across on anti-discriminatory practice with young children, *Anti-Bias Curriculum* (Derman-Sparks, 1989), a book teeming with good suggestions, and especially strong on disability.

Of course there are many other forms of discrimination and stereotyping. One which should certainly be given more attention by early years educators is ageism. People are also discriminated against for being poor, unemployed, choosing to wear their hair in an unconventional style or living in vans instead of houses. In this brief discussion we have only been able to indicate some matters for the staff group agenda and suggest sources of further advice and information.

SUMMARY

In the third year children are constantly striving to assert their increasing autonomy and to make sense of the world around them. The tool of understanding is their growing command of language, which they need ample opportunity to practise. To ensure that this happens in a group care setting requires careful attention and planning, based on the key person system.

The third year is also a time when awareness of diversity develops. Early years workers have a unique opportunity to counter prejudice and discrimination and to help children feel good about themselves and develop positive attitudes to all the different groups of people who make up our society.

10 Mealtimes

Where there is no enjoyment and no fun the food is beige-coloured.
Raymond Blanc, *chef*

When a friend tells us about their holiday, describes where they stayed and what they did and recommends that we go to the same place, perhaps the first thing we ask is 'What was the food like?' Food is not only to do with survival but also with enjoyment and companionship. We need to give mealtimes special attention both for the children's sake and for our own.

Only someone who has actually conducted mealtimes for a group of young children fully understands the kind of stress which this can mean and the detailed and complex organization needed. In this chapter we first consider how caregivers can look critically at the way meals are run so as to make them more enjoyable for the children and for themselves. We then review points of practical organization, and especially how effective use of the key person system can make the period around the main meal less stressful for children and adults and provide valuable learning opportunities. In the last section, we discuss the role of nurseries and day care centres in laying the foundations for healthy eating and the importance of taking a multi-cultural approach.

RAISING AWARENESS

In order for practice to change, people first have to become aware of what habit may have led them to take for granted. As an illustration of how this might be done, here is Elinor's account of an exercise she ran as part of a training course for senior staff in charge of day nurseries in a social services department. She had the help of the two under-fives advisers who had invited her to run the course as well as the collaboration of the kitchen staff in the day nursery where the course was taking place. It was agreed that the participants would have lunch in the nursery on two days in successive weeks.

The kitchen staff helped me to lay on a really beautiful meal. The tables for four were set out attractively with cloths, a small pot of flowers, water jugs and coloured paper napkins. There was comfortable space for everyone, no sense of hurry, no clatter. The food was well-presented and attractive in appearance, ready waiting for us when we sat down, with the two nursery advisers and myself at different tables. Knowing there a whole hour for lunch engendered a mood of relaxation, and conversation flowed. We almost forgot that we were on a training course!

After the meal was over the participants in pairs were asked to make a list of the good and enjoyable features of the meal that they had just finished. On the basis of these criteria they were asked to consider how the meals were run in their own nursery, taking point by point and deciding on a scale of 0–10 how the meals actually experienced by their staff and children measured up to the quality of the meal they had just had. It was made clear that this assessment was to remain a private matter between themselves and their own nursery staff. No-one was asked to share their judgements with the other members of the course.

The group then came together and I asked them during the following week to look at exactly what was going on in their own workplace and to consider how they could use the day's experience to initiate change. We ran over together the good points that we were agreed on, from which it was clear that in many instances it was attention to detail which lay behind a good result.

The following week we spent the morning working on another theme unconnected with mealtimes. We were all engrossed and at half past eleven we were startled by the noisy, bustling entrance of the two under-fives advisers (duly primed) who moved into our circle saying, 'Come along now, put your things away. We're a bit late, so don't bother to finish what you're doing'. Our group felt somewhat irritated but were compliant, and obeyed the instruction of the advisers to get along to the bathroom with the comment 'Sorry there's only one available so you'd better stand in line and don't play about'. We duly followed each other and crowded into the bathroom to take our turn as directed, though everyone (except me of course) felt very puzzled and vaguely rebellious.

What happened next, quite spontaneously, was that in different ways, some more active than others, everyone began to 'behave badly'. Someone, laughing, began to muddle up the staff's outdoor shoes lying by the lockers, another turned on a tap and began squirting the water about.

One of the advisers coralled us into the dining room, insisting that we form a 'train' holding each other's waists. All twelve of us sat at one long table with no cloth, with chairs crowded up together, some too high and some too low for comfort. The advisers stood about telling us to be quiet and sit still and a wait of 15 minutes began before the food came.

Everyone wriggled about and rocked their chairs. The advisers, exchanging looks of exasperation, gave us books to look at, but most of them were dropped on the floor. The noise level rose and only quietened after the arrival of the food trolley, which was greeted with clapping and banging on the table. The advisers, standing by the trolley, doled out the food rather slowly, heaping the same amount on every plate. One adviser insisted that each person said 'Thank you' before she would put down the plate. No choice or refusal was allowed.

The food was good in quality but quite monotonous in appearance – steamed white fish, mashed potatoes and cauliflower. The advisers sat either end of the long table, and talked to each other about their holidays. They did not address the participants except to tell them to sit still and eat up their dinners.

The advisers had to get up three or four times to pick up a fork from the floor and wash it before giving it back because there were no extra forks on the trolley. It was evident from their faces and movements that they were not particularly enjoying their own meal.

The second course was served only when everyone had finished and two 'slow ones' made everyone feel irritated. Again there was some delay as there were two plates short and one adviser had to go to the kitchen to get another. The pudding consisted of rice pudding with stewed pears.

Somebody asked for water but was told they could only have a drink when they had finished what was on their plate. There was a jug of water on the trolley but the glasses had been forgotten and an adviser had to get up again to get them from the kitchen.

As can be imagined, as the meal went on everyone had seen the point of the exercise. We were all laughing and making suggestions as to how it could have been made even more awful! Direct experience focused attention on detail in a way that no amount of talking would have done. People noted with interest, and some surprise, the way in which they reacted to being ordered around even though they had obviously realized quite early on that it was a 'game'. We then went on to discuss some of the problems they had observed in their own nurseries during the previous week and they quickly began thinking of practical steps which could be taken to improve matters.

PRACTICAL ORGANIZATION

The transition time from playing to shared use of the bathroom to mealtime is a difficult period but it can be made easier by careful planning. The description of the key person system in Chapter 3 sets out how each staff member can act as the central focus for her own small group of children during the period from the end of play activities, through the meal and until those who are going to sleep are comfortably on their beds or mattresses.

One of the underlying reasons for ensuring that washing and pre-dinner time are spent in a small group is to calm the atmosphere before the meal. This eliminates to a great extent noise and tension, and makes it possible to avoid the disastrous situation of children being forced to sit down and wait at tables before the dinner trolley is brought in. The training exercise described above highlights all the elements which go towards the successful conduct of a meal. Here are some points to consider when planning how to make mealtimes enjoyable for children and staff alike:

Predictability

Uncertainty, and the confusion which it brings, can be avoided if all the children know which is their table and their place at it.

Good relations

Understanding and collaboration between the cook, ancillary staff and nursery workers in the group rooms are essential. This will be more likely if the nursery staff show thoughtfulness and consideration for their fellow workers and always explain the educational reasons behind any decisions which will involve more work for them. The cook needs to understand what the group room staff are aiming for in the organization of meals. Whoever is responsible for setting up the trolleys will need to know just why it is so important that the right amount of cutlery (with extras in case needed at table), water jugs, mugs and all other items are always to hand. A member of the domestic staff should bring in the trolley so that no nursery worker is obliged to absent herself from her small group.

Tables

A separate table is needed for each key person and her small group, with chairs which are the right height so that children can rest their feet on the floor and their elbows are at table height. If a child's face is too near her plate, because her chair is the wrong height she will have added difficulty in manipulating her spoon. She will have to raise her shoulder to bring the spoon to her mouth since small children do not flex their wrists as we do when using a spoon or fork.

Staying still

The key person, once she is seated with her group, should be able to remain seated, with everything to hand. Each key person should have, within easy arm's length, a side table, the top of a low piece of furniture or a shelf of the food trolley on which can be put both the food for her table and all the equipment she will need during the whole meal.

Food containers

There should be individual containers for each table so that the key person can serve her own group whose appetites and likes and dislikes she will know. Second helpings can always be given to children who want them, and in this way waste is avoided. The separate containers will mean more washing up for the kitchen staff, and this needs to be negotiated if it has not been the practice in the past.

Drinking

Water for drinking must always be available and actively offered, especially to the children who do not yet have language. Mugs should have a wide base. As soon as children can pour for themselves they should be encouraged to do so. Often a child, when she has finished drinking, will put her mug on the very edge of the table; tipping over will be avoided if the adult quietly moves the mug forward to a convenient place in front of her.

PROVIDING FOR YOUNGER CHILDREN

If the key person has a group of mixed ages she will generally have near her any younger ones who need help with eating. Luckily today it is understood that fingers came before forks, and that in the first stages of independence in feeding a child should feel quite free to eat with her fingers everything that can be conveniently picked up. When a child can accept help as she learns to use a spoon, it is important for the adult to have an extra spoon so that there is no need to take the child's own spoon from her hand.

A real trap for the adult is the temptation, when a child has one mouthful, to put a loaded spoon again to her lips. This can be a harmful practice because it means that we are pressurizing the child to gulp down what she has in her mouth in response to the waiting spoon we hold. Older children are always being told off for eating too fast and not chewing their food properly. Perhaps the roots of such behaviour lie in earlier adult impatience.

Some children, particularly the younger ones, may not be accustomed to sitting down at a table. It is especially important for them that we organize carefully to maintain an atmosphere of tranquil efficiency, and make mealtimes, which inevitably involve some restraint on their activity, an enjoyable time for them.

Being with young children who eat slowly can impose a quite stern discipline upon us not to let 'institutional rush' take over the meal. Any works or office canteen will remind us what this rush and noise does to our digestion.

In one nursery, where there was a harmful and disturbing sense that the meal had to be 'got over with', we traced it to the fact that the kitchen staff who did the washing up had a contract which meant they had to finish by 1 p.m. This deadline had a kind of 'ripple effect' right back to the moment when the children sat down at their tables. It was not possible to change this arrangement immediately, but at least we had identified one source of the problem of 'rush'. We studied small ways in which the staff in the group room could reduce work for the kitchen staff after the meal, for example, by making sure that the trolley went back to the kitchen with the plates well scraped and stacked and the dirty cutlery already standing up in a plastic jug with a little water and detergent to start the cleaning process. We found that if there were always a kitchen-roll on the trolley, or a non-drip sponge handy, the staff member could neatly wipe up bits of rice or mashed potato spilled during the meal so that any gluey or sticky substance did not make extra work in subsequent cleaning.

Another detail which can often create stress for small children, seated expectantly at the table, is when a container of something hot arrives. Quite often a whole portion is put on a plate, but it is too hot, and the hungry child, already coping with the complex manoeuvre of handling her spoon, is faced with yet another obstacle to eating. The solution is for the nursery worker to put a very small amount on the plate. The food will cool immediately because the plate is cold. When the child has finished she can have a second helping, by which time it will be at the right temperature for eating.

Sometimes, in their anxiety that children should eat well, nursery workers give over-large helpings which can lead to unnecessary waste. It is now fully recognized that, however much the adult feels that a child ought and needs to eat, there must never in any circumstances be pressure. That is not to deny that children who refuse to eat create severe stress for their caregivers (see Chapter 13).

A useful exercise is to arrange for each member of staff in turn to be freed from responsibility for her table and to sit apart as an observer during one mealtime, making detailed notes of all that happens. Comparing these observations at a group room meeting will highlight problems which otherwise can remain unnoticed. As a result of one such exercise a staff member commented that Peter, a child who was partly feeding himself with his fingers and partly being fed, had food around his mouth; the adult scraped this off with the spoon. This was repeated many times, and the observer noted that each time the child winced slightly. In the group room meeting staff tried doing it to each other to see how it felt. As a result they vowed never to do it to a child again.

When the staff in a group room have decided to operate a key person system with (say) three tables for five or six children and three staff, it can happen that at one table three children are absent. One nursery worker remarked that if that happened she felt very guilty when she had only two children and her colleague at the next table had her normal number of five or six. Then there is a tendency to put the two tables together.

The question we must ask is, how do the two remaining children feel, being deprived of the attention of their key person? It would be on just such an occasion that they could enjoy a more intimate time together which is not possible in a larger group. We could say that the nursery worker with the fewer children has more cause to feel guilty if she does join up with her colleague at a moment when she has a rare opportunity to give close attention to two children for whom she has special responsibility.

At other times of the day when there is food and drink – at breakfast, mid-morning juice or fruit and at teatime – it is easier to be more relaxed, though it is still essential to plan every detail if these moments are to be enjoyable breaks in the long day. At breakfast and teatime there may be parents present so that attention needs to be given to their comfort, particularly in seeing that there are suitable chairs for them to sit on. Being informal does not mean being disorganized.

HEALTHY EATING

So far we have said nothing about the food which is provided for children and staff to eat, and often surprisingly little thought seems to be given to this, although if the food is not good nobody will enjoy the meal however well organized it may be.

Some social services day nurseries face the great problem of not having their own kitchens and being obliged to accept meals centrally provided and delivered in containers, with little direct control over the content. Worst off of all are those whose meals come frozen in individual portions, bearing no relation to personal preferences and likes or dislikes. For them the following points may at least offer a basis for negotiating better arrangements.

The type of food provided for children in day care centres is important, not only for its immediate impact on their health and development but because it lays the foundation for future eating habits. Ideas about nutrition have changed significantly over the past twenty years, but many nurseries still offer an extremely traditional menu based on outdated principles, with too much sugar, salt, fat and protein and not enough fibre or fresh fruit and vegetables.

The way that children's tastes develop depends very much on what they are offered, and this is particularly true of sugar. Adults tend to give small children sweetened food because that is the way they themselves prefer it, but this is a learned taste and can be unlearned, as anyone will know who has given up sugar in tea and coffee. Eventually it tastes better without. The diet of British children is usually far too high in sugar, often causing obesity and tooth decay. Sugary drinks are of course especially bad for teeth, but even unsweetened fruit juices can be damaging because of their acid content. Water is the best drink and should always be freely available.

There has been a lot of publicity about the possibly harmful effects of artificial colourings, flavourings and preservatives, but 'natural additives' like sugar and salt may do just as much damage in the long run. One implication of this which some staff may find difficult is that they should not be seen by children adding salt and sugar to their food, any more than they would light up a cigarette at table.

There is no shortage of advice on healthy eating, on the lines of Islington Health Authority's excellent *Under Fives Nutrition Training Pack* (Islington Health Authority, 1988). However, just because food is such a fundamental issue, it is essential not to make drastic changes without full consultation. A necessary first step is to create the motivation for change, which means ensuring that all staff understand the principles involved, and then engaging everybody in a critical examination of current practice. How does the food served in the nursery over the past month match up to criteria for a healthy diet? This can be calculated quite precisely by comparing the carbohydrate, fat, protein and fibre content with the recommended amounts for children of different ages: a good topic for a training day.

Having assessed the quality of the diet currently offered, it should be possible to reach agreement if change is necessary. What can be done immediately, and how far is complete rethinking necessary? Of course it goes without saying that the cook and kitchen staff must be fully involved in this discussion.

Substantial improvements can often be made very quickly, for example, the substitution of wholemeal bread for white, fresh fruit for sweet puddings, carrot sticks or unsweetened rusks for biscuits. More fundamental changes will take longer, but can at least be established as a goal to work towards.

The objection is often raised that the nursery cannot expect children to eat food which is too different from what they are used to at home. This makes two assumptions: that we know what children eat at home and that parents are ignorant of what constitutes a healthy diet. In fact Berry Mayall, in a study of what mothers do to keep their children healthy, found that most had a clear idea of which foods were good or bad for their children, but were often prevented by low incomes or poor living conditions from putting their ideas into practice (Mayall, 1986). What children eat is a matter of great concern to mothers, as research by Hilary Graham (1984) has also shown. Nurseries can help by accustoming children to foods that are cheap and convenient as well as healthy and that parents could also offer them at home.

TAKING ADVANTAGE OF CULTURAL DIVERSITY

Every country has its distinctive style of eating, and the food offered in day care centres is usually a scaled-down version of the typical adult meal. This is immediately obvious if we look at nursery menus from another country. In Italy, instead of 'meat and two veg.' and pudding, Italian infants are offered a first course (*primo piatto*) of pasta, thick vegetable soup or rice, followed by a second course (*secondo piatto*) of meat or fish and salad or a vegetable, usually ending with a piece of fruit.

Our eating habits are a very basic expression of our cultural identity, and nursery meals ought therefore to reflect the backgrounds of the children in the nursery. All should have the experience of eating some food which is familiar from home and some which is new to them. This needs to go much beyond the occasional 'multi-cultural' evening event when a special meal is provided, though these also have their place. Food is an important element in all the feasts and festivals which will be celebrated as part of the nursery's commmitment to anti-discriminatory practice.

However, food from many different cultures and national cuisines can be introduced as an integral part of nursery meals and will greatly increase their interest and variety. Chapattis, wholemeal pitta bread, unsweetened yoghurt, brown rice, yam and plantain, can become regular components of nursery menus. Pasta is a particularly suitable food for small children. Even in this country it can easily be obtained in dozens of different shapes and sizes, some of which, like butterflies and shells, seem to have been thought of with children in mind. Although some kinds of food may need adapting to suit children's more delicate tastes, it is best to have the real thing and not an anglicized version of it.

Where many different ethnic groups are represented in the nursery, the best resource is the parents (usually but not always mothers). They might be asked to suggest some dishes that they serve to the family at home which would be suitable for nursery meals and to come in to show the cook how to prepare them. If they are working during the day, they may be willing to invite a nursery worker into their home for the purpose.

Sometimes adults from different ethnic backgrounds continue to eat in their accustomed way but give their children 'English' food because 'they like it better'. This is unfortunate for two reasons: one that it is likely to lead to the children having a less healthy diet, but also because it suggests that the nursery has failed to convey respect and appreciation for different life styles, of which food is so important a part, and this may in turn lead to children devaluing aspects of their own culture.

Children's acceptance of new foods

Some children come into the nursery having been used to a very bland and restricted diet. It may be difficult at first to persuade them to try new types of food, even such a small change as wholemeal bread. However, they will gradually accept unfamiliar tastes and textures if these are first offered in very small quantities and they see other children eating with enjoyment. Of course parents need to be involved in this process – which most will welcome – and great care should be taken that any dietary restrictions, whether for religious or health reasons are thoroughly understood and respected by all staff.

INTRODUCING A NEW APPROACH

As with all significant changes in nursery practice, there are bound to be practical difficulties associated with a new way of thinking about food. Especially if the unit does not have control over its own food budget or purchasing, an ethnically sensitive approach to food may create problems, so the staff group and organizer need to have a clear view about why it matters and think of ways to get round obstacles. We know a family centre where herbs and spices, unobtainable from central stores but easily available in local shops, are bought out of the petty cash – a little goes a long way.

It is advisable to prepare the ground carefully, first by ensuring that the change has full backing from staff and parents, and then by seeking allies outside the nursery, such as the health education officer, the centre for multi-cultural education, and local government officers responsible for equal opportunities and anti-discriminatory policies.

Inevitably cooks and domestic staff as well as child care workers will vary in their receptiveness to new ideas. If they have been in post for many years and are accustomed to a particular range of foodstuffs and style of cooking they are not always prepared to learn new ways. A lot will depend on how fully integrated they are as members of the staff team (see Chapter 4). We have come across situations where the resistance of the cook has completely blocked progress towards healthier eating and cultural diversity. Sometimes such resistance may stem from anxiety and lack of confidence, which can be overcome with help and training. Very occasionally the only solution may be for the cook to change her job.

SUMMARY

The content and conduct of meals have a very significant influence on staff wellbeing and job satisfaction. It is an area which needs much more attention than it has received in the past. Close attention to detail is the key to making mealtimes an enjoyable and educative experience for children. Introducing more interesting and varied food which reflects cultural diversity offers a valuable opportunity for staff and parents to collaborate. Since it will often be the staff who are learning from the parents, it can also make a contribution to creating a more equal relationship.

11 Out of doors

Thrice happy he who, not mistook,
Hath read in nature's mystic book.

Andrew Marvell

Many of us have childhood memories of dandelion clocks, hoar frost
suspended in a spider's web, frozen puddles, grass wet with morning dew.
Children living in cities are often deprived of such simple experiences,
spending a large part of their early years indoors or in uninspired man-
made environments. Carefully planned outdoor space can provide
countless opportunities, not only for play and social experience but for
first-hand learning about living things that no book can teach.

In Australia the garden of a child care centre is known as the 'outdoor
teaching area', and much thought and care goes into its planning and
organization. In this country the potential for children's learning and
enjoyment offered by outdoor space tends to be overlooked. Too many
nurseries are surrounded by featureless rectangular patches of grass and
asphalt.

Nursery workers often wish the outside area were more interesting but,
having no clear idea of what they want, feel unable to push very hard for
improvements. There is no model of good practice such as the British
nursery school tradition to some extent provides for indoor activities,
and compared with the vast literature on indoor play and learning, there
is little useful material on planning and using outdoor space. One
exception is the excellent book by an Australian, Prue Walsh (1988),
Early Childhood Playgrounds. We have drawn on some of her
suggestions in this chapter as well as on creative ideas that we have seen in
centres in Italy and in this country.

The chapter falls into three sections. We consider, first, the organization of outside activities for small children and some ways in which the
garden area could be used to better effect. Second, we suggest a strategy

for taking maximum advantage of what the neighbourhood has to offer. This will obviously be especially important for nurseries and child minders with no access to their own outdoor space. For the third section we have enlisted the help of a landscape consultant who has designed a number of original and attractive garden playgrounds for small children in London.

We have tried to provide enough practical information to enable a nursery staff group to plan a transformation of their outdoor area. Money, of course, is bound to be a problem, but if the staff themselves are convinced of the need to create a genuine outdoor learning environment for the children they care for, they should be able to persuade their funding organization to make some at least of the necessary financial outlay. Moreover, the project is an appealing one for fund-raising, and much of the physical work could be done by volunteers. A local garden centre might be approached to sponsor the undertaking, or at least to supply plants free or at special prices.

MAKING THE MOST OF OUTDOOR SPACE

Changing attitudes

Although there are often practical obstacles to the flexible use of outdoor space – for instance an upstairs group room with no direct access to the garden – we are inclined to think that attitudes, sometimes unconscious, are an equally important barrier.

Ask anyone for their memories of their primary school playground and their answer will fall into one of two categories. Either they remember the blessed release from the confinement of the classroom, the chance to run and jump, fight, shout and play games or they had the very different experience of being the odd one out, hanging about by the railings with nobody to talk to. In the midst of all the activity was the teacher in charge, often visibly bored and having little communication with the children. Invariably the whole class, often the whole school, went out and came in together so that for much of the day the playground was an unused space.

Echoes of this model persist in day nursery practice and need to be re-examined. The first step is to get away from the idea of a mass exodus to 'let off steam'. Once nursery workers grasp the idea of the outdoor space as a place for learning, they will want to go out with their own small group and act in a facilitating rather than a supervisory role.

When the idea is first suggested, however, it may not be greeted with universal approval. Staff may have been used to the welcome respite offered by all the children going out together, with one or two colleagues looking after them, while they used the time to clear up or to take a break. They may need to have some good experiences of working actively with the children outside before they can appreciate the value of the new arrangement.

The very mention of the garden may induce a mood of pessimism and despondency. In some areas vandalism is a problem; paper and plastic rubbish may get blown in or thrown over the fence, accumulating in the corners. Sometimes an unkempt look develops, which no-one would tolerate in their own front garden, and which staff and children find very depressing, though they may not express this. Staff may feel they have quite enough to do in their group rooms without taking on the outside area as well.

One way of creating a hospitable climate for change is to look in detail at how the space is used at present, both at how nursery workers guide the children's activities outside and how the children behave in the freer context that the garden offers. A staff-meeting discussion could focus on how everyone sees the value of the garden area and their own role during outdoor play. This discussion is almost certain to throw up a number of frustrations and negative feelings which should be noted as problems to be solved rather than as excuses for inactivity.

Closely observing individual children can be particularly revealing in undertaking an assessment of the use of outdoor space. If the key person system is working well, each nursery worker could be asked to make a detailed observation of one child in her group during outside playtime. Students and parents, if available, could also be asked to do this. Putting these observations together should provide a good idea of the quality and variety of experience which the outside area already offers, and also where it falls short.

Some questions that the observers might have in mind are: what do equal opportunities mean for boys and girls, younger and older children, the outgoing and the timid? How do the social strains of being in a group outside differ from being indoors? Do some children always dominate the equipment, such as swings or climbing frame, while others seem unable to assert themselves? How do the children learn to negotiate and take turns, and what is the adult's role in this? Are there opportunities for the children to experiment and take small risks to test and extend their abilities, and which children will take advantage of them?

THE OUTDOOR SPACE AS A LEARNING AREA

Types of activity

Large-scale motor activity – running, jumping, climbing, sliding and using wheeled toys – obviously has its place in outdoor play. However often this is the *only* type of activity observed in a nursery garden. Classifications of play in terms of its contribution to cognitive development usually rate this type of activity lowest (Sylva *et al.*, 1980; Smith and Cowie, 1991), and this needs to be considered, especially in centres where many of the children may have been referred because of 'lack of stimulation' in their home backgrounds.

Here we want to look more closely at a few of the activities that can be undertaken by a worker with not more than three or four children at times when the garden is not in full use. This gives more opportunity for conversation between adult and children as well as reducing the pressure of numbers within the group room.

Garden equipment

Implements for use in the garden should be kept in suitable boxes or baskets in a recognized space, preferably a shed, and should be of appropriate size. Basic requirements are an adult-sized rake and broom, small rakes with short handles, small brooms (real ones, not toys), wheelbarrows, watering cans, trowels and small forks.

Care and maintenance

As with the group room, children can make a real contribution to keeping the garden looking well cared-for and attractive, at the same time as enjoying themselves. As already mentioned, rubbish can be a real problem for nurseries in urban areas. Even very small children can join in picking up waste paper, raking and sweeping leaves and piling them into a wheelbarrow with hands and trowels. Cleaning up can lead to conversation about keeping the environment free of litter.

Growing and tending plants

Many nurseries grow beans, carrot tops or cress on indoor plant tables but make less use of the outdoor area. Children can join in planting bulbs and bedding plants to enhance the general appearance of the garden (see Figure 11.1), but the most interesting thing, if there is space and consistent interest from the worker is to create individual gardens for children.

One way of defining the space is to use small car tyres (easily

Figure 11.1 Activities in the garden: growing and tending plants.

obtainable from garages specializing in changing and supplying tyres), half-embedded in the earth. This kind of individual plot is manageable both for the child and the worker – rather like the way some people will happily tend a hanging basket but feel overwhelmed by a whole garden. The group of children can be helped to sow different types of flower and vegetable seeds, to water their own tiny plots and watch the results. When the plants come up they can be compared with the pictures on the packets or in flower books or postcards.

In using re-cycled tyres for this purpose or to create play structures there are some practical points to take into account. Steel belt tyres should be avoided as they may eventually wear, exposing steel bands; tyres should be checked for broken rims before use; when filling them with soil, the earth should be packed tightly into the casing before laying and filling the centres.

Figure 11.2 Activities in the garden: learning about living things.

Learning about living things

Long before they reach their third year many children will already have learnt to dislike and fear crawling and flying insects. Their immediate response to an insect seen in the garden may be to stamp on it. By expressing our own interest in and respect for 'minibeasts' we can play a significant role in re-education, and the children will soon pick up our very different attitude. Bees, wasps, ants, beetles, spiders, earwigs, ladybirds, woodlice, centipedes, snails, caterpillars, worms and butter-flies all offer scope for conversation, and some for close examination (see Figure 11.2).

Each child in the small group needs a plastic magnifying glass and the older ones will like to identify the insects they have seen in a well-illustrated book. Of course this activity takes place under close supervision, but children quickly learn to distinguish between insects which must on no account be touched, such as wasps, and those that can safely be picked up (gently) and inspected at close quarters.

Children old enough to appreciate the need for quiet and stillness will enjoy observing birds if the garden is provided with a feeding tray and bird-bath out of reach of local cats. The children can help to put out different types of food to attract a range of birds. Describing them helps to develop vocabulary – what colours are their heads, beaks, wings, do they run or hop, what sound do they make, which bird in the book looks most like the one in the garden, and what is its name?

Other animals

Pets such as rabbits and guinea-pigs can be an asset in a nursery, provided the children are involved in their care and feeding and one or more staff members is prepared to take clear responsibility for their wellbeing and especially for care at weekends and holidays. This needs to be someone who really loves animals and does not have to be persuaded to do the job as a tiresome obligation. If there is no such person on the nursery staff, it is better to do without pets altogether. An adequate hutch and run are needed, so space is another consideration.

Play equipment

When a nursery or centre has the opportunity to design from scratch or remodel the outdoor area, equipment for large-scale physical activity will be a key element. In this section we will only make a few suggestions about equipment already to be found in most nursery gardens. Natural materials with natural finishes – wood, bark, stone and metal – weather gracefully and look good far longer than the plastic equipment in garish colours to be seen in some playgrounds, which quickly starts to look grubby and stained.

Lengths of tree trunk are infinitely versatile, and can often be obtained from municipal Parks Departments, which may be willing to cut them into specified lengths. These can be laid horizontally or on end as steps or stepping stones. They can be used for climbing, balancing, jumping off and imaginative play. A useful idea is to set an old car steering wheel into one end of a tree trunk. Branches can make a cat-walk in a grassed area.

If possible it is better to have two smaller sandpits rather than one large one so as to reduce crowding and occasions for conflict between the children. Smaller ones are also more easily protected from cats as the covers will be more manageable to take off and replace. Sand needs maintenance and this makes a useful outdoor activity for a worker with a small group. Raking and sieving will be enjoyed, and the sand can be disinfected and kept damp using small watering cans – filling and spraying are water play with a purpose. As with the indoor sand tray, there must be plenty of sand and not too much equipment, and this should be checked regularly and stored, not left cluttering up the pit, which can quickly develop a neglected and uninviting aspect.

USING THE RESOURCES OF THE NEIGHBOURHOOD AND COMMUNITY

Here we are less concerned with major outings than with small-scale expeditions, usually at a short distance from the nursery or at least no further than the town centre. There are both negative and positive reasons for building these into the centre programme. On the negative side there is the fact that many children in day care spend most of their waking lives in one room. If parents are working full time they may be too occupied with domestic tasks at weekends to take the children out on leisurely shopping trips or child-paced walks.

Parents of children in local authority nurseries are sometimes too poor, demoralized or overburdened to think of taking the children out when they are not at the nursery. Either way the children may miss out on quite ordinary experiences and live in a world limited by the walls of the nursery and their own home.

There are also positive reasons: first, the opportunities that even the most ordinary neighbourhood offers for interest, learning and conversation and second, the advantages to the nursery or centre in getting to know the local community and making friends. This is especially important when, as is often the case, most of the staff do not live in the district where the nursery is situated.

Visits and outings

Successful outings depend on good organization and preparation, a small group of children, and enough adults to ensure safe supervision – at least one to every two children, which will probably mean involving parents, volunteers or students. Every neighbourhood has its own particular features: parks, markets, fire station, railway station or bridges, museums, libraries, swimming pools. What seems quite unremarkable to an adult – builders at work with a cement mixer or mechanical digger, a crane, traffic lights or the different types of fruit and vegetables on display outside a greengrocer's, can all provide a focus of interest.

It is important that all the adults involved are in clear agreement about the purpose of the outing, which is to provide enjoyment and learning opportunities for the children, not to achieve some adult objective which has little meaning for the child. The going matters as much as the arriving (which can if necessary be postponed for another occasion). Thus, the nursery worker's intention may be to visit a particular place, and she should build in plenty of time to get there without hustling the children, but if on the way they become engrossed in something else, a tree just shedding its shining chestnuts, for instance – she should be flexible enough to negotiate a change of plan with the children and her colleagues.

If one of the adults has a camera, he or she can take the occasional photograph, which can be used later by the key worker as a way of reviewing the experience with her small group and as a focus for conversation. A group photograph album is also useful for keeping parents informed and sharing nursery experiences with them (see Chapter 12).

When planning an outing, it is a good idea for the nursery worker to do a dummy run and talk to any outside people she plans to involve. For example, if she intends to take the children to visit shops of various kinds, they are likely to get a very different reception if they go at a time of day when business is slack rather than at a peak period, and she can also find out which shopkeepers are prepared to be friendly and helpful.

Trips to the local children's library can start very early in a child's life, whenever possible involving a parent too, reinforcing the interest and pleasure in books which the nursery has created. The nursery will probably already have a good relationship with the Children's Librarian and may have an arrangement for a stock of books changed periodically. Some parents may need convincing that a child is never too young to have a book borrowed on his behalf and read or shown to him at home.

Museums and art galleries are not often thought of as places to take very young children, but are full of objects and pictures which can hold great interest for them. Obviously the visit should be scaled to the attention span of the child. The nursery worker leading the outing should discuss with the person responsible for the educational work of the museum or gallery what is likely to appeal to small children and ask if possible for a guided tour. She can then make her own selection from her knowledge of the children and compile a list of exhibits to last over several visits, taking the children to look at no more than two or three different things on each occasion. This of course is entirely different from most people's past experience of visiting museums, either in school parties or as tourists, when we tend to rush round the whole place ending up exhausted and with no clear impression of what we have seen.

Swimming

Another possibility worth consideration, though it may take some effort to set up, is swimming. Children can learn to swim from a few months old and get great pleasure from it. This is commonplace in California, where the ubiquity of private pools makes it necessary for children to be 'water-safe' from an early age. The Vanessa Nursery in Hammersmith has a pool incorporated in the building, and the ACE parents' co-operative nursery in Cambridge also includes swimming as part of its programme (Elias, 1972; March, 1973), but swimming is not usually considered as a pre-school activity in this country.

One difficulty is that pools are often kept at too low a temperature for small children, but where there is a separate learners' pool it is sometimes possible to negotiate warmer water for particular sessions. Another is the need for an adult with each child, which can be difficult if most parents are working, unless the nursery is supported by a very strong group of voluntary and occasional helpers willing to go in the water with the children.

As swimming is likely to happen at best once a week, it is unrealistic to hope that many of the children will learn to swim unless they are also taken regularly by their parents at weekends. However, they can learn to feel happy and confident in their armbands, to propel themselves using dog-paddle, and become used to putting their faces in the water, so that they will learn to swim more easily when they are older. If the local pool has an instructor with a special interest in young children and if one of the nursery staff is a keen swimmer, a more ambitious programme may be possible.

Occasionally parents who would be available to help with swimming seem reluctant to join in. The key person needs to be very tactful in finding out the reason. It could be that a mother cannot swim herself, has no suitable costume or is self-conscious about her appearance, all obstacles that can be overcome with patience and sensitivity on the part of the worker. The mother may be asked to come along to the pool just to watch at first, so that she can see that the adults have their feet firmly planted on the bottom and don't need to swim themselves. Swimming is an activity with good potential for involving men, so it is always worth asking if a father might participate even if the mother is unable or unwilling.

Transport

Outings have a useful function in introducing parents to the resources of the neighbourhood and to activities they might undertake with their children which will also be enjoyable for themselves. However, transport is likely to be a difficulty if they live in the country or in outlying districts of a town. For a nursery, use of a minibus, perhaps shared with another centre, greatly widens the scope of possible outings, providing much pleasure and stimulus to the children. Staff members with their own cars may also be willing to use them provided the necessary insurance arrangements are made.

PLANNING OR IMPROVING AN OUTDOOR LEARNING AREA

Most of the following suggestions for designing or transforming a nursery centre garden have been contributed by a professional landscape consultant, Judy Hackett (see Figure 11.3). However, she emphasizes that, although it is wise to seek expert help, ideas must be evolved in close collaboration with nursery staff, management, and those who will be responsible for future outdoor maintenance to ensure that the design responds to the needs of everyone who will be running and using the nursery.

Aims and priorities

These will differ to some extent with the age of the children and whether, for example, there is space for a separate under-twos outdoor area or the garden must serve the needs of a wider age group. Other considerations are the size of the nursery, budget and the amount of voluntary help available. Ideally a garden might be designed to meet all the following requirements:

- Create a range of stimulating play and learning opportunities for children of different ages and abilities.
- Provide freedom for children to play without inhibition, as well as areas where they can be quiet and private.
- Accommodate group and individual play and occasional larger events (for example a parents' picnic).
- Provide for sensory experiences, exploring scale, space, light, shade, colour, sound, shape and scent.
- Provide some material which can be brought indoors such as flowers, leaves, seedheads, fruit, 'minibeasts'.

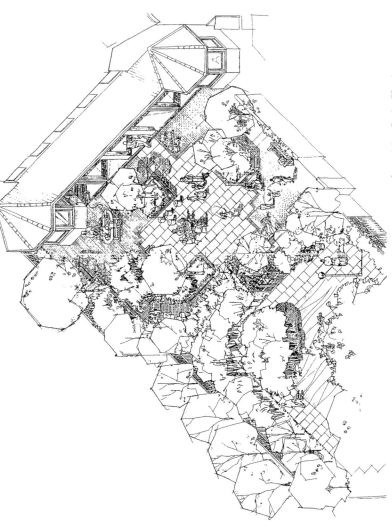

Figure 11.3 Lea View House Community Centre, day nursery garden, designed by Judy Hackett

The illustration opposite shows how Judy Hackett was able to meet many of these aims in her design for a community-centre day nursery garden.

Investigating the space and planning layout

Every outside area has its own unique opportunities and constraints, and it is important to identify these right from the start.

If the area is cold and windy it will not be an attractive place to play and learn. Shelter and enclosure must therefore be early considerations. Are there any existing trees and plants, and how do these influence your space? Are there views into and out of the playspace which you might want to enhance or screen? Are there any legal constraints which you should be aware of?

It is important to know what lies under the site – water, electricity, gas, telephone lines and any obstructions such as old sewers or foundations. A further consideration is how the garden will be maintained – whether outside assistance will be provided or if maintenance will fall almost entirely on the nursery staff, children and volunteers.

The size of the space should be assessed in relation to numbers of children and the need for nearby seating for adult carers. The general arrangement of the space should allow children to be reasonably visible to the carers at all times, though this does not rule out providing 'secret places'. There should be space for quiet, thoughtful play as well as active, noisy play. A covered area is needed for use in wet weather and shade for hot weather.

The special needs of children with disabilities should be considered. Ideas incorporated at the planning stage for the benefit of disabled children can be valuable for other children too – for example, enhancing the sensory impact of a play environment. Providing smooth-surfaced, wide pathways for access by wheelchairs and ramped alternatives to steps will also facilitate play with wheeled toys. Raised sand play areas or water containers, walkways or mazes with kerbs and handrails for guidance, designed with visually handicapped children in mind, are fun for the others as well.

Levels and contours

A small space need not be a disadvantage. The most modest contouring will increase play value and add variety to movement patterns, which makes it all the more surprising that so many nursery gardens are relentlessly flat. Children love abandoning themselves to the force of gravity and a grassy slope will encourage many motor activities such as rolling, balancing, swinging and jumping. Likewise the smallest bumps and wrinkles will become hills, valleys, mountain ranges or river canyons. What better than a grassy hollow, perhaps combined with shrub planting, for a secret hiding place or den? Mounds can be used as a planning device to create enclosure, provide shelter from the wind or to separate different play activities.

Planting

Plants are a source of many sensory experiences – colours, smells, textures, sounds. Their leaves, flowers, bark, twigs, cones and fruit can also be used as improvised play material.

Apart from many practical applications such as for screening, to create enclosure or to provide shade, much imaginative use can be made of planting to create child-scale fantasy play spaces. Shrubs and small-scale trees can be planted to become mini-jungles, to dramatize paths or clearings or form leafy tunnels. A weeping tree is invaluable as a play house or hiding place.

Children's gardens should be full of eye-catching and interesting plants, designed to stimulate curiosity both in the plants themselves and in the wildlife that visits them. Areas for energetic activities should be planted with robust shrubs or trees which will survive the impact of play, while other areas can aim for visual interest, fun and sensory stimulus throughout the year. Apart from the general principles related to play impact, some possibilities to be borne in mind when designing a planting scheme are:

Bold foliage shapes
Interesting textures
Flowers and seed-heads with intriguing shapes
Evocative names
Winter flowering plants
Plants for drying or use indoors
Strong scents
Bright colours
Decorative vegetables or fruits (including fruit trees)
Arches, pergolas, leafy tunnels
Plants which attract wildlife
Jungle planting using massed shrubs

Working out a planting scheme is a job for someone who has a real inclination and feel for horticulture, or an interest in learning about it.

There may be someone like this on the nursery staff who can work closely with a landscape consultant, supported by the head of the unit.

Another possibility is to involve a volunteer, either by a general appeal – a local newspaper will probably be willing to publish an article on the subject – or through a gardening club.

Wildlife

A variety of trees, shrubs and flowers will also attract many birds and insects, and this can help children to overcome their prejudices about creepy-crawlies. If space is limited, climbing shrubs grown on walls or fences can substitute for trees. Flowers should be chosen with strong scents and single (rather than double) blooms to attract butterflies and bees. If you also introduce a small rotting log or tree stump in a shady spot in the garden, this will soon harbour colonies of 'minibeasts' such as woodlice, beetles and dragon-like centipedes.

Grass

No other material can compare with grass for its restful and visually harmonious qualities. It can be tailored to fit any layout or ground shape and provides an informal surface on which children enjoy sitting, rolling, lying and running. As grass will degrade with intensive use it should be used with discretion and in conjunction with other surfaces to give year-round access. Grass is not a suitable impact-absorbent safety surface beneath and around play equipment.

Water

Water is very popular with children, but obviously safety must be taken carefully into account. A nature pond for fish, frogs, snails, water beetles and plants can be a valuable educational resource that will capture children's imagination and promote much enquiry and conversation. To reduce the likelihood of a child falling or stepping into it, such a pond can be constructed above ground level (400–500mm. (16–20in.)), and as an additional safeguard a wire mesh can be fixed just below the water level. In principle no pool should exceed 200 mm. (8 in.) in depth.

An asset for any playspace is an outdoor tap fitted with a hose and a selection of spray attachments which can be used for special fun events in the summer, as well as for garden maintenance (see Figure 11.4). Outdoor paving could feature drainage channels which a child can fill with water to create a stream. Other play use of water might include scope for damming, diverting the flow, creating waterfalls, mixing water with earth or sand, sailing toy boats.

Seasons, weather and time

The fall of snow, buds bursting out, flowers, autumn leaves, shadows of different lengths: a garden provides endless opportunities for demonstrating seasonal change, weather and the passing of time at a level which small children understand and remember. Add to the scene a sundial, weather vane, windmill or flag and children will be intrigued and delighted. All offer much scope for conversation and discussion.

Play equipment

This has the effect of formalizing and focusing activities. It is unfortunate that play equipment is almost always located in unimaginative settings isolated from natural features. However, many play structures now on the market consist of a flexible kit of parts enabling fixed equipment to be tailored to particular needs and to suit a particular space so that landings, ladders, steps and slides can be integrated with the surrounding terrain.

When space is limited, it is important to choose fixed equipment carefully, taking into account the surrounding safety zones required. Any existing equipment should be assessed in terms of both play and educational value. Is it the right size and scale in relation to the children's ages? Will it help them develop better co-ordination so that they acquire skills of climbing, swinging, hanging, spinning, jumping, balancing, crawling? Will it give them a sense of real movement in their bodies? Will it heighten their sense of spatial awareness? Could they use it as an adjunct to fantasy play? Is it flexible enough to be used in different ways? Is it durable and safe?

Such considerations should also be applied to any existing equipment. Your evaluation may conclude that an existing structure would be better located in an alternative place or even scrapped altogether.

The use of a variety of materials within a structure provides greater stimulation and interest. A combination of very simple fixed structures which can be linked and varied with the addition of ropes, nets, tyres, platforms and interchangeable swing assemblies offers most scope for variety and challenge. Detailed specifications are given in the book referred to earlier (Walsh, 1988). It shows how equipment more usually found in adventure playgrounds, such as a 'flying fox', can be scaled down to suit small children.

Figure 11.4 Water: the Primrose Hill Schools Centenary Garden, designed by Judy Hackett.
Source: Conservation Foundation, 1 Kensington Gore, London, SW7.

SOME PROBLEMS AND CONSTRAINTS

Apart from the obvious limitations of space and money, some other aspects which have to be thought out very carefully in designing an outside learning area are safety, the impact of play on planting, access, and maintenance.

Safety

There are British and European standards for children's play equipment, but these are intended for unsupervised playgrounds and are not primarily concerned with play value, so they should be considered as guidelines rather than absolute rules. Children need challenges and over-safe equipment may lack excitement and interest – on the other hand it is clearly important to minimize any risk of injury. The following checklist summarizes the main points to be considered:

- Well-designed equipment – construction, fixings and finishes, heights above ground, safety rails to recommended standard, slide profiles related to age.
- Planned layout and circulation – siting of equipment, safety zones round equipment, separation of active play from quiet area, angle of slopes and steps adapted to ages.

- Ground surfaces and finishes – impact absorbent materials below play equipment, durable slip-resistant surfaces to paths and paved areas.
- Controlled use of water – close supervision if deeper than 200mm., ponds raised and small-scale.
- Low-risk planting – avoidance of allergy-causing species and plants with poisonous roots, leaves, flowers or berries (reference material on this should be kept in the nursery).
- Regular maintenance – prompt repairs and replacements, care of whole area, daily clearance of leaves, berries, squashed fruits from paved areas, tree surgery repairs and replacements of planting.

Impact of play on landscape

Natural resources are to a greater or lesser extent fragile, and can be degraded by children's play. Planting in particular needs to stand up to considerable abuse and consideration must be given to its design and to the vulnerable period of establishment.

- Where active play is envisaged robust plant material should be used – vigorous, fast-growing trees and shrubs, large in size.
- Planting should be dense and massed.
- Paths or steps should be incorporated within planted or grassed slopes where heavy use is expected (for example, for access to a built-in slide).
- Prickly species should be incorporated on boundaries to deter access and reinforce site security.
- Newly planted and grassed areas should be fenced off until well established and an alternative play focus provided.
- Small-scale planting or fragile herbaceous species should be incorporated in raised beds or clearly defined by kerbs as non-play areas.

Access

Paths and paved areas should be spaced throughout to enable access at all times of the year, and these need to be durable, non-slip and wide enough to manoeuvre prams, pedal cars, tricycles and wheelchairs. Children love to follow tracks and trails, and the more interesting these can be the better. There could be a path which vanishes through a planted area or follows the gradient of a slope. Stepping stones could lead into a secret corner or be laid in grass between trees. Recommended surfaces are paving slabs, brick (not slippery engineering quality), tarmac, asphalt, brushed concrete, but *not* loose gravel or reinforced grasscrete.

Beneath and around play equipment there should be all-purpose, all-weather surfaces. The main suitable safety surfaces are loosefill (tree bark, sand or peagravel), rubbercrumb or rubber sheet or tiles. All have their assets and drawbacks which need to be considered in relation to their situation and expected use. For example, loosefill surfaces are more difficult to maintain and are not suitable for scuff points, such as under swings and at the ends of slides. Rubber surfaces become less impact-absorbent as they compress and wear out. Moulded rubber is non-porous and puddles can collect unless the ground is flat and well drained. Professional advice will be needed to decide on the best combination of surfaces for the intended use of the space.

OUTSIDE AREA FOR UNDER TWOs

Ideally the smallest children should have their own outside space, opening out of their group room with a covered terrace area. It is best situated next to the older children's garden with a low fence or hedge and a connecting gate so that the children can see each other and sometimes play together. Unlike the older children, they do not need a large active area or fixed equipment, but they do need space because they are constantly on the move, walking unsteadily and erratically, tumbling over and bumping into things. This means eliminating unnecessary hazards, sharp edges and protrusions, providing smooth surfaces and flat junctions between them.

Children in their second year love to jump off low heights, climb on and off tyres and boxes, empty and fill containers, crawl through and under things. This can all be accommodated with a range of light, moveable equipment such as cardboard boxes, balls, bean bags and cubes to hide in. The basic requirements are a flat space to push toys, a section with earth mounds or slopes with a one in three gradient, a shaded sand pit, not too big, with a wide sweeping edge to minimize the risk of tripping, and a low climbing platform with a run-up ramp or two steps which can also be used as a setting up point for moveable equipment.

Small children, like older ones, need a quiet area where they can come to a pause for a moment and just watch what is going on. They also need the reassurance of a close adult presence, so sitting places for nursery workers are essential. If possible, the quiet corner should be situated on a slight rise so as to give the adult a view of the whole play area, but be given a limited sense of enclosure by a low curved hedge or wall, or failing that by an arrangement of mats and cushions.

Planting should be designed to create interesting shapes, some shade and small enclosed spaces, but needs to have especially in mind the tendency of under twos to put anything small in their mouths.

SEEING THROUGH THE CHILD'S EYES

The educational and play value of a nursery garden, however well designed, will only be as good as the use the adults make of it. A serious deterrent in this country is the absence of any dependable period of fine weather and the long winter months when it never seems to stop raining. This is where nursery workers should try to put themselves back in the place of a child, who is not only indifferent to rain but often positively enjoys it until he takes on the negative attitudes of adults. Short forays into the garden with a small group of children during or immediately after rain can be highly enjoyable and provide many opportunities for observation and conversation. The key point, though, is that the group must be *small*. Drying out four sets of boots and jackets is a very different proposition from dealing with twenty.

Sometimes nursery staff feel reluctant to take children outside in winter because they feel that they themselves will be cold, uncomfortable and bored. This goes back to the attitudes discussed at the beginning of the chapter, with the adult in the playground in a passive, supervisory role, instead of actively facilitating play and learning with a small group. The activity needs to be carefully planned to suit the weather, perhaps running about together for 5 minutes in an exhilarating high wind, using rain for water play or experimenting with different materials in the sun to see which get hot fastest. In all this the adult needs to consider her own comfort and interest as much as that of the children. Only if the nursery staff genuinely enjoy working in the outside learning area will it be effectively used.

SUMMARY

Outdoor space is often an underused asset. This chapter shows how it can become a resource for children's education and pleasure and provide much interest for adults too.

The first section suggests ways in which, given positive staff attitudes, the garden can become a genuine 'outdoor learning area'. The second explores the possibilities offered by the surrounding neighbourhood for visits and small-scale outings. In the third section, landscape consultant Judy Hackett shows how even a small outdoor area can be transformed by well-planned contouring and planting into a place with infinite possibilities for children's learning and enjoyment.

12 Working relations with parents

The joys of parents are secret, and so are their griefs and fears.

Francis Bacon

The way that caregivers and parents talk, behave and feel about each other is inevitably influenced by the reason why the child is receiving day care away from home, and the function of the unit. But whatever the setting, nursery managers and workers have to make a conscious effort to build a bridge between the centre and each child's home and family over which information can flow freely both ways, and people, too, can cross from one side to the other, so that there is as much consistency and continuity as possible between the child's two worlds.

The key person has the essential task of setting up an effective channel of communication between the home and the day care setting. Her relationship with the parents will do much to determine the quality of the child's experience, yet it contains inbuilt tensions which have to be recognized and managed.

The centre has to be clear exactly what it is offering to the child and parents, and misunderstandings are less likely if this takes the form of a written agreement. There are many different ways in which nurseries and family centres can support parents and in some circumstances enrich their lives. We describe in this chapter how some centres are able to help parents manage their children with less stress and enjoy them more. The relationship is not all one way, however. Finding ways for parents to become effectively involved in the life of the centre can greatly extend staff resources, reveal unexpected skills and talents, and generate energy for new developments.

THE ROLE OF THE KEY PERSON

The key person system plays a crucial part in creating and maintaining good working relations with parents. The relationship should be established at the earliest opportunity, preferably, by the key person making a home visit before the child starts attending the centre, as described in Chapter 3.

Although the primary purpose of this first visit is not to obtain or provide more than basic information, the nursery worker is sure to come away knowing a good deal about the home and family, and it is sensible to record this immediately afterwards. She will need an early opportunity to share her impressions with a colleague or senior and discuss how the nursery can best provide a service to the child and parents within the limits set by available resources.

The key person and parents in the nursery

During the home visit arrangements will be made for the parent(s) to visit the nursery. First impressions are very important. The key person needs to check, for example, that welcoming messages on the noticeboard include the language of the family she is expecting.

Clearly it is essential that they are warmly greeted when they arrive and that the key person makes herself free to give them her full attention. After showing them round the building and introducing them to a few of the other staff (too many new people at once can be overwhelming), time needs to be made for a full discussion on how parents and nursery can work together to give the child the best-possible experience. If there is a real question mark over the parents' capacity to care for the child adequately, it is advisable for the social worker or a senior staff member to be present at this interview, but the key worker should take the lead, with the other person there to observe and support.

Much of this discussion will inevitably be taken up with practical matters: what hours and days the child will attend, who will be bringing and collecting her, what happens if she is ill, how much, if anything, the parents will be asked to pay towards fees and/or meals. Expectations and obligations on both sides need to be clear but realistic. It may be easy for parents with their own telephone to let the nursery know by nine in the morning if their child is too ill to come, but impossible for a single mother to leave a sick child to find a public call-box.

It is important not to offer more than can be delivered. For example, nursery workers anxious to be open and available to parents will often say 'Feel free to come in and talk to us any time'. This creates the situation where the nursery worker feels obliged to drop whatever she is doing (when she might be engrossed in an activity with a group of children) and give priority to a parent who wants to talk to her. Not only does that convey an unfortunate message, that children matter less than adults, but it disrupts the work and probably means that the caregiver will have half her attention on what the parent is saying and half on keeping order among the children. If the matter is important, it is better to ask the parent to sit down (on one of the comfortable, adult-sized chairs with which the room is provided) and wait until the nursery worker can make herself free, or fix an appointment for another time. Of course this does not apply when the parent is acutely distressed or there is a real emergency, when the key worker will have to ask a colleague to cover for her.

It is essential to state rules and boundaries firmly and then operate them with regard to individual circumstances rather than leave parents floundering, trying to guess what is expected of them and what really matters or doesn't. For example, if, as we would hope, the nursery or centre has a 'No smoking' rule, this needs to be made quite clear, certainly not allowing parents to smoke at the first interview with the mistaken intention of putting them at their ease. Another boundary which needs to be firmly adhered to right from the start is collection times. It can be very upsetting to children and cause great inconvenience and irritation to staff when a parent persistently turns up late at the end of the day. When parents have gradually slipped into the habit of collecting children after the official closing time, it is much harder to reinstate the rule, and nursery workers may as a result become angry and hostile, like the staff group mentioned in Chapter 4 who wanted to punish the parents by taking away the children's places.

Communication between home and nursery

The key person needs to plan how she will know what is going on in the child's home life, keep the parents informed about their child's progress, and sort out any difficulties. Depending on the shift system in the unit, she should always be able to exchange a few words with them on arrival or with whoever comes to fetch the child. It should be standard practice that the person who hands the child over at going home time, knows either directly, or from the key person, what the child has been doing that day and can tell the parent. However, we know, both from research and experience, that such conversations can be very conventional and convey little information. 'She's been a really good girl and ate all her dinner' may be reassuring but not much else.

One family centre gives each family an attractively bound 'link' book which goes backwards and forwards between home and centre. Each day the key person makes brief notes of how the child spent the day, describing the occasional incident or achievement at greater length. The family (which can include brothers and sisters or grandparents) usually write about what they did at the weekend, record amusing sayings or describe aspects of the child's behaviour. Any significant family events can also be recorded.

A regular time needs to be scheduled for more reflective discussion about the child's progress, to which the parent(s) make a full contribution. This will be more useful if it is based on systematic observation both at home and in the nursery. The link book provides one device for encouraging this.

Time should be allowed for at least half an hour's uninterrupted discussion when the key person can arrange for a colleague to cover her work and take telephone messages. It may sometimes be necessary for the nursery worker to raise topics for discussion, but she needs to be careful not to fall into the trap of doing all the talking herself. This kind of implicit discounting of the parents' knowledge of their own child is an experience which will be only too familiar to anyone who has attended a school open evening. However, it can often be helpful to have a structure to work round, for instance, by asking the parents to help complete a developmental assessment schedule. Meetings of this kind provide a chance to discuss everyday matters that need a co-ordinated approach. Toilet training is one example. Another, which often causes ill-feeling between parents and nursery workers, is sleep. Most nurseries expect under-threes to sleep, or at least rest, after the midday meal, but some children refuse to sleep again until late in the evening if they have an afternoon nap, causing much inconvenience to their parents. It is, of course, impossible to keep a child awake when she needs to sleep, but there may be scope for negotiation and the timing and length of the rest.

It sometimes happens that parents have problems in their own lives, for example, with relationships, debts, housing or welfare rights, and are more interested in talking about those than about the child. They cannot be brushed aside, but the key person has to be clear that she is not a social worker or counsellor. However sympathetic she may be, she has to set limits to the amount of time she can give. She needs to know or find out where the parent(s) can go for help, and guard against offering possibly ill-informed advice herself.

The focus of attention can sometimes be brought back to the child by helping parents to consider what they can do to reduce the harmful effects that their difficulties may be having on her.

The key person and the parent

Parents are generally in favour of the key person system because they like to feel that their child is especially important to someone in the nursery, and they also find it easier to relate more closely to one staff member than ten, but this feeling sometimes has elements of ambivalence in it. The mother (less often the father) may worry that the child will come to prefer the key person. A study of mothers returning to work after four or five months' maternity leave found that this anxiety was not uncommon: 'I'm jealous – I want my own to want me', one mother said, and a similar reason is often given for preferring group care to child minding: 'I feel I'd mind the baby having a relationship with one other woman – at the crèche he prefers certain women but it doesn't bother me because there are so many' (Brannen and Moss, 1988).

All nursery workers need to be very sensitive to this point. For example, if the parents' circumstances make a painful separation unavoidable at times (see Chapter 3), it is not helpful for the key person to tell the mother on her return 'Oh, she didn't miss you at all after the first few minutes' when what the mother wants to hear is 'She missed you very much but I was able to comfort her after a while'. One detail which helps the mother not to feel that the key person is taking her place is if the caregiver, when holding the child in the mother's presence, as must occasionally happen, makes a point of having the child's face *outwards*, towards the mother. It is also better for the nursery worker not to feed or change the child in her mother's presence, unless specifically asked to do so.

AGREEMENTS WITH PARENTS

A distinction is sometimes made between day care places offered to families on a contractual basis and those where a place is provided for a child with no conditions attached. In practice there is always an implied agreement and the difference is one of how explicit this is made, the precise conditions, and the sanctions for failing to comply with them.

There is everything to be said for being quite clear what is expected on both sides and putting it in writing. This applies just as much to private day care centres where parents are paying high fees and to child minders as it does to local authority day nurseries with most of the families living on welfare benefits. The agreement has to be negotiated, and if necessary renegotiated later, in the clear understanding that its primary object is to promote the wellbeing of the child.

The content of agreements

What should such an agreement include? We have already mentioned times of taking and fetching and meetings with the key person. Other important matters are any special dietary requirements, whether for religious or health reasons, practical arrangements for payment, daily routines and bodily care, and methods of control and management. If the child has been referred by social services with a requirement that one or both parents spend some time with her in the nursery, it needs to be clearly stated when this will happen and how any changes can be negotiated. It also needs to be set out how parents can make suggestions or complaints, initially to the key person and, if still dissatisfied after discussion, to the head of the unit.

It is important that nursery staff do not regard conditions proposed by social workers as written in tablets of stone. For example, if in their judgement what an overburdened mother most needs is relief from child care to enable her to generate some energy to deal with her problems, it is pointless to put pressure on her to attend the nursery with her child until she is in a state to gain some benefit from it. If she is able to find a job, her renewed sense of competence and self-esteem, to say nothing of the money, may do more to improve her care of the child than any amount of talk about parenting skills. If, on the basis of their daily observation of child and parent(s) nursery workers disagree with the social worker's assessment, they should say so and negotiate a change.

CONSULTING PARENTS

As we noted in Chapter 1, despite the rhetoric of partnership, very few day care units give parents any opportunity to participate in their management. All important matters tend to be decided from above and most social services-run centres do not even have a management committee. For different reasons private day-care centres are equally unlikely to allow any real influence to parents. However, voluntary organizations and community nurseries usually have committees made up of staff or trustees of the funding body, local interests, the unit organizer and parent representatives. Sometimes there is a separate parents' committee, but too often its functions are restricted to discussion of fund-raising activities. That can be useful of course, but fails to provide the users of the service with any way of expressing their ideas about its policy and operation.

Usually only a minority of parents want to become involved at this level. For them it is often a valuable experience, enabling women especially to recognize unexpected abilities, learn important skills and feel a new sense of their own competence. There is a risk, though, that this group of parents will be seen as an elite from which the majority feel excluded (Daines *et al.*, 1990). Other ways of consulting parents also need to be found, such as group-room meetings, suggestion boxes, 'ideas' boards and mini-referenda, offering choices between alternatives.

A difficulty is that the unit staff may have very narrow bounds within which to operate, being limited by the policy and financial resources of the agency, and this can be hard for parents to understand. Parents often have different priorities from the staff. They are not always tolerant and accepting of each other and may want to be tougher on rule-breakers than the nursery workers are prepared to be.

There is no doubt that involving parents in this way is liable to mean more work for staff though it can also be a source of valuable new ideas and produce new resources for the nursery. It does, however, need careful thinking through: creating opportunities for parents to express their views and then ignoring them is bound to lead to trouble.

Keeping parents informed

Direct participation in running the nursery is usually limited by the time and effort it takes to bring up a young child in our society. Working parents are likely to have very little time to spend in the day care centre once the child is settled. Nursery workers need to recognize that the fact that parents are not inclined to linger reflects the reality that they are either rushing not to be late for work or are trying to fit in a bit of shopping or get to the post office before dashing home to prepare the evening meal. It does not mean that they are not interested in talking or hearing about their child. In Sweden parents are entitled to paid time off work to visit and observe in their child's school or day care centre (Melhuish and Moss, 1991). Until we have that kind of enlightened legislation here, most parents will not be able to make such arrangements unless they take a day's leave, which they may not be able to afford.

Nursery staff can show that they understand the situation and find ways of keeping parents informed. For example, a simple monthly newsletter is a good way to let everyone know what is going on in the unit and about plans for future activities. (It can also make a good collaborative project for parents who are not working.) Parents who never have a chance to see what their child does in the nursery often enjoy watching short sequences of video showing her at play. If the nursery has a video camera or can borrow one this is a useful thing for the key person to do.

The parents' room

In local authority day nurseries the majority of parents have been offered a place for their child because of their living conditions, social or personal problems, and this presents a great challenge to day care staff who may have no personal experience of, say, unemployment or living on an inadequate income and whose basic training has usually given them little preparation in coping with such problems. Nevertheless the nursery can play an important part in helping to tide families over what may be an especially difficult period in their lives. In some areas the day nursery or family centre is what a staff member described as 'the one oasis in a cultural desert'.

Increasingly nurseries are designed or reorganized to incorporate a parents' room. Though some units are desperate for space and can only find places for parents to get together occasionally for specific purposes, a designated area is coming to be recognized as essential, especially in centres where a high proportion of the families are disadvantaged.

Quite often this space when it exists, is not well used. It is discouraging to find a 'parents' room' which is dark and dismal, with blank walls, and which has become a dumping ground for unwanted toys and items for the next jumble sale. It is hardly surprising to be told that 'the parents don't use it much'. Clearly there is no point in having such a room unless it is warm, attractively decorated, comfortably furnished and equipped for tea- or coffee-making and preferably washing-up. It may also offer facilities that can be useful to parents on low incomes, such as a sewing machine and ironing board.

It should be supplied with a large noticeboard on which can be posted information about local events of interest to families with small children, items for sale or wanted, offers of services on an exchange basis. Even if staffing resources do not allow for organized activities to go on in the room, it can have a useful function as a social meeting place and help to reduce the isolation suffered by so many mothers of young children.

It is essential for one member of nursery staff to take responsibility for seeing that the parents' room is kept in good order, and, in the interest both of health and maintenance, that the no-smoking rule is firmly enforced, otherwise the environment can quickly deteriorate. If the parents' room is used for other purposes, such as group sessions, cookery classes, work with small groups of children or individual meetings with parents, this should be clearly indicated on the door, so that parents can see when it is available for social use and do not feel themselves to be intruders.

CHANGING PARENTS' BEHAVIOUR

How far is it a legitimate aspect of the nursery or family centre's task to change the way parents handle their children? This is a question that arouses strong views. We are not talking here about the relatively unambiguous situation where attendance of both child and parent(s) at the centre is a condition of her being allowed to remain at home (see Chapter 14). If the nursery is primarily offering a service to working parents, or a better play and learning environment to children living in cramped conditions, do the workers have any right to impose their own ideas about bringing up children on families who may come from a different class and possibly a different culture from themselves? To some extent this is an unreal question, as most research shows that persuading people to change their child-rearing practices is very difficult. However, there is one aspect of child care where professional early years workers can give a clear lead, and that is in relation to physical punishment.

In five European countries this is forbidden by law (Sweden, Finland, Denmark, Norway and Austria), but in this country hitting children by parents is both socially and legally accepted. A recent survey found that almost two out of three mothers admitted smacking babies under a year, and nearly all 4-year-olds were smacked, often several times a day (Newson and Newson, 1989). Peter Newell has pointed out that this is a gross invasion of the child's physical integrity (Newell, 1991). Our tolerance of assault against children is yet another indicator of the low value given to them in our society.

Some progress is being made, and the campaign to end physical punishment of children (EPOCH) is gaining increasing support. Obviously it will be made clear that hitting children is not acceptable in the nursery, but nursery workers have an important educational role in helping parents to understand the reason for this and to find more effective ways of controlling and guiding their children's behaviour. The topic is one which always provokes lively discussion in parents' group meetings, and it can be very satisfying to see attitudes shift as people come to see behaviour which they had previously taken for granted in a different light.

We argued in Chapter 1 against categorizing parents into those who are competent and those who need help. Almost all parents feel the need of advice and support at some time, especially in the early stages. They turn for guidance to older relatives, more experienced friends, to books and magazines. There are many ways in which nursery workers can be helpful. In particular, they can offer reassurance that a child's behaviour is normal for her stage of development (if it is). When there is a real cause for concern, they can discuss with parents what action might be taken. Some of the ways that nurseries and family centres can help children and families in difficulties are described in the next two chapters. Also, they can help parents to enjoy their children in the nursery, whatever may be the stresses of their life outside.

RELATIONSHIP PLAY WITH CHILDREN AND PARENTS

Little children need a great deal of close physical contact with adults who care for them if they are to develop trust and a sense of security. With a strong key person system the nursery worker is likely to feel an intimacy with her small group of children that makes it seem legitimate to engage in the kind of physical play that is usually a natural part of family life. However, sometimes carers feel that anything more than an occasional cuddle is inappropriate with children who are not their own.

For the majority of children any deficits in the care setting are compensated for at home, but if one or both parents are also inhibited about relaxing physically with their children, the implications are more serious. It would be a pity if our present heightened awareness of the danger of sexual abuse to even very young children were to prevent close bodily contact between children and adults that can be so pleasurable to both.

A few parents, although they say they love their children, find this hard to express physically. They may rationalize their reluctance by saying that the child is 'not cuddly' or resists contact. Relationship play is particularly valuable to parents who are not physically comfortable with their children, especially if things have gone wrong and the family has been referred to the Centre for reasons of abuse or neglect, but it also has value in its own right, whether the child is partnered by a nursery worker or by her own mother or father.

What is relationship play? It is a system of physical interaction between two people in which power, size, strength and ability become irrelevant. It produces a sense of trust, intimacy and mutual enjoyment between the people concerned, which may be temporary or part of the process of building a long-term relationship. It also helps a child to develop a sense of her own body, physical agility and confidence. It provides a non-verbal means of communicating with children but is also an effective way of increasing their vocabulary, since words associated with physical experience are more likely to be absorbed and remembered.

The method, based on the theories of Rudolf Laban, was developed by Veronica Sherborne, working with a complete spectrum of children from toddlers to adolescents, including those with special needs. Through Veronica's teaching on the Bristol post-qualifying course for day care managers it has come to be used in a wide variety of nurseries and family centres. It is unlike anything else we do with parents and has the potential to free even the most tense and overburdened to be relaxed and loving with their children, at least for a short time.

Many studies have shown that fathers are much more likely than mothers to engage in physical play with their children. Not only do women tend to give up most forms of sport and physical recreation in adolescence, but once they become mothers they may be so preoccupied with getting through their daily tasks that they come to feel that play for its own sake is not a legitimate way of spending time. Their enjoyment when 'given permission' to play is striking.

Relationship play is also a good way of involving mothers who may lack confidence to participate in other activities, and in day care centres where most of the mothers are working it can be a relaxing and fulfilling one-off session, perhaps at the end of a day. With very young children it is essential for each child to be paired with an adult. If some parents are unable to be present, this may allow the child to join in with a staff member, preferably his or her key person.

One great advantage of relationship play is that no equipment is needed. Veronica Sherborne herself preferred to work in a large open room with a smooth, uncarpeted floor, such as a school gymnasium or untiered college lecture theatre, but we have seen very enjoyable sessions in cramped, carpeted day nurseries. It is important, of course, to fit the activity to the space available as too many adults and children together in a confined area can lead to accidents.

The leader for the session should have a clear plan of the activities to be included in, say, a 40-minute period, and when several people are taking part for the first time may need to demonstrate first, with a child or another nursery worker, to show that nobody will be asked to do anything difficult or alarming.

Relationship play falls into three categories: caring, shared and 'against', the third type only to be introduced when the partners have developed a strong sense of mutual trust and confidence, perhaps after experiencing several sessions. Here we describe a few of the simpler activities in each category, but for a fuller description and explanation of the underlying developmental theory you will need to consult Veronica Sherborne's book, *Developmental Movement for Children* (Sherborne, 1990).

Cradling

This is always a good way to begin and end a session, with the older partner giving a sense of security to the younger and becoming comfortable with close bodily contact with the child. We sometimes call it 'making a house' (see Figure 12.1).

The child sits between the adult's outstretched legs and is rocked gently from side to side, supported by the older partner's knees, thighs and arms. When the partners achieve a rhythm that is satisfactory to both, the side-to-side movement is harmonious and calming. The ability to contain the child in a secure but unrestrictive way, so that the experience is one of comfort and security, is a skill that has to be learned and requires considerable sensitivity to the child's reactions and almost imperceptible physical signals. It is often noticeable how much more comfortable and relaxed the partners look when the cradling is at the end of a session and they have become better acquainted with their own and each other's bodies.

Rocking

The adult sits with the child between her legs, both facing forwards, and grasps the child under the knees (babies and small children can sit on the adult's thighs). The caregiver then tips backwards and forwards as far as the child wants to go. Eventually the child may be upside down with feet in the air and older ones, when sufficiently confident, will enjoy turning a complete somersault, landing on knees or feet behind the adult's head. Less confident children may prefer a variant of cradling, increasing the sway until adult and child fall over in a heap together. These activities usually produce much laughter and enjoyment, for adults and children alike.

Figure 12.1 Relationship play: cradling.
Photo: Clive Landen

Supporting and rolling

The adult lies on his or her back with knees bent up and the child sits astride, leaning back on her partner's thighs. The adult bounces the child gently up and down. Alternatively the adult can lie face down with the child astride the back and hump her up and down in that way. In this position the child is the dominant partner and is not obliged to make eye contact, which is sometimes helpful with insecure or shy children in the early stages.

Rolling is something which most little children do spontaneously. To start with the adult can sit with the child lying across her thighs and can then roll the child down to the ankles and back up again. Then she can lie back and roll the child right up to her chin and, coming up into

Figure 12.2 Relationship play: shared activity.
Photo: Clive Landen

the sitting position, all the way down to her feet. The way a child and parent relate to each other in this exercise can be very revealing, with a great difference between the way a confident, well-loved child will roll freely, adapting to the parent's body, and the rather stiff, awkward movements of a child who is less secure.

One way of giving even a very small child a sense of power and control is by encouraging her to roll the adult. Of course it requires a good deal of co-operation from the older partner but the child need not be aware of this.

Tunnels

This is a very popular activity which can be carried out either in individual pairs or groups. The adult makes a 'horse' on all fours, with knees well apart, and the child (or children) goes through the spaces, under the arms, between the legs and under the arch. A group of adults can make a long tunnel or one with bends in it and the children have the opportunity to exercise choice and initiative.

Children enjoy balancing on an adult's body in different ways: standing on the partner's thighs with hands supported, sitting on her back while she makes a 'horse' and subsides to the floor again (see

Figure 12.3 Relationship play: flying.
Photo: Clive Landen

Figure 12.2), or best of all 'flying', where the adult lies face up and supports the child on her shins, holding the child's shoulders (see Figure 12.3).

Rowing the boat

An activity which encourages eye contact comes into the category of shared relationships. The partners sit on the floor facing each other with legs outstretched – a very young child can sit on her mother or caregiver's legs. The child holds the adult's wrists while the adult grasps the child's elbows. Each takes it in turn to lie back and then sit up and lean forward while the other partner lies back on the floor. The child and adult alternately support and pull each other, with the child contributing to the shared activity. The adult obviously helps when it is her turn to sit up, but allows the child to feel she is exerting all her strength. This is another equalizing exercise, with the child and adult alternately higher than each other. There are many other balancing and see-saw activities which can be introduced as children and their adults gain experience and agility.

Focusing energy

The third type of activity involves the child in testing her strength against an older partner. The task of the adult is to feed in experiences of strength to the younger partner, encouraging effort and determination, and allowing the child to be successful only as a result of using all the energy of which she is capable. For most mothers and fathers this comes quite naturally, but parents whose relationships with their children are potentially abusive often find it hard to allow children, particularly their own, to be successful against them. They quickly lose their perception of themselves as adults and of their strength relative to that of the child. They forget that the activity is intended to be lighthearted and enjoyable, and in their desire to 'win' may even inflict pain. Clearly 'against' games are not without an element of risk, but they can also provide a valuable opportunity for the parent to learn that allowing the younger partner to test herself against a controlled resistance represents strength in the adult, not weakness.

Examples of 'against' activities are 'rocks' and 'prisons'. The 'rock' assumes various shapes, depending on whether the person sits with knees bent up and feet apart, lies spreadeagled on the floor, or kneels on all fours, but the task of the other partner is to force it to move. The adult pushes just hard enough so that the child has to use all her strength to resist, but not hard enough to move her off her base. When the roles are reversed the adult judges the moment to collapse or fall over, to the child's great delight.

In 'prisons' the partners adopt the same position as in cradling, but in this case the older partner's arms and legs grip the child, who is encouraged to struggle hard to escape. If the escape is too easy it is unsatisfying, and the adult has to make a sensitive judgement of the child's strength and ability to tolerate frustration.

We have seen relationship play used successfully with depressed mothers, with parents known to have abused their children, with inexperienced nursery workers and with social workers who find difficulty in communicating with small children. It is one of the most effective forms of direct work with parents who are hard to influence by discussion-based methods, and since there is no right or wrong, no winners or losers, it provides an opportunity for modelling without undermining the confidence of parents.

SUMMARY

In this chapter we have discussed some of the practical issues which arise when the daily care of a young child is shared between parents and an out-of-home setting. Whatever the reason for the child's attendance, lines of communication need to be carefully worked out and expectations clear on both sides. The key person plays a very important role here.

In some centres relations with parents will not go much beyond this. Others have extended their function to involve mothers, and occasionally fathers, in a whole range of activities, of which relationship play is one. We have touched on some of the problems which may arise even in ordinary relations with parents, but which can usually be overcome with goodwill and some skill in negotiation. In the next two chapters we go on to consider children and families with more serious difficulties.

13   Children in difficulties

The hearts of small children are delicate organs. A cruel beginning in the world can twist them into curious shapes.

Carson McCullers

The handling of young children with difficulties is the subject of countless books and articles, generally relating to problems which happen within the family. Very little has been written to help nursery workers or child minders who are looking after children outside their own homes. We know that a high proportion of children in local authority day nurseries are likely to have problems of behaviour or development (Bain and Barnett, 1980; McGuire and Richman, 1986). This may not only reflect the way priorities are applied in allocating places, but also learning from peers, so that the clustering of severely disadvantaged children in particular settings may, as Moss and Melhuish (1991) suggest, turn them into 'training schools in problem behaviour'.

However, any child can find himself in difficulties, if only temporarily, not only those with obvious problems in the family. We should not forget that the way the care setting is organized also has a powerful effect on child behaviour, as Richman and McGuire found in a study of six London day nurseries (1988).

Problems which a child already has can be accentuated by being in a group, and in some instances may even be created by the way a group is run. We start by considering general principles of managing behaviour in a group care setting and then look at some varieties of difficult behaviour which may cause problems for nursery workers.

DIFFICULTIES GENERATED BY THE SETTING

As adults, we can think of situations, such as being squeezed up in an overcrowded bus or waiting endlessly in an outpatient department, when we feel oppressed and frustrated and have to exert great self-control not to express our anger too openly.

For the child in a day care centre, equivalent situations are having to sit for a story in a too-large group with no room for his legs, being given a puzzle with two pieces missing or a doll with no clothes on and lacking an arm, sitting at a table on a chair which is much too low and so finding his chin in his plate. When nursery workers are finding a child's behaviour difficult, it is essential to ask if the environment we provide may be making matters worse, especially if the child obviously has a good deal to cope with already. In this way we can often avoid conflicts which would otherwise produce tears and uproar. It is always better to anticipate confrontation with children rather than react negatively once a problem has arisen.

Of course setting limits is part of the process of socialization which occurs as the baby, entirely dominated by his physical needs, develops and matures. For his caregivers this means striking a balance between two kinds of interaction with the child: on the one hand affection, approval, tolerance, sympathy, protection, understanding, reassurance and encouragement; on the other making requests, forbidding certain behaviour, expressing displeasure, giving responsibility.

When nursery workers are rushed and overpressed they may find themselves doing too much on the control side, giving a stream of orders, or constantly rebuking the child, which can produce either rebellion or withdrawal. There is a danger that a child in difficulties may receive little communication of a positive kind, either at home or in the nursery, and this will have a very damaging effect on his self-concept and thus on his behaviour and development.

Sometimes we say 'no' rather carelessly when under pressure, realizing afterwards that our prohibition was really not necessary. If we are not interested in 'winning' and know that we made a mistake, we can say so honestly, showing the child a genuine person who isn't afraid to correct a wrong decision.

REACTIONS TO STRESSFUL EVENTS

When a child who is normally well-adjusted and co-operative suddenly starts behaving in an uncharacteristic way, he is quite likely to be responding to some important event in his family. Where the key person system is in operation his special adult will be able to give him extra affectionate attention at this time. A typical instance is when a child in his third year experiences the birth of a younger brother or sister. One study found that 93 per cent of first-born children showed an increase in unco-operative and demanding behaviour after the arrival of a second child (Dunn, 1984), so that a temporary change in behaviour can be regarded as entirely normal. The important thing is for the adults to avoid reacting in a punitive way.

Even though a child has been well prepared and a favourable expectation created, the actual reality of a baby who displaces him and receives everyone's attention can be too hard to bear. He may express his resentment by being thoroughly awkward and screaming for what is thought to be no reason. He may clamour to have a bottle again when he had quite given it up. He has powerful feelings to cope with and, as yet, very limited means of expression. Unless his close adults can help him through this genuine crisis, their exasperation with his behaviour will quickly give him the idea that he is bad.

Adults sometimes get very anxious about admitting that jealous feelings exist and a child can be continually hearing how wonderful it will be to have a little brother or sister to play with. When the baby arrives it is not wonderful at all, quite the opposite, and the child, understandably from his point of view, can feel isolated and angry about the denial of part of the reality he is living at that time. It would be remarkable if he did not *feel* jealous and we can only help him not to *act* jealous.

Other circumstances may also produce a shift in attention away from the child, with similar effects, such as for example the death of a grandparent, a sudden financial crisis or the parents' decision to separate.

The situation at home will be known when a key person system is working well, and the child will gain confidence from knowing that there is a nursery worker who has special concern for him and will support him when he finds himself in trouble of some kind. When a young child is going through a period of what he may experience as environmental upheaval, a familiar routine and contact with a substitute attachment figure have been found the most effective way of reducing distress (Arnold, 1990).

HANDLING DIFFICULT BEHAVIOUR

Temper tantrums

Temper tantrums are extremely common in very small children, probably related to their inability to recognize their own wants, the frequent frustrations they experience, and their limited command of language. It is estimated that nearly 20 per cent of 2 and 3-year-olds have a tantrum at least once a day, and a much higher proportion of children display the occasional tantrum, often unpredictably (Jenkins *et al.*, 1980). Although a temper tantrum does not directly affect the other children, it is upsetting to the group because of the noise and confusion it can cause.

Sometimes a tantrum will happen quite suddenly and a child will throw himself on the floor screaming and beating his feet. At moments like this it is clear that words are quite useless, in fact any attempts to check the tantrum generally make things worse.

The most helpful thing for the adult to do is to stay near the child, perhaps sitting down, attentive and available but not intervening, until the child is quiet again. It is often noticeable that the other children watch the nursery worker very carefully and are reassured that she stays calm and, once the tantrum has passed, helps the child, with a drink of water and quiet words, to feel all right again.

Some children who have frequent tantrums may have learned that this is the best (or only) way to get what they want. It is of course very important not to reinforce this behaviour, and for the key person to discuss with the parents how to discourage it at home.

Aggression against other children

Aggressive actions which distress, disturb and sometimes injure other children, such as snatching, pushing and pulling, kicking and hitting, pulling hair and throwing play equipment, are particularly testing for staff in group settings. Although it is the child who has got hurt to whom we give our immediate attention as we intervene to stop the conflict and comfort the victim, it is important to notice how the aggressor is looking, which is often pretty unhappy. How we then relate to him also needs our understanding; there is little point in asking 'Why did you hit her?', a question to which a child is most unlikely to give an answer which has any meaning. Some kind of statement is more likely to be of help to the child, such as 'I know you're angry but you can't get what you want by hitting her – let's see what the trouble is'. In this way the feeling is recognized but it is made clear that the action is not acceptable.

Imitation has been shown to be a very influential factor in aggressive behaviour, so that children who habitually attack others are probably reflecting discord and disharmony in their home. Boys in particular have been found to show increased aggression when they have witnessed violence by one parent against another (Arnold, 1990), which makes it all the more important for the nursery to offer an alternative model.

One of the problems about handling aggressive behaviour in groups is to give the aggressor the attention he or she needs without reinforcing the behaviour. The key person, in consultation with other staff members, can work out a care plan to ensure that such children get regular positive attention when they are playing co-operatively with others and that desirable behaviour is rewarded with warm approval.

Conflicts between children

We may recall from our own childhood the way that the adult often arrived on the scene and told us off for some angry response when in fact they never saw how the quarrel had begun. Often the other child had provoked us in the first place and we felt the injustice of being the only one to be blamed for a conflict for which we were only partly responsible.

When two children have tight hold of the same toy and are screaming 'Mine, mine!' they often turn furious faces to the nursery worker whom they expect to take action. The temptation is to quell the noise by intervening immediately, insisting that one or other child relinquish the toy. However, if the adult can stay quietly beside the contending couple and just wait, the children may come to their own solution when they run out of steam, prevented from injuring each other by the worker's attentive presence.

Sometimes a young child will accept another toy in place of the disputed one. If not, the worker as negotiator/mediator can offer her help saying 'You and I will do something together while we wait for your turn'. Such an offer must of course be faithfully honoured. When one child has relinquished his toy to another we can make a point of thanking him, which shows him that the effort he has made is appreciated.

If there has clearly been an aggressor and the adult is sure that she saw the doll being grabbed from the pram another child is wheeling, then a quiet intervention to restore the doll needs to be made.

Conflict over playthings is a good example of the type of behaviour which can easily be increased or reduced by practical arrangements. In a heuristic play session, as described in Chapter 8, where there is a calm atmosphere and an abundance of material, this type of dispute seldom occurs.

Biting

Biting probably arouses more anxiety than any other form of aggression. Being bitten is very painful and arouses intensely hostile feelings not only in children but in adults. One still occasionally hears the suggestion that the adult should 'bite the child back to teach him what it feels like'. A (male) child minder told Sonia how he went to a meeting of the Pre-school Playgroups Association where the question of biting was discussed and told them he believed in this method. 'One of the ladies looked at me in astonishment and said "dogs bite, people don't" '.

Another common but undesirable approach is that the child who bites is pressed immediately to 'make up for it' by kissing the child he has just bitten. This mixes up aggressive and loving gestures and is simply confusing to children.

Biting tends to go in waves when young children are in groups, and staff need to decide amongst themselves how they can try to prevent it and how they will respond when it happens. The key person is central here because she needs to help the child to control his impulse to bite and yet at the same time not to take on a picture of himself as being the bad person feared by others. She must try to convey her affection and concern at the same time as setting limits. The worker can underline the proper use of teeth: 'let's look at your nice strong teeth in the mirror, let's see how sharp they are – they're for biting food *not* people'. Sharing an apple or a raw carrot with the child, she can talk about the pleasure of biting a hard, crisp thing, making a clear distinction about what is for biting and what is not. Everyone dealing with the child needs to understand that punishment and isolation will not be effective in bringing about the kind of self-control that is needed.

Biting often occurs at moments of rising tension and when children have for some reason become crowded up and jostling each other in a group. Staff, by being observant and sensitive at risky moments, can often prevent a child biting another if they are alert to the situation.

The key person's help to the parents both of the biter and the bitten child is worth thinking about carefully. She may well feel embarrassed and perhaps defensive when she has to face the parent of the victim at the end of the day. The parent may be outraged and certainly distressed at the large weal on her child's cheek or arm. She may feel guilty about having left him at the nursery if this sort of thing is going to happen. She is likely to feel angry not only with the biter, whom she not unreasonably will want to identify, but also with that child's parents even though they were probably not present at the incident. Angry words and accusing looks can be exchanged while the biter looks on, silent and guilty. The key workers for both children need to be in harmony in explaining what happened and what are the approaches they use to deal with such incidents.

It may be worth reminding ourselves that though we adults have learned to inhibit physical biting, we can still inflict painful wounds with our tongues. A 'biting' comment that reaches its target may be remembered for many years, when teeth marks would have long since faded.

Victims

We need to think about the child who always seems to be on the receiving end of any aggressive acts. They, too, are in difficulty, and need special understanding and support.

We can probably think in our adult lives of individuals to whom disappointments and disasters always seem to happen. When we hear about something of this kind we often say, 'Oh dear, it would happen to *him*!'. Such people can easily be exploited by their peers and sometimes become scapegoats in a group.

There are children in the nursery who, because of their home experiences or because they are physically rather unwell for much of the time, either withdraw and are unwilling to take part in what is going on, or cry very easily and seem depressed. Stronger, more aggressive children may take advantage of them – pushing them off the slide or snatching their toy. A sad, restless child can severely test his key person's patience and understanding when he does not respond to her attempts to stimulate and involve him. However, it is the key person's continuing affectionate attention which will enable such a child to take courage and feel that there is someone on whom he can rely to make time for him and to listen to what he has to say. In addition, the key person's good relationship with the child's parents can create a trustworthy bridge between nursery and home, giving him hope and confidence to face the world.

Overactivity and restlessness

Children often come to a day nursery labelled as 'hyperactive' or having been diagnosed as suffering from attention deficit disorder. In our view these terms do nothing either to increase our understanding of a child or help to improve what we are able to offer him during a nursery day.

It is important for nursery workers to know that the whole subject of hyperactivity is intensely controversial. In the United States the phenomenon has been considered largely as a medical problem and treated with powerful drugs. Only recently has the alternative view been proposed that this is learned behaviour, socially and environmentally caused (Tyson, 1991).

Even in this country the tendency is to focus on the child's behaviour rather than considering his daily experience from his own viewpoint. Children differ temperamentally in their level of activity, and parents differ in what they are able to tolerate. What one parent will define as normal curiosity and a sign of intelligence, another will consider 'being a nuisance'. Some so-called overactive children may be victims of inappropriate expectations, such as being asked to sit still for long periods, or simply have too little to interest them in their environment. In only a very small minority of cases is the behaviour due to neurological impairment.

Once children are provided with adequate attention and activities the behaviour may disappear; on the other hand, it may have become very firmly entrenched as the only way that the child has found of attracting adult attention, or the nursery programme may not offer enough to engage the child's interest. The key worker needs to make an assessment of the child's level of ability in control of his own body, his manipulative skill, his command of language, his use of available material in constructional and imaginative play, and the quality of his relationships with other children and the other nursery staff.

It may emerge from this assessment that the child is capable and energetic but bored and frustrated because he has exhausted the possibilities which the nursery can offer. The limitations of the nursery can be very real, but an improvement can be made by seeing that the interests and abilities of the child are understood and stretched. This may mean that nursery workers need to introduce more advanced activities, such as simple carpentry, the use of clay for the child to make real objects which can be fired and painted and used in play, making life-size 'houses' with cartons and glue or making papier-mâché for puppets and setting up a theatre to use them in. The child's interest in books, which will give him independence, can be strongly encouraged, as can his exploration of the possibilities of musical instruments. Such children are often capable of helping in the care and cleaning of the room and the outdoor or garden area, and this kind of responsibility can be very helpful to them.

More difficult is the type of child who seems unable to concentrate on any activity, is destructive of play material, and rushes noisily about, disturbing and irritating everyone. Sometimes, by agreement with other staff members, the most effective way of helping a child like this is to give him very concentrated attention for a certain period of time, taking him on his own into the garden if he seems to need to 'let off steam', or sitting beside him while he plays, trying gradually to increase the length of time he can focus on a particular activity. The attention of his key person gives him emotional anchorage and the control which he needs to gain if he is to join in with the activities of the nursery day.

Sometimes children are referred for urgent admission to day nurseries with little information provided other than a vague assurance that they are to be seen by a paediatrician for assessment at a later date. The tendency then is to put off any hard thinking about what to do with the child while waiting for a diagnosis.

Elinor was asked to help with Janet, 22 months, who, from the moment when her exhausted mother left, ran frenetically round the rooms and passages of the nursery, creating disturbance and anxiety for everyone. In consultation with staff an immediate course of action was agreed which enabled them to feel more confident and less frustrated. It was decided that Helen, Janet's key person, should make a list of all the things that Janet could do, starting with running. This list turned out to be surprisingly long, and in discussion the nursery workers were able to move from a total focus on Janet's disruption of the group to consider some of her capabilities.

Starting from her ceaseless running, it was suggested that Helen might use the garden to run round obstacles with Janet, holding her hand. The object of this was to slow the child down and enable her to gain greater skill and control in movement, in close relation to her adult. Another approach was for Helen to hold Janet in her arms until she relaxed and then encourage her to explore the Treasure Basket, picking objects up, mouthing them and putting them down, as if she were a much younger child. Later she would offer receptacles for Janet to put objects in and take them out. Concurrently, the organizer spent time with Janet's mother, helping her to understand what Helen was trying to do.

Within a few days of this intensive attention, Janet's level of activity began to subside to a level closer to that of a normal, energetic 2-year-old. The staff realized that there were many practical steps that they could take to calm her down and engage her in activity, based on their own knowledge of child development. They had no need to wait for a diagnosis, which would still leave them to find ways of turning the information into everyday practice.

Non-compliance

Children in their second and third year frequently go through phases of refusing to do what they are asked by an adult as a way of asserting their independence. This is different from the child who habitually ignores adult requests or goes out of his way to do things which have been specifically forbidden. One possibility that needs to be excluded is that the child is suffering from intermittent hearing loss, which is extremely common, particularly among children from disadvantaged homes. There is no guarantee that standard audiometric screening will pick this up (Bamford and Saunders, 1985).

If the child's hearing is normal, the problem probably lies in the way his parents have handled him. For example, some parents give instructions to their children without either checking that the child has understood what is wanted, or ensuring that the desired behaviour actually happens. The child quickly learns to ignore such communications. Another common situation is where the child gets attention only when he is making a thorough nuisance of himself.

Parents need help to understand that attention, however negative, is rewarding to a child and will therefore make the undesired behaviour more likely to persist. Together with the parents, nursery workers can analyse the child's behaviour in detail and identify a particular problem to be worked on. Sometimes the difficulty can be eliminated by altering the conditions, as suggested earlier, or by considering whether what is being asked of the child is necessary or reasonable given his stage of development.

When it is agreed that there really is a problem, the key person can help the parent to identify precisely how she would like the child's behaviour to change, and tackle one step at a time. Small successes may enable the parent to develop a strategy for managing their child more effectively and with less stress. Charles Gibb and Peter Randall (1989) in their book *Professionals and Parents* explain very clearly the theory behind the behavioural approach and suggest many useful techniques for using it with parents and young children.

Feeding difficulties

These can cause staff a good deal of anxiety. They may have their origins in very early relationships or they may be connected with the way that the child feels about his experiences in the nursery. If the first, then the nursery worker doing a home visit before admission will have heard about it from the parent or the parent will talk about it while she is with her child during the settling-in period.

Sometimes a child will eat well at home and find difficulties in the nursery or vice versa. One of the first things to find out is whether, in spite of eating apparently very little, the child is in fact gaining weight in a reasonable way and is generally healthy. This can easily be checked by using a growth or centile chart. A child whose weight falls below the third centile would be diagnosed as suffering from 'non-organic failure to thrive' (organic causes for the feeding difficulties having been excluded), which is a very serious condition, certainly requiring expert help (Jenkins and Milla, 1988). However the majority of children with feeding problems are not seriously underweight and continue to grow normally; these are usually categorized as 'behavioural feeding problems', and are often a reason for referral for day care.

As with all behaviour termed 'difficult', it is important to see it against the background of the child's experience at home and in the nursery. The first point to consider is that children come from a variety of family circumstances. A child may not be accustomed to sitting down at a table but is used to being fed on someone's knee or moving about while he eats. Inevitably eating at the nursery will mean a big change for any child to which he has to accustom himself, adapting not only to the different taste and appearance of the food but also to the arrangements for eating.

We adults are often very cautious and reserved about food with which we are not familiar (think of how we react on holiday when we are offered octopus, blackbird pâté or frogs' legs) so that it is not surprising that some children are the same. Adults are allowed to say they just don't feel like eating and this is understood and accepted. If children are not allowed the same freedom, mealtimes can develop into a battle, which is invariably counter-productive.

Another possibility is that the child may be responding to a number of unsatisfactory mealtime experiences such as a noisy chaotic period before the meal, confusion and delay in serving it, uncomfortable and crowded seating and so on (see Chapter 10).

When a child is reluctant to eat we can gently offer him a very small amount on his plate and, if he does not eat, take it away, again with gentleness; this is a message of care and concern which is conveyed without words. Taking an uneaten plate of food away can be done in a quiet understanding way or in an exasperated or punitive way and the child's face will tell us exactly how he is feeling about it.

With a well-functioning key person system a child who has difficulty in feeding will not go unnoticed. If the child has eaten little or nothing, we need to be able to do in the nursery what we would do at home, have some fruit or raisins or raw carrot (for example) available so that if he is hungry later on in the day we can unobtrusively offer something to him. This does not mean offering alternatives during the meal, which is the trap that parents often fall into at home and is very likely to lead to faddiness (Douglas, 1989). This suggestion can cause outcry in a nursery because the organization requires that the children eat only at fixed times. On the whole the children conform; however, we are dealing with people and not with robots and we need to have the courage to be flexible when necessary. As with other behaviour difficulties, all the staff who will be handling a child with feeding problems need to be agreed on their approach.

Comfort and tension-relieving behaviour

Thumb-sucking, head banging and masturbation are kinds of behaviour which create difficulties for the adults rather than the children in the first instance, but can become a problem between them if unwisely handled.

Thumb- and finger-sucking

Over and above the sucking which is involved in feeding, it seems that babies need quite a substantial amount of 'non-nutritive' sucking as part of their development (Douglas, 1988). The sucking of thumbs or objects by babies and very young children is an emotive subject which sometimes arouses all sorts of anxious and aggressive feelings in adults. However, it is an activity which is energetically pursued and evidently enjoyed by each generation of babies. We can see the baby Jesus with two fingers in his mouth in Renaissance paintings, and some babies are born with a little red mark on one of their thumbs, which indicates that they have been sucking comfortably even before they were born.

Over the years, the discussion around 'thumb or dummy' has ebbed and flowed. There are times when a dummy is helpful, but unfortunately it lends itself to misuse by adults as a too-convenient 'gob-stopper', cutting off the communication the child is trying to make and inhibiting vocalization and early speech development. The advantage of a thumb is that it is always *there*. It does not fall on the ground to be picked up and wiped on the adult's skirt or sucked before restoring it to the baby's mouth. Neither does it get lost in the folds of a blanket, causing frustration and outcry.

Another advantage of the thumb is to do with a baby's growing capacity for exercising choice. Learning to make choices begins very early. When a baby who is already sitting up is sucking his thumb, rather than a dummy, it means that at some moment he will have to choose between using his hand (and thumb) for continued sucking, or alternatively for manipulating some toy which attracts him. This can present him with a real dilemma: 'Shall I enjoy the immediate pleasure of sucking or shall I release my hand for the more advanced satisfaction of playing with the toy?'

Masturbation and sexual play

A young child is full of curiosity about his own body and discovers very early that he can gain comfort and pleasure and also release of tension in exploring it. This has carried a heavy load of misconception and disapproval in the past, and probably in the childhood experiences of many adults. This means that we need to have accurate information and confidence in our own attitudes (and those of the other staff) in deciding how we respond.

Children in the day nursery will come from a number of cultural and social backgrounds where family attitudes will vary widely. They will have differing degrees of freedom in their families to explore their bodies, to see the differences between men and women and boys and girls, and to know what to call their tummy, breast and navel, penis and vagina. As they grow up they absorb the taboos which belong to their culture and their family relationships. The nursery worker needs to find out as much as possible about parents' attitudes and think how to respond when they differ from her own.

Not so long ago masturbation was regarded as having the most dire physical consequences, such as blindness. Children were faced with violent threats and punishments, increasing the anxiety which they were attempting to alleviate in their own way. Now that attitudes in this country have generally changed, the preoccupation with the subject in, for example, A.S. Neill's famous book *Summerhill* (1960) seems quite strange. However, we have to remember that it takes more than one generation for previous ideas to disappear, so that not only parents but some nursery workers may still have misconceptions carried over from their own childhood. Caregivers need to be clear that masturbation in childhood (and beyond) is a universal practice with no adverse physical effects. The reasons for discouraging it are social and must never be done in such a way as to make the child feel he is bad. There are sometimes inhibitions about discussing this in the staff group, but it is important to have a collective view.

Masturbation, like excessive thumb-sucking, is a form of comfort-seeking which may indicate that the child is experiencing tension or boredom. If his key person becomes aware of this, she can offer him companionship and an alternative activity. Persistent masturbation associated with withdrawal from social contact over long periods requires further investigation and consultation with parents, and possibly outside experts. As always, physical causes, such as itching caused by infection or inflammation, should be ruled out, if necessary by arranging for the child to be examined by a doctor.

Play with sexual connotations can similarly be a cause of anxiety to caregivers, partly because they may suspect associations with sexual abuse (discussed in the next chapter). This is not necessarily so, but when playing at doctors and hospitals or fathers and mothers, children can become very excited and agitated, and the nursery worker, by talking sensitively, joining in their conversation, can see the way to calming the atmosphere. The children will be quick to respond to the mood which she is seeking to create.

Sometimes children become very confused about sexual matters. They will puzzle over incidents at home which they have witnessed and half understood which cause them stress and anxiety. Children will certainly have noticed pregnant women, if not their own mother, and in indirect ways try to figure out how the baby gets in and comes out. Mercifully the gooseberry bush and doctor's black bag are less in use as a cover for the adult's embarrassment, though we still see in newsagents birth-announcement cards depicting a stork flying with a cloth held in its beak carrying a baby. Children take very seriously what their adults say and the phenomenon of birth is impressive enough not to need trivial wrappings.

Because children are so attuned to perceiving adult feelings, they are very quick to pick up embarrassment or evasion and will tend not to pursue their questions if they sense a rebuff. A straightforward answer, giving no more and no less information than the child requires at that moment, needs to be combined with sensitivity to the fact that deep feelings may be involved.

Rocking and head-banging

These are not uncommon as a form of self-comforting behaviour associated with going to sleep, but in the nursery it often indicates that a child has been severely deprived of stimulation and attention at home. It was very characteristic of children in residential nurseries providing physical care and not much else, and can still be seen, sadly, in child-care institutions in poor countries. Like any other undesired behaviour it is important not to reinforce it by attention, and it tends to disappear quite quickly if the child is given a great deal of loving care and active play with his key person. Meanwhile, of course, it is important to protect him as far as possible from injuring himself.

Toilet training

This is rarely a problem in a nursery provided it is recognized that children differ quite widely in the age at which they achieve bowel and bladder control, and that temporary regressions (often associated with stressful events at home) are treated in a matter-of-fact way. A quarter of 3-year-olds are still wetting during the day (Richman *et al.*, 1982), so that in the age group we are talking about many children will not be reliably dry.

Two particular difficulties that nursery workers may encounter are potty phobia and encopresis (soiling), both of which may be associated with harsh and punitive toilet training or being forced to sit for prolonged periods on the potty (Douglas, 1988). Both problems need to be tackled in collaboration with parents.

The child who has developed an acute fear of the potty may start screaming as soon as any attempt is made to persuade him to sit on it. The only solution is to abandon any attempt at toilet training for the time being and for the child's key person very gently and gradually to reintroduce the idea in a way the child can tolerate, for instance by taking him to the bathroom with the other children but not at first suggesting that he uses the pot or toilet.

Failure to achieve bowel control in children who come to the nursery in their third year may be due to the fact that no-one has taken the trouble to train them, and is usually quite easily overcome. More worrying is secondary encopresis in a child who has previously been clean, which is liable to provoke angry and rejecting responses from adults. The problem is well discussed by Douglas (1989). Quite often the child may be perceived as deliberately soiling when more likely the cause is a combination of severe constipation with a leakage round the impacted mass of faeces. A vicious circle is set up in which the child is frightened to pass a motion because he knows it will be painful and so becomes more constipated.

Medical advice is essential, and parents may need support in requesting referral to a consultant paediatrician as the prescription of laxatives by a GP may simply make matters worse. Although psychological and emotional factors may have contributed to the problem in the first place, there is now a physical one. The child is lethargic and irritable, has no appetite, and is prevented from playing by his pain and discomfort. He may constantly scream to go to the bathroom but be unable to do anything when he gets there.

All this is both tiresome and distressing for his key person, who needs support for herself if she is to remain calm and sympathetic while feeling powerless for the moment to do anything to help. Before a normal pattern of excretion can be achieved, the child may need hospital treatment to clear out the blocked bowel, and many months of patience and understanding may be required before the problem is finally overcome.

WHEN PARENTS ARE PRESENT

The behaviour of children is often specific to particular situations so that a child may present no problem to nursery staff or to his child minder and yet be very difficult for a parent to manage. Feeding difficulties, for example, are much more likely to appear at home.

A child who is perfectly willing to comply with a request from a nursery worker may be irritable and resistant with his mother. This puts the worker in an awkward situation when the mother is in the centre and the child 'plays up'. Usually it is best for her to withdraw tactfully for a few moments. If she intervenes, it makes the mother feel incompetent; on the other hand the parent may be embarrassed by the child's behaviour and react with disproportionate severity. The worker needs to show her understanding that children behave very differently with their own parents, and maintain an uncritical attitude. On the other hand, it has to be made clear that certain forms of control, such as hitting or shouting at a child, are not acceptable in the nursery. If the situation looks like getting out of hand it is probably best for the worker to lead the child a little way off, allowing the parent to recover his or her dignity and composure, and then suggest some way out of the difficulty. If the incident is symptomatic of general problems in child management, this will need to be tackled separately.

WORKING TOGETHER AS A TEAM

One of the problems of being a member of a team of nursery workers who all handle the same children for some part of the day, is that unless all the adults really understand the thinking which lies behind any one person's treatment of an individual child, there may be spoken or, worse, unspoken criticism of a colleague as being 'too soft' or 'spoiling their favourite'.

This can be very destructive and create further problems for the child, who may feel more insecure, and without knowing it, play one staff member off against another, just as they sometimes do with parents. Here again, a key person system which works effectively should avoid this kind of complication, for there is then one staff member who takes responsibility for explaining her approach and gaining her colleagues' understanding and co-operation. In this way staff can become more mature professionally and their work become more interesting and effective.

SEEKING OUTSIDE HELP

Some children may not come to the notice of social services until they have already endured months or years of damaging experiences. Social workers sometimes have unrealistic expectations of the capacity of even very sensitive, high-quality day care to help such children recover and develop normally. Their behaviour can be discouraging and dispiriting to nursery workers. Local authority nurseries often have visiting speech therapists, psychologists, play therapists and others who work directly with children and sometimes parents. Their usually infrequent visits are of limited use unless the child's key person is closely involved, and it is essential to allow for this in the nursery's organization.

When there are many children with severe difficulties in a centre, the most effective way to use outside help is to negotiate a regular visit from a psychologist who will not work with individual children but act as a consultant to the nursery staff. A key worker who is particularly worried about an individual child might ask the psychologist to observe him for a while, or staff members might take it in turns to present for discussion a child whose development or behaviour is causing them concern. Of course many of these children will also be discussed in regular staff supervision sessions, and as we emphasized in Chapter 4, it is important that the head of the unit, who will often be offering support to nursery workers in very stressful situations, also arranges appropriate support for herself.

SUMMARY

In considering the difficulties which children present in the nursery, the significant thing is to see each particular kind of behaviour as part of the child, not isolating the symptom of his trouble but trying to understand what he is trying to say to us. It may be the environment and not the child who is causing the problem.

Many behavioural and emotional difficulties in children of this age can be fairly easily overcome if sensitively handled, and others may diminish or disappear with time as the child achieves more control over his situation. However there is always a risk that problems ignored at this stage may lead on to increasingly severe difficulties through childhood and sometimes into adulthood. A day care centre can play an important role in preventing this from happening, both by providing affectionate, consistent care and stimulating experiences for the children and by helping parents to understand and look after them more effectively.

What the key person can offer will inevitably have its limits and there will be aspects of a child's family circumstances which we can do little to change. However, it is easy to underestimate the value to the child of spending at least some hours of the day in a calm, well-ordered environment, being looked after by adults who are sensitive and responsive. By carefully examining our own practice and agreeing a plan for the child with colleagues and outside advisors it may be possible to help him to overcome at least some of his difficulties and lay a better foundation for future development.

14 Families in difficulties

> Poverty is a great enemy to human happiness; it certainly destroys liberty and it makes some virtues impracticable and others extremely difficult.
>
> Boswell's *Life of Johnson*, 1782

The acute shortage of day care facilities in Britain, as noted earlier, has led to a situation where publicly funded nurseries are reserved almost entirely for families facing serious difficulties. Places are allocated by social services managers on the basis of priorities laid down by the local authority. A typical list of criteria might include:

- Child on Child Protection Register
- Child at risk of removal from family because of emotional rejection or poor physical care
- Mother suffering from severe depression or mental illness
- Very substandard accommodation (e.g. temporary housing or 'bed and breakfast' – a single room in a 'hotel' for the homeless).
- Child has disability or serious developmental delay
- Single parent with other social needs

The effect of concentrating this extremely disadvantaged group of children all together is not helpful to them or to those who look after them. The quality of play and language in the unit tends to be impoverished. Caregivers lose their sense of developmental norms and accept a low level of progress and achievement. They may also become discouraged and overwhelmed by the scale of the problems which these children face in their daily lives.

Some organizers and managers have successfully argued for a more balanced nursery population by reserving a proportion of places for families where both parents want to work or for single parents with no obvious social problems. However, in many areas the problems of young families are so acute and so many children are in urgent need that it is hard to justify allocating scarce places to families who seem to be coping relatively well. Even family centres with a commitment to offering a service to the neighbourhood and maintaining open access find themselves under constant pressure to accept more and more families with serious difficulties.

The Children Act (1989) for the first time gives statutory recognition to the importance of day care in improving children's quality of life, protecting them from abuse or neglect and helping them to achieve what is described in the Act as 'a reasonable standard of health or development' (Part III, Section 17 (10) (a)). It gives local authorities powers to provide day care for any child under five and not attending school, but it is clear that this is still intended to be a targeted and not a universal service. The emphasis on children *in need* remains, and the wording of the Act is such that a local authority will have considerable scope to widen or restrict the number of children for whom it provides services (Shaw *et al.*, 1990). Some may simply define 'need' to coincide with the old priority categories, but even in areas which make a policy decision to broaden access to local authority day care, the geographical location of most day nurseries and family centres makes it likely that a high proportion of the children will still come from families under stress.

DAY CARE AND CHILD PROTECTION

Among the families in difficulties who use day nurseries and family centres or have sponsored places with child minders, a small proportion will have admitted or been convicted of harming their children, and a much larger number will have been referred by health visitors or social workers who believe there is a risk that abuse might occur. Day care is nearly always mentioned as a resource by writers on child protection, but it is obvious that few have more than a passing acquaintance with nurseries. As a result the impact on day care providers of this aspect of their work has been overlooked.

One of the few exceptions is Julia Gilkes's valuable article on the problems that nursery workers face in coming to terms with sexual abuse (Gilkes, 1988). She writes of the shock and disbelief which workers experience when they encounter evidence that children as young as two or three have been sexually abused and the emotional stress this causes.

Training and support are essential. All nursery workers, not just the organizer, need to be familiar with local guidelines and procedures in relation to child protection. Most social services departments have provided a much-increased level of training related to the implementation of the Children Act but this does not always extend to nursery workers. The organizer needs to be insistent that all staff have access to training, not just about procedures or recognition, but to enable them to become familiar with current thinking on the nature of child abuse and approaches to treatment.

For example, because child abuse was first identified and described within a medical setting there was an emphasis on diagnosis – was the injury accidental or not? – and on the characteristics of parents, who were seen as disturbed and abnormal. There is now a much better understanding that child abuse is socially and culturally defined. A theoretical shift has taken place which allows child abuse increasingly to be seen in the context of the wider community and society. Poverty and powerlessness are more important determinants of the way people treat their children than are their personal characteristics or family history, although all these factors interact to produce the phenomenon which we call abuse (Jackson, 1992).

Owen Gill (1992) has written a vivid account of family life in a single street on a Bristol housing estate which shows how difficult it is to be a 'good' parent in the circumstances these families have to contend with. Nearly all were unemployed (no jobs, no day care), had very low incomes from state benefits, made lower by deductions at source, and lived in flats not designed for families with children. Their immediate environment was rubbish-strewn and dangerous, and they could not afford any relief from child care or recreation for themselves. Like Gil (1973) and Parton (1985), Owen Gill argues that it is society as a whole that is guilty of abuse, by failing to provide parents with an income adequate to the demands of bringing up children or an environment conducive to their emotional, physical and intellectual development.

Nursery workers need these wider perspectives if they are to maintain a non-judgemental attitude and not fall into the trap of blaming the victims – who are the parents as much as the children (Andrews and Jacobs, 1990). This does not alter their basic responsibility to protect the child, but underlines the importance of looking at the whole life situation of the family rather than focusing exclusively on the parent–child relationship.

THE FUNCTIONS OF DAY CARE FOR FAMILIES IN DIFFICULTIES

A factor which complicates the task of staff in a day centre with a high proportion of children whose families face severe problems is that the nursery serves different functions for the child, the parent(s) and the referring agency. Some of the dilemmas which arise for nursery workers spring from attempting to negotiate the conflicting needs and demands of these three groups.

Looking first at referrers – doctors, health visitors, social workers and other professionals – day care is the most effective resource they have to offer, and a first line of defence against the ultimate disaster, the death of a child for which they might be held responsible. For social workers, day nurseries occupy a halfway position between leaving a child in a possibly dangerous family and taking him or her into local authority accommodation or seeking a care order. The nursery functions that are most important for them are providing respite for the parents, which may enable them to cope better, and monitoring the child for signs of abuse or neglect.

For the parents – mostly mothers – the nursery can fulfil many different purposes. Overwhelmingly the most important is to provide relief from 24-hour responsibility for child care. This is true even in centres which insist that parents stay with their children. At least while in the centre they are not responsible for the child *on their own*. The nursery is important, too, as a social centre, a place to meet others in the same or similar situations and exchange problems and ideas. The nursery can also be very useful as the most accessible place to make contact with a knowledgeable professional who is prepared to listen and to offer advice.

If there is work available in the neighbourhood, a nursery place may transform the life of a single parent by making it possible for her (usually her) to go out to work instead of living on social security.

Although parents generally welcome the opportunity which the nursery gives their child to play more freely than in cramped home conditions, to run about and shout in the garden without annoying neighbours, the child's experience, provided she is not obviously unhappy, is often a secondary consideration for them. Very low down on their agenda is likely to be any idea of acquiring parenting skills, an objective beloved of social workers and health visitors. Poor parents are usually clear that they could look after their children perfectly well if their living conditions were not so difficult. So one problem that arises for nursery staff is that parents and social workers may have very different ideas about why the child has been offered a place and what her attendance is supposed to achieve.

There is some risk that when the focus is on work with adults, the child's needs may be largely overlooked. This has clearly happened in some nurseries and family centres we have seen where staff resources have been overstretched and the quality of care and education offered to the children has suffered. It is crucial for nursery workers to remember that their central task is the same for the child of a family in difficulties as for any other: to offer affectionate, individualized, responsive care.

The educative function of the nursery is even more important for a child who has had a poor start and this is as true for babies as for 4-year-olds. It may require special patience and planned effort. For example, most babies of 9 or 10 months, even those of a naturally cautious disposition, will start to explore the Treasure Basket within a few minutes of being sat down beside it. A child whose instinct to explore has been roughly suppressed may need much gentle encouragement and reassurance before she will feel confident enough to reach out to grasp an object.

Sharing responsibility with parents

Most nursery workers are well aware of the danger of 'taking over' from parents and leaving them feeling even less competent and in control of their lives than before. The difficulty is that families under severe stress are often too preoccupied with their problems to keep an overall view of their children's development and undertake tasks essential to their wellbeing.

Most mothers, for example, give high priority to 'keeping children healthy' (Mayall, 1986) and generally succeed, often against considerable odds, but a few fail to notice that a child needs medical attention or lack the energy to do anything about it.

There are many reasons why parents may be reluctant to take a child to the doctor. These range from a general mistrust of professionals to a specific fear of criticism. The parent may know that the problem has existed for some time and is fearful of being blamed for not having come to the doctor before. A more sinister reason may be the fear that a medical examination will reveal marks and scars caused by injuries inflicted by parents or other adults.

Sonia visited a family centre run by a voluntary organization and headed by a social worker with a strong commitment to 'empowering' parents. The organizer took the view that it was the mother's job to take her child to the doctor and that any initiative on the part of the centre workers would undermine the parents' self-esteem. There were children in the centre covered with sores, one with an unrepaired hernia, another in obvious pain from an ear infection (a frequent occurrence according to one of the nursery workers). It was unsurprising to learn that the centre had recently suffered a serious outbreak of dysentery.

Although this was an extreme case it does illustrate the danger of sticking to a theoretical position which flies in the face of common sense. If a parent is unable or unwilling to protect the child's health, it is the clear responsibility of the nursery to take action. This of course was the primary purpose of day nurseries when they were first set up, but has sometimes been lost in the transfer of management from Health to Social Services.

ACTIVE WORK WITH PARENTS

Children on the Child Protection Register or at risk of removal from their families are often referred to nurseries or family centres by social workers with a stated expectation that the Centre will 'work with' the parents, but what this work consists of is often left very vague. There is also a strong tendency for social workers to reduce their contact with a family once a day nursery place has been allocated, leaving the nursery staff to cope on their own. This is understandable, but unless the centre has its own social worker, an agreement to continue to work together is likely to lead to a better outcome for child and family.

Who are the parents?

An important point to establish is who are the adults whose relationship with or behaviour towards the child the nursery might be attempting to modify or change? In the past it was simply assumed that parent equalled mother, and only recently has this begun to be challenged. Looked at from the viewpoint of risk to the child, an approach which focuses exclusively on the mother is clearly inadequate. Although more women than men are implicated in child abuse cases, this is mainly beause they spend far more time with their children and are much more likely to be bringing them up on their own. Cases of serious injury or death almost invariably involve a man, and of course the preponderance of men among sexual abusers is overwhelming. Despite this, studies of on-going work following child abuse case conferences show that male adults are rarely involved (Corby, 1987).

The Children Act, 1989, greatly extends the categories of adults who are recognized to have a legitimate interest in a child: grandparents, aunts, uncles and family friends, older brothers and sisters. Nurseries are sometimes critical of families when different people turn up to collect a child. Some even go so far as to insist that only the mother or father, or only an adult will do. This is to ignore the varied patterns of caregiving which prevail in different cultures, but also fails to take advantage of the opportunity to meet and make links with members of the child's natural support network. Active work with families implies identifying the significant adults in a child's life and may sometimes mean, in collaboration with a social worker, reviving potentially useful links which have weakened for lack of encouragement and contact.

For most children 'parents' will mean whoever is responsible for their day-to-day care, usually the mother and any other adults who live in the same household. Clearly the most likely 'other' person is the mother's male partner, whether or not he is the father of the child. As we pointed out in Chapter 12, the nursery organizer and key person play a critical role in determining the man's attitudes to the nursery. There are bound to be ambiguous situations, for example, when the relationship is relatively new or in a fragile state, but it is virtually impossible for a man to remain detached from his partner's young child. The constant need of young children for physical care and protection, and their power to annoy and disturb adults by crying or by innocent but destructive exploration, ensures that any adult in the same household will share the task of parenting either positively or negatively.

It is therefore essential that when the child's attendance at a nursery is based on an agreement or contract, which is especially desirable in situations of perceived risk or where the child is on the Child Protection Register, this should explicitly include the father (or father-substitute). Any new approach towards the handling of the child needs to be consistent and cannot succeed unless all the adults are in agreement.

Nursery workers also need to be clear about the position when the parents are separated or divorced. Sometimes there may be a court order restricting access, but if not, the natural father (assuming the mother has day-to-day care) is also entitled to know about his child's experience in the nursery, and this needs to be managed in consultation with the mother and social worker if there is one. Family centres often provide facilities for access visits, which enable staff to get to know the father, but if the child spends weekends or holidays with the father and perhaps a new partner, nursery workers may have no contact with these significant people in the child's life unless special efforts are made.

Changing behaviour

Nursery workers have to recognize that they have only limited possibilities of achieving fundamental changes in the way people treat their children. That does not of course mean that they should make no effort to improve relationships or modify behaviour. There are a number of different approaches directed to the same broad objective: first, to help parents enjoy their children instead of experiencing them as an irritating burden; second, to enable them to learn more about child development and so to find their own children more interesting and have more realistic expectations of them, and third, to build up their self-esteem and awareness of their primary role in the child's development.

In practice these aims are interlinked. For example, modelling is one of the most effective ways that nursery staff can expose parents to different ways of behaving. If nursery workers always speak to children in a quiet, affectionate voice, parents who spend any time in the centre will gradually adjust their own style of communication. They will see that other forms of control are more effective than shouting or hitting, which anyway, it will have been made clear to them, are not permitted in the nursery. The approaches to child management discussed in the last two chapters may need more explanation and demonstration when they are very different from the way the parents have been accustomed to relate to the child.

Some parents find it hard to show physical affection to their children, even amounting to a real dislike of touching them except to give the minimum physical care. One technique for overcoming feelings of this kind is the relationship play described in Chapter 12 (Sherborne, 1990). Another is to adopt a behavioural approach.

Darren, aged 2, had been admitted to the nursery suffering from serious physical neglect and emotional deprivation. The family social worker had considered placing him with foster carers and was not optimistic about his single mother's ability to look after him. The mother, Susan, insisted that she wanted to keep the child, but Darren's key person noticed that she seemed to shrink from physical contact with him. Susan later confided that she longed for a baby she could cuddle, but Darren had always been 'unloving'. She realized that her reluctance to touch Darren had contributed to the neglect and wanted to change but couldn't see how.

The key person undertook to tackle this problem with Susan while the social worker took practical measures to improve Susan's home situation and ensure that she received the welfare benefits to which she was entitled.

Together the key person and Susan made a list of all the forms of touching and closeness which might occur between a mother and child, and Susan ranked them in order of difficulty for her. Each week they made a plan for Susan to do the next most difficult thing. If Darren resisted when, for example, Susan took his hand as they walked, she was to let go and try again later. To begin with progress was slow, and the key person had to give much encouragement and think of ways in which contact could occur almost by accident. But gradually Darren began to respond to his mother's changed behaviour, and Susan unexpectedly found this so rewarding that she raced through the later stages of the programme and was quite soon able to respond with a kiss and a cuddle when Darren spontaneously climbed into her lap. She began to take much more interest in her own and her son's appearance. It was easier for her to do this once her social worker arranged for her electricity to be reconnected.

Changing perceptions

Some parents, especially those who are very immature and have suffered harsh and inconsistent treatment in their own childhood, have a negative view of their children, seeing normal, childish behaviour as deliberately hostile and designed to annoy them. They avoid interaction whenever possible, thus provoking attention-seeking behaviour which they find irritating and to which they respond abusively.

One technique which can help to break into this cycle is the use of video. Through a video camera parents seem to see the child with different eyes, as someone with a separate identity from themselves, an independent person. They may, for the first time since she was a baby, see the child as lovable. They usually greatly enjoy both the filming and watching the playback with their key person.

If the video session is repeated several times over two or three months, they have a chance to observe and take pride in the child's developing abilities. It also enables them to see that the child can play in an active way without being destructive or disruptive.

The key person can video the mother and father playing with the child, feeding, bathing or changing her. Viewing the tape, parents have little difficulty in spotting weaknesses in the way they interact with the child, the severity with which they control her or override her attempts to assert her wishes. The nursery worker, however, only comments on the positive aspects of their behaviour – the parent making eye contact with the child, responding to non-verbal cues, speaking to the child in a warm tone of voice.

For parents who find it difficult to have any peaceful contact with their own children it may be necessary first, to ask them to take charge of the camera while the key person plays with the child, talking about what she is doing and modelling attentive responsiveness.

Some parents are so uncomfortable playing with their child that they can only sustain the activity for a few minutes at a time, so that the early sessions need to be kept very short, gradually building up to more challenging and complex activities. The most important principle is to avoid any implication of criticism, which would probably evoke either aggressive defensiveness or apathy and withdrawal. Self-criticism can be accepted objectively, but related to a positive. For example, reviewing the video, Sally could see that she was constantly interfering with her little boy's play and imposing her ideas on him:

> Oh dear, I can see I shouldn't have taken away the yellow brick like that – it made him cry. Only I didn't want him to spoil the pattern.

> Yes, perhaps he was thinking of a different pattern. Didn't he look pleased when he waved his hand at the green brick and you gave it to him? It was good that you understood what he was saying to you.

A great deal is contained in this brief exchange. The key person confirms Sally's perception of her son as an individual with his own ideas even if he cannot yet express them in words. Sally is praised for attending and responding to her baby, so she is more likely to do the same in future. The underlying message is that children's communications are important and that if adults make an effort to understand them, they will be rewarded with smiles instead of crying.

Video is proving to be an effective tool in assisting parents to be sensitive to their children's development and to learn how to manage their own and their children's behaviour without resorting to coercive methods. Because of its distancing effect it seems to be less threatening to parents who already feel themselves under attack than more direct methods. It is already widely used in family centres and in child abuse prevention schemes in Canada (Wolfe, 1991). In the Netherlands there is a well-established video home-training programme in which specially trained workers take the video into the homes of families with child-rearing problems (Barker, 1991).

Groupwork with parents

Many nurseries and family centres build their parent involvement programme around groups, but very little has been written about the use of groupwork in day care settings with families in difficulties. Discussion groups about alternative approaches to bringing up children and ways of handling problem behaviour are quite prevalent, but here we want to focus on the less usual groups which contain children and parents together. Two rather different types, though with features in common, are *nurture groups* and *communication groups.*

Nurture groups derive from the theory that some mothers are unable to recognize or meet the needs of their children because they have experienced so little love and care in their own lives. The group is designed to provide some of that experience for the mother and child together.

One family centre runs a weekly nurture group for ten 2-hour sessions in a room apart from the main activity area. Three or four pairs of mothers and children attend with one nursery worker. The room, warm, carpeted and comfortably furnished, is set out in advance with different activities, suited to the ages of the children. Each session begins with relationship play, as described in Chapter 12, and ends with relaxation to music. In between the mother and child play together with each activity in turn (though they can take time out to read a story or just have a cuddle). The mother's instructions are to follow the child's lead and respond to her signals. The session is always followed by a communal meal in which the atmosphere of calm and warmth is maintained by careful pre-planning (see Chapter 10).

Feedback from mothers who participate in this group is very appreciative. Some feel that they have really enjoyed playing with their children for the first time. They are surprised at how long the children can concentrate with the attentive but unobtrusive presence of an adult beside them, and how much they find to talk about, even if the child is still at a pre-verbal stage. They come to trust the group leader and be more receptive to her suggestions, and they also get to know each other well and make friendships which in some cases continue outside the centre and constitute the beginnings of the social network that they so badly need.

The style of the leader in this group would probably be described as authoritative in that, although her manner is very gentle, she determines the form and content of the sessions, arguing that part of the nurturing consists in setting clear boundaries and relieving mothers temporarily of the need to take decisions.

A different kind of group, set up in a London family centre with a high proportion of children known to have been abused, focused on communication and used a more democratic style of leadership. In this case the centre was committed to interprofessional work and the sessions were co-led by a nursery worker and a social worker.

The value of groups in aiding communication is well documented (Brown, 1992; Heap, 1985), and inhibition of communication is a typical feature in families who abuse their children (Dale *et al.*, 1986). The parents often have difficulty in expressing their feelings and ideas, misinterpret their child's signals and behaviour, and give them confused messages. Dale suggests that in these frustrated and inarticulate families, physical violence and sexual abuse sometimes represent desperate and distorted attempts at communication with children.

The five families who took part in the group all acknowledged communication problems with their children and wanted to work on them. With their key worker they each identified personal goals which they hoped to achieve through their participation in the group. At the first group meeting they agreed on the aims of the group and how it should be run (the limits of confidentiality was one of the difficult issues, given that all the families were on the Child Protection Register). The sessions included group games involving collaboration between parents and children and between the different families, within-family tasks related to individual goals, observations of children engaged in activities selected and set out by parents, and relaxation, using various techniques and types of music.

Music was also used as a form of non-verbal communication, and parents, especially men, who were reluctant to participate in group games which they saw as childish, happily combined to produce a musical performance.

The parents who took part in this group made some progress towards achieving their personal goals. They were surprised by the children's participation in the relaxation exercises and by the fact that they kept as quiet as the adults, having previously seen them as always noisy and disruptive. Most parents grasped the idea of active listening to their children and felt supported by seeing other parents doing the same thing. Paradoxically, through the group exercises, they became aware of their difficulty in communicating constructively with other adults, which most had not previously recognized as a problem.

The workers felt that running the group was an effective form of intervention and an economical use of their time. It gave the families the opportunity to learn from each other and to use each other's strengths; they felt less pressured and isolated and more hopeful of being able to change. The key elements in its success were very careful pre-planning by the two co-workers and the project leader and a determined effort to include the families at every point – setting the agenda, agreeing objectives, deciding content, evaluating outcome. This kind of work cannot be done without full management support, allowing time for planning and evaluation and adequate space and equipment.

WORKING WITH OTHER PROFESSIONALS

Running groups such as those described above requires skills and experience which may not be available within the nursery or family centre team. In-service training in groupwork should be built into the staff development plan. Another way for nursery workers to acquire groupwork skills is to work with other professionals. In addition, every child abuse enquiry since Maria Colwell (1976) has emphasized the need for interprofessional collaboration if children are to be adequately protected. For very young children the nursery plays a key role as the agency which has most frequent and regular contact with the child and parents and is in the best position to co-ordinate services in their interests. Failure to attend the nursery is often the first sign of something going seriously wrong.

When a child has been returned home 'on trial' following an incident of abuse or a period in local authority accommodation, and a day nursery or family centre place is offered as a form of support, the child's key person needs to work very closely with the social worker and be clear on what conditions the child has been placed at home and what is the contingency plan if the family is not able to provide an acceptable level of care.

This is a highly vulnerable group of children, as Farmer and Parker (1991) have shown in their study, *Trials and Tribulations*. Once the decision has been made to allow a child home there is a reluctance to remove her again even when there is obvious cause for concern. The nursery worker's professional view can be a vital source of support to the social worker in this situation.

The organizer needs to establish an expectation that social workers do not hand over families to the nursery and then withdraw. Both at individual and group levels the work can be much more effective if tasks are shared, as they were in the case of Susan and Darren. Co-leadership of groups is also strongly recommended (Brown, 1992), and has many practical advantages – fewer demands on nursery staff, a wider range of knowledge, and a chance for the social worker to increase his familiarity with the nursery setting.

Some children as a result of having suffered abuse in the past are acutely disturbed when they come into the nursery and very difficult for parents, foster carers or nursery workers to handle. A psychologist may be asked to come and observe the child in the nursery and help staff and carers work out a treatment plan. Play therapy may help the older ones, though most therapists prefer to work with children over four. An increasing number of play therapists are developing special expertise in working with severely abused children (Cattanach, 1992; West, 1992), but there are problems in that the timescale tends to be long and behaviour may deteriorate in the early stages, which can be very difficult in a group setting.

WHEN DAY CARE IS NOT ENOUGH

Many official inquiries into cases of fatal child abuse have remarked on the risk of collusion between social workers and parents. A notorious instance was the case of Jasmine Beckford (Brent, London Borough of, 1985) where the report commented that the most favourable interpretation was always put on the parents' behaviour even while the children were suffering horrific cruelty. The same risk exists with the daily contact which occurs between the key person and parent in day care. The parent is likely to see the key person as a friend, and though initially aware that her role is partly one of surveillance, that can quickly be forgotten.

On her side the nursery worker may be torn between her sympathy for the parents, with their debts, relationship problems and miserable living conditions, and her awareness of the vulnerability of the child. She is in a better position than a social worker to see signs of physical abuse in the process of providing normal bodily care, and sexual abuse is frequently revealed through children's play and drawing (Briggs and Lehmann, 1989). However, the indications are often ambiguous and there is a great temptation to ignore them or wait for more evidence in order to postpone the need to take action. Especially if a family has been coming to the centre for several months, good relationships have been built up and there is a sense of some achievement, it can seem like a defeat to set in train a process which may well result in the child's removal from the family and probably also from the nursery.

In this situation it is essential for the key worker to share her anxieties with a senior member of staff immediately. She will need to write a careful description of what she has observed – bruises, burns, sexualized play, verbal disclosures, making a precise record of dates, times and names. The most appropriate action can then be decided on, in consultation with the child's social worker and in line with procedures laid down by the Social Services Department.

The key person may have had to work hard at the time of referral to overcome initial feelings of anger and disgust towards parents known to have abused a child. Having come to know them as individuals, and perhaps even to like them, it can be extremely painful to have to give evidence against them in a case conference or in court, and to experience their anger at what they are likely to see as a betrayal.

The staff member in this position needs several kinds of support. The opportunity to discuss feelings of disappointment, inadequacy and sadness in supervision and within the staff group is important both for herself and for other nursery workers. The organizer also needs to remember that any staff group may include one or more people who have themselves experienced abuse. Depending on how the discussion is handled, a disclosure may be liberating or traumatic. Unresolved personal issues may need to be tackled outside the nursery, by encouraging the worker to seek counselling or to join an incest survivors' group.

When there is only one male member of staff, as is not uncommon, he may feel under particular pressure during discussion of sexual abuse. Some social services departments have recognized this by setting up support groups for men working in early years settings.

Apart from the emotional stress, there are also problems for nursery workers arising from their low status. Of all the people involved with the family they are likely to have the most detailed knowledge of the child and the best understanding of children's needs. They will certainly be the most skilled in communicating with very young children. Yet their expertise is often undervalued by other professionals and their opinions given little weight compared with those of social workers or psychologists who may have seen the child and family on only one or two occasions.

Nursery workers need training to participate effectively in case conferences and to express their point of view clearly and forcefully. Giving evidence in court requires specific preparation and rehearsal for the particular case, as well as familiarity with the setting and with the relevant law.

THE ROLE OF DAY CARE IN CHILD PROTECTION

In this chapter we have considered the vital part played by nurseries and family centres providing day care in supporting families under stress, offering an alternative to separation when abuse has occurred or the child is considered to be at risk, and helping the rehabilitation process when children are returned to their families. Potentially day care is by far the most effective treatment resource if the long-term plan is for the child to remain in her own family. However, much more research and thinking needs to go into what actually happens after the child is offered a place. While some centres offer well-thought-out programmes to build parents' self-esteem and competence and help them to make better relationships with their children, others flounder for lack of guidance and support, to say nothing of staffing ratios that take no account of this very demanding and time-consuming aspect of their work.

It is essential to recognize that day care has limits. Nursery workers cannot undo the effects of a violent childhood or stop parents from misusing drugs or alcohol or give them an adequate income or rehouse them. The nursery cannot make a dangerous family safe – even with a full-time place the child will spend much more time at home than in day care, and most abuse occurs at weekends or in the evenings.

Nevertheless it is important for nursery workers to recognize that they have something valuable to offer the child irrespective of their success or failure in helping parents. There are many reasons why it is hard for people to change established patterns of behaviour and even social workers and psychiatrists who are very expert in working with abusive parents often have to admit defeat. For the child, however, a good experience will not be wasted, and may provide the foundation for a successful future placement.

There is a danger that the welcome emphasis in the Children Act on supporting children within their own families could lead to unrealistic expectations of day care. Experienced nursery workers are in a unique position to assess the quality of the relationship between the child and her close adults. For a few of those children their contribution may be to advise that the best option for the child is a permanent substitute family placement. Sometimes the critical thing is to know when to let go.

SUMMARY

Many family difficulties spring from structural factors such as low income, poor housing, unemployment and educational disadvantage, which all limit parents' ability to provide good care for their children. Nursery workers face problems when a high proportion of children in the centre come from such families.

Day care is potentially the most important resource for social workers trying to help families stay together. Nurseries and family centres provide respite, social contact, advice, and help in changing perceptions and relationships. They need much more recognition for this important work and better training and support to cope with the stress it involves.

The good experience they give the child will never be wasted, but it is important to be realistic and acknowledge that attempts to support parents and help them to change their behaviour may not be enough to provide adequate protection. In such cases a clear understanding with social workers and other professionals involved is essential.

15 Looking ahead

Not just rewriting the law is needed, but a social vision, expressed in policy and in the community, which recognizes the condition of childhood and seeks to plan for its best present and better future.

Brian Jackson, 1979

The previous chapter underlines the fundamental weakness of the British child care system. Because children are seen as the responsibility of their parents, not of society as a whole, help is only given to those who fall below a minimum acceptable standard instead of being provided as a universal service like clean water or roads.

Rather than taking positive measures to reduce the stress of parenting, which in extreme cases leads to abuse, a series of governments have redistributed income from poor people to richer ones and from families with children to those without. Nothing has been done to share the costs of bringing up children, and publicly funded day care for children of working parents has almost dispeapeared. Although the proportion of mothers in paid employment with children under five has risen steadily, fewer than two in a hundred now have places in local authority day nurseries. This is hardest of all on single mothers, of whom only 6 per cent are in full-time employment, and is one of the major causes of child poverty. It also limits women's opportunities for study, involvement in public activities, and recreation.

It is in the vital early years that children are most likely to be cared for by parents under economic stress, in unsuitable accommodation and with least outside support, yet the resources allocated to them are minimal, and what services there are continue to be hopelessly fragmented. The pattern of British pre-school services has often been likened to a patchwork quilt. That is a charitable image. To us it looks more like a rediscovered Roman pavement with large chunks missing, where we can only guess at the original design.

The failure to provide publicly-funded child care has not, as the government intended, been compensated for by other forms of provision. Community and co-operative nurseries are still thin on the ground. Workplace nurseries have been hit by recession and are mostly provided by public-sector employers.

The only significant increase has been in private day nurseries. However, most are finding it difficult to offer good quality care and remain commercially viable. To do so they are obliged to charge fees which rule out lower-income families and put a severe financial strain even on those who are better off. Nevertheless, together with child minders, they are likely to be the main source of provision for children under three with working parents. This means that they will become increasingly important as employers of nursery workers. Local authorities, if they take seriously their responsibilities under the Children Act, 1989, will have to recruit more staff with early years expertise or retrain existing staff to inspect and support private day care centres and provide training.

The already marked trend for local authority day nurseries to rename themselves family centres and redefine their functions, offering a much greater variety of services and facilities, is likely to continue. However, with severe limits on local authority spending there is extreme pressure on centres set up to offer a resource for the community as a whole to accept more and more referred cases from social workers and health visitors. The arguments against providing facilities exclusively for very disadvantaged children and families have been considered earlier. It will be unfortunate if definitions of 'children in need' under the Children Act are drawn to exclude under-threes whose parents are struggling to provide good care for them despite difficulties, but whose quality of life and opportunities for learning and development could be much better with adequate support.

Overall the picture is not very encouraging. The official position has remained virtually unchanged since the notorious Ministry of Health circular in 1945 which stated that 'the right policy to pursue would be positively to discourage mothers of children under two from going to work' and that day nurseries should only be provided for 'children whose mothers are incapable for some good reason of undertaking the full care of their children'. Good reason in 1945 did not include going out to work to raise the family income above poverty level, nor does it in the official view today. The reality is different.

As increasing numbers of mothers with young children have

continued to work, motivated by economic pressure, a sense of their right to pursue professional careers, or the desire for regular time away from housework and child care, we hear less overt condemnation of working mothers. Public attitudes have certainly changed. However, despite years of intensive lobbying, there is still no commitment to make child care a public service, nor to allocate the resources it needs, even though these would be recovered in taxation within a relatively short period (Pugh, 1992b).

People under three, having no vote, are politically negligible, a point vividly illustrated by the General Election of April, 1992, when children simply did not figure on the active agenda. Until the majority of people in Britain are prepared to vote for a government that sees young children as a better investment than obsolete weapons or empty offices, we will continue to have the sense of running to stand still.

All this might be seen as cause for despondency, but on balance the message of this book is a hopeful one. Even within the profoundly unsatisfactory structure of services for young children in Britain today, it is possible for those working within the system to make substantial improvements in the quality of children's experience.

Day care for very young children can be loving, responsive and individualized. It can provide a good foundation for future relationships with other children and adults, within and outside the family. Recognizing that education begins at birth, it can create opportunities for exploration and learning from the earliest months. By enabling women to work outside the home, it can improve the family's standard of living. It can extend its functions to offer support, advice, social, educational and recreational opportunities to the parents of children who use nursery and family centres. It can recognize their right to be involved in decision-making and management.

Despite the reluctance of government to engage in fresh thinking, there are signs that the framework of pre-school services, so long frozen in an outdated pattern, is at last beginning to shift, opening up the possibility of new forms of provision. The 1989 Children Act provides a legislative framework within which this can happen, and for the first time treats day care for young children as part of the child care system as a whole.

The inadequacies of existing forms of preparation and training for early years work, with their limited scope and narrow professional focus, have long been recognized. There is an ever more insistent demand for an integrated foundation for work with young children and their parents which recognizes the need to understand child development in its family, cultural and social context. We now see clearly that no one academic discipline or profession provides an adequate basis for an 'ecological' approach to early childhood.

Traditional barriers are hard to overcome and progress is slow, but visible. A new training and career structure is beginning to emerge in which child care knowledge and skills can be set in a wider educational framework and people can progress through different levels. Bristol University now offers an interdisciplinary degree course in Early Childhood Studies, drawing together relevant elements of Psychology, Sociology, Social Policy, Education, Social Work, Law and Child Health. Graduates may move directly into child care, specialize in early years work within other professions, or go on to do much-needed research. As other institutions follow this lead, the status of early years work will begin to rise and exert more influence on public opinion and policy-making than it has succeeded in doing in the past.

The strongest force for change in the future is likely to come from our increasing awareness of thinking about child care in other countries. Instead of endlessly debating the obvious shortcomings of our own muddled and incoherent system we can now look to other models. Taking an international perspective, we can see that Britain stands between the countries of Scandanavia and Northern Europe, where children are far more highly valued and universal services are taken for granted, and the United States, where provision for under threes is left to private enterprise, whether commercial or philanthropic. Comparative studies leave no doubt which provides a better quality service for children. At least in Britain we still have a legal and administrative structure which would enable us to change direction should we wish to do so. Closer contact with European countries can only underline the inadequacies of our own services and generate more effective pressure for improvement.

Another significant step is the British Government's ratification of the UN Convention on the Rights of the Child, belated and grudging though it was. Clearly, Britain does not meet the requirement of Article 18(3) 'to ensure that children of working parents have the right to benefit from child care services and facilities for which they are eligible'. However the important point is that under the Children Act, 1989, this Article of the convention could be fulfilled by local authorities if they were given the necessary resources.

A major expansion of this kind would force re-examination of the divided responsibility for day care and children below school age both at central and local government levels. The logical solution, already initiated by a few authorities, is to transfer services for under-fives to the education department. This is a move in the right direction for two reasons: first it underlines the point that we have emphasized throughout this book, that children's experience before the age of three is, for better or worse, just as much part of their education as anything that happens in schools. Second, because state education is available to all, it may work against the present stigmatized image of public day care as a service offered only to the most disadvantaged children.

Defenders of the existing system can usually find only one thing to be said for it, that is its diversity. In present circumstances the diversity is largely a sham, since although many different forms of provision exist, in any one area a family is likely to have little choice. However, this variety has provided experience of many different patterns of provision which it would be a pity to lose. An example would be the recognition of the importance of parents and experience of engaging them at different levels, which is much less developed in most European countries.

We also recognize that the demand for day care is closely linked with general employment conditions and provision for parental leave, which are outside the scope of this book. The trend in other countries is to take positive action to enable parents to care for their own children in the first year of life, by enhancing financial entitlements, not by restricting provision of care. This is a sensible recognition of the difficulty and high cost of providing sensitive group care for babies, and of the fact that many mothers prefer not to work away from home when their children are very young. We should remember, too, that group care is not the only model. The scope for a much more highly developed form of family-based care has hardly been explored, but properly resourced and supported it could have advantages, especially for the youngest children.

In the long run demographic trends may force us to value our children more highly and accept that their care and education from birth is a public as much as a family responsibility. That is for tomorrow, and may still be a long way off. What we have tried to show in this book is that there is no need to wait: there are a thousand things we can do to give our least regarded citizens, people under three, a better experience *today*.

Suggestions for further reading

Brenda Crowe (1980) *Living with a Toddler*, London, Allen and Unwin.

Although addressed to parents, this lovely book is just as relevant to those caring for other people's children. It gives a vivid picture of the child's experience and sensible, practical advice on how to cope with what can be an exhausting stage of development.

Louise Derman-Sparkes and the ABC Task Force (1989) *Anti-bias Curriculum, Tools for Empowering Young Children*, Washington, DC, National Association for the Education of Young Children.

One of the few books about anti-discriminatory practice that combines a clear, jargon-free explanation of the theory with guidelines and suggestions for activities and materials. Unusually, it gives as much attention to disability as to race, colour and gender. It includes some good suggestions about informing parents and involving them in the work. The illustrations and examples are American, but easily transferable to a British early years setting.

David Evans (1978) *Sharing Sounds: Musical Experiences with Young Children*, London, Longman.

Shows how making and listening to music, just like speech, grows from the child's relationship with close adults and from everyday experiences. No special skills or equipment are needed. Many practical illustrations and charming anecdotes drawn from the author's family and professional experience.

Charles Gibb and Peter Randall (1989) *Professionals and Parents: Managing Children's Behaviour*, Basingstoke, Macmillan Educational.

This book, by two educational psychologists, explains clearly and simply the basic principles of learning theory and shows, with many practical illustrations, how it can be used to help parents experiencing problems with their young children's behaviour.

Fraser Harrison (1985) *A Father's Diary*, London, Fontana.

A moving account of a father's day-to-day experiences in intimate relationship with his small children. Helpful in providing a balance to the exclusive focus on the mother's viewpoint in much early year's work.

John Holt (revised 1988), *How Children Learn*, Harmondsworth, Penguin.

Learning for young children is as natural as breathing, but as John Holt showed in his earlier book, *How Children Fail*, educators can often get in the way.

Gillian Pugh (ed.) (1992) *Contemporary Issues in the Early Years: Working Collaboratively for Children*, Paul Chapman/National Children's Bureau.

A collection of papers by leading British early childhood educators, discussing policy, research and practice in a readable style. It provides an excellent overview of current thinking on a wide range of topics concerning young children and their caregivers, and some useful descriptions of good practice.

Peter Moss and Edward Melhuish (eds) (1991) *Current Issues in Day Care for Young Children*, London, HMSO.

Covers some of the same ground as the previous book, but with a stronger emphasis on policy and research. Includes a valuable discussion of international comparisons and useful statistical data.

Veronica Sherborne (1990) *Developmental Movement for Children: Mainstream, Special Needs and Pre-school*, Cambridge University Press.

An indispensable book for anyone wanting to understand the theory of relationship play, introduced in Chapter 12. It gives detailed instructions for a planned programme of activities, illustrated with many expressive photographs.

Anne Stonehouse (ed.) (1988) *Trusting Toddlers: Programming for One to Three Year Olds in Child Care Centres*, Melbourne, Australian Early Childhood Association.

One of the best books available on group care of under threes. It has a well-documented research base, drawing mainly on American sources, but reflects the strength of early years work in Australia. It is a treasure house of imaginative suggestions for planning and programming, and particularly good on multi-cultural perspectives.

Prue Walsh (1988) *Early Childhood Playgrounds: Planning an Outside Learning Environment*, Melbourne, Robert Andersen/Australian Early Childhood Association.

A step-by-step guide to site assessment, planning, building and equipping an outdoor learning area. Many imaginative ideas equally applicable to conditions in this country.

Burton L. White (1985) *The First Three Years of Life*, New York, Prentice Hall.

This book is a distillation into practical terms of thirty years of findings by one of the world's leading early years researchers. It argues that the period from eight to thirty-five months is of unique importance in the development of a human being, and that the informal education which a child receives before the age of three makes more of an impact on her total education than the whole of the formal education system.

Videos

Infants at Work (1989)
The Treasure Basket explained and presented by Elinor Goldschmied. Shows sitting babies at play, individually and interacting with each other.

Heuristic Play with Objects (1992)
Directed by Elinor Goldschmied and Anita Hughes. The principles and practical organization of heuristic play, demonstrated by children in their second year from four London day nurseries.

Both videos available from National Children's Bureau, 8 Wakley Street, London EC1V 7QE.

Child Studies
Produced by Kirin Davids. A series showing children's development from birth to five in the home environment. Summaries at the end of each section list important milestones.

Restraining Small Children
Feeding Techniques with Toddlers
Childminding
Imaginative Supervised Play at Home
Supervised Learning and Playing at Home
Children Learning Through Play
Fathers Handling Small Children
All useful for staff development and parent discussion groups. They are genuinely multi-cultural and avoid intrusive commentary.

Available from Kirin Davids, 3/20 West Parade, Norwich NR2 3DW, Tel: 0603 613879.

'I Don't Need Toys': Children Under Three Years at Play at Home
Produced and directed by Anita Hughes.

Available from 1 Oakland Close, Shalford, Surrey GU4 8JL.

Let's Play Colour (1991)
East Birmingham Health Education Department. A training video for use with early years students or staff in day care settings. Suggests strategies for dealing with racist incidents and developing anti-racist practice.

Available from Daycare Trust, Wesley House, 4 Wild Court, London WC2B 5AU.

References

Ainsworth, M., Bell, S.M. and Stayton, D.J. (1974) 'Infant–mother attachment and social development', in *The Integration of a Child into a Social World*, Cambridge, Cambridge University Press.

Andrews, K. and Jacobs, J. (1990) *Punishing the Poor: Poverty under Thatcher*, London, Macmillan.

Arnold, L.E. (1990) *Childhood Stress*, New York, Wiley.

Aspinwall, K. (1984) *What are Little Boys Made of? What are Little Girls Made of? A Discussion Paper for student nursery nurses*, London, National Nursery Examination Board.

Bain, A. and Barnett, L. (1980) *The Design of a Day Care System in a Nursery Setting for Children under Five*, Occasional Paper No.8, London, Tavistock Institute of Human Relations.

Bamford, J.M. and Saunders, E. (1985) *Hearing Impairment, Auditory Perception and Language Disabilities*, London, Edward Arnold.

Barker, W. (1991) *The Video Home Training Programme*, Early Childhood Development Unit, University of Bristol.

Bee, H. (1985) *The Developing Child* (4th edn) New York, Harper & Row.

Bowlby, J. (1953) *Child Care and the Growth of Love*, London, Penguin.

Bowlby, J. (1969/82) *Attachment and Loss*, vol.1 (2nd edn) London, Hogarth Press.

Bradshaw, J. (1990) *Child Poverty and Deprivation in the UK*, London, National Children's Bureau.

Brannen, J. and Moss, P. (1988) *New Mothers at Work: Employment and Child Care*, London, Unwin Paperbacks.

Brent, London Borough of (1985) *A Child in Trust: Report of the Panel of Inquiry Investigating the Circumstances Surrounding the Death of Jasmine Beckford* [The Blom–Cooper Report].

Briggs, F. and Lehmann, K. (1989) 'Significance of children's drawings in cases of sexual abuse', *Early Child Development and Care*, 47, 131–47.

Brown, A. (1992) *Groupwork* (3rd edn), Aldershot, Ashgate.

Bruner, J. (1980) *Under Five in Britain: the Oxford Pre-school Research Project*, Oxford, Grant McIntyre.

Bryant, B., Harris, M. and Newton, D. (1980) *Children and Minders*, London, Grant McIntyre

Cattanach, A. (1992) *Play Therapy with Abused Children*, London/

Philadelphia, Jessica Kingsley Publishers.

Chandler, T. (1990) 'Men caring for young children: a personal account of a male worker in a childcare setting', in Rouse, D. (ed.) *Babies and Toddlers: Carers and Educators: Quality for Under Threes*, London, National Children's Bureau.

Clarke-Stewart, A. (1991) 'Day care in the USA', in Moss, P. and Melhuish, E. (eds) *Current Issues in Day Care for Young Children: Research and Policy Implications*, London, HMSO.

Clyde, M. (1988) 'Staff burnout – the ultimate reward', in Stonehouse, A. (ed.) *Trusting Toddlers: Programming for One to Three Year Olds in Child Care Centres*, Melbourne, Australian Early Childhood Association.

Cohen, B. (1988) *Caring for Children: Services and Policies for Child Care and Equal Opportunities in the United Kingdom*, Report for the European Commission's Childcare Network, London Family Policy Studies Centre, 1988.

Commission for Racial Equality (1990) *From Cradle to School: a Practical Guide to Race Equality and Child Care* (2nd edn) London, CRE.

Corby, B. (1987) *Working with Child Abuse: Social Work Practice and the Child Abuse System*, Milton Keynes, Open University Press.

Dale, P., Davis, M., Morrison, T. and Waters, S. (1986) *Dangerous Families: Assessment and Treatment of Child Abuse*, London, Tavistock.

Daines, R., Lyon, K. and Parsloe, P. (1990) *Aiming for Partnership*, Ilford, Barnado's.

Derman-Sparks, L. and the ABC Task Force (1989) *Anti-bias Curriculum, Tools for Empowering Young Children*, Washington DC, National Association for the Education of Young Children.

Dixon, B. (1989) *Playing Them False: a Study of Children's Toys, Games and Puzzles*, Stoke-on-Trent, Trentham Books.

Douglas, J. (1988) 'Behaviour disorders: principles of management', in Richman, N. and Lansdown, R. (eds) *Problems of Preschool Children*, Chichester, Wiley.

Douglas, J. (1989) *Behaviour Problems in Young Children: Assessment and Management*, London, Tavistock/Routledge.

Drummond, M.J., Lally, M. and Pugh, G. (eds) (1989) *Working with Children: Developing a Curriculum for the Early Years*, London, National Children's Bureau Under Fives Unit.

Dunn, J. (1984) *Sisters and Brothers*, London, Fontana.

Elias, E. (1972) 'The nursery swim school', *Where*, 68, April, 1972.

Erikson, E. (1955) *Childhood and Society*, Harmondsworth, Penguin.

Evans, D. (1978) *Sharing Sounds: Musical Experiences with Young Children*, London, Longman.

Farmer, E. and Parker, R. (1991) *Trials and Tribulations: Returning Children from Local Authority Care to their Families*, London, HMSO.

Ferri, E. (1981) *Combined Nursery Centres*, London, Macmillan.

Ferri, E. (1992) *What Makes Childminding Work? A Study of Training for Childminders*, London National Children's Bureau.

Ferri, E., Birchall, D., Gingell, V. and Gipps, C. (1981) *Combined Nursery Centres: a New Approach to Education and Day Care*, London, Macmillan.

Freeman, N. and Cox, M. (eds) (1985) *Visual Order: the Nature and*

Development of Pictorial Representation, Cambridge, Cambridge University Press.

Freud, A. (1965) *Normality and Psychopathology in Childhood*, New York, University Press.

Gibb, C. and Randall, P. (1989) *Professionals and Parents: Managing Children's Behaviour*, London, Macmillan.

Gil, D.G. (1973) *Violence Against Children: Physical Child Abuse in the United States*, Cambridge, MA, Harvard University Press.

Gilkes, J. (1988) 'Coming to terms with sexual abuse: a day care perspective', *Children and Society* 3, 261–9.

Gill, O. (1992) *Parenting Under Pressure*, Cardiff, Barnardo's South Wales and South-West.

Goldschmied, E. (1974) 'Creative play with babies', in Jennings, S. (ed.) *Creative Therapy*, London, Benbow Press.

Graham, H. (1984) *Women, Health and the Family*, London, Harvester Press.

Heap, K. (1985) *The Practice of Social Work with Groups*, London, Allen & Unwin.

Holmes, E. (1977) 'The education needs of children in care', *Concern*, 26, 22–5.

Hopkins, J. (1988) 'Facilitating the development of intimacy between nurses and infants in day nurseries', *Early Child Development and Care*, 33, 99–111.

Hutt, C. (1979) *Play in the Under Fives: Form, Development and Function*, New York, Brunner/Mazel.

Islington Health Authority (1988) Health Education Department and Nutrition and Dietetic Department *Under Fives Nutrition Training Pack*, London, Islington Health Authority.

Jackson, B. (1980) *Starting School*, London, Croom Helm.

Jackson, B. (1984) *Fatherhood*, London, Allen & Unwin.

Jackson, B. and Jackson, S. (1979) *Childminder: a Study in Action Research*, London, Routledge & Kegan Paul.

Jackson, S. (1987) '(Fathers in) Great Britain' in Lamb, M. (ed.), *The Father's Role: Cross-cultural Perspectives*, New Jersey, Erlbaum.

Jackson, S. (1988) *The Education of Children in Care*, Bristol Paper No.1, Bristol, School of Applied Social Studies.

Jackson. S. (1989) 'Assessing outcomes in child care', in Hudson, J. and Galloway, B. (eds) *The State as Parent: International Perspectives on Interventions with Young Persons*, Dordrecht, Kluwer.

Jackson, S. (1992) 'Benign or sinister? Parental responsibility in Great Britain', in Close, P. (ed.) *The State and Caring*, Basingstoke, Macmillan.

Jenkins, J. and Milla, P. (1988) 'Feeding problems and failure to thrive', in Richman, N. and Lansdown, R. (eds) *Problems of Preschool Children*, Chichester, Wiley.

Jenkins, S., Bax, M. and Hart, H. (1980) 'Behaviour problems in pre-school children', *Journal of Child Psychology and Psychiatry* 21, 5–19.

Joshi, H. (1987) 'The cost of caring', in Glendinning, C. and Millar, J. (eds) *Women and Poverty in Britain*, Brighton, Wheatsheaf.

The Lancet (1985) 20 July.

Lane, J. (1990) 'Sticks and carrots – using the Race Relations Act to remove bad practice and the Children's Act to promote good practice', in Bennington, J. and Riley, K.A. (eds) *Local Government Policy Making*, vol.17, no. 3, London, Longman.

Leaves, C. (1985) 'Volunteers in a family centre', Unpublished Development Project Report for Univesity of Bristol Postqualifying Diploma in Work with Young Children and Families.

McCrae, S. (1986) *Cross-class Families: A Study of Wives' Occupational Superiority*, Oxford, Clarendon Press.

McGuire, J. and Richman, N. (1986) 'The prevalence of behavioural problems in three types of preschool group', *Journal of Child Psychology & Psychiatry* 27, 455–72.

March, L. (1973) *Swimming Under Five*, Cambridge, Advisory Centre for Education.

Marshall, T. (1982) 'Infant care: a day nursery under the microscope', *Social Work Service* 32, 15–32.

Mayall, B. (1986) *Keeping Children Healthy: the Role of Mothers and Professionals*, London, Allen & Unwin.

Mayall, B. and Petric, P. (1983) *Childminding and Day Nurseries: What Kind of Care?*, London, Heinemann Education for the Institute of Education, University of London.

Meadows, S. (1986) *Understanding Children's Development*, London, Unwin Hyman.

Melhuish, E. and Moss, P. (eds) (1991) *Day Care for Young Children: International Perspectives*, London, Routledge.

Menzies, I. (1960) 'A case-study in the functioning of social systems as a defence against anxiety', *Human Relations* 13, 95–121.

Millar, J. (1989) *Poverty and the Lone Parent Family: the Challenge to Social Policy*, Aldershot, Gower.

Milner, D. (1983) *Children and Race: Ten Years On*, London, Ward Lock Educational.

Moog, H. (1976) *The Musical Experience of the Pre-School Child* (trans. from German by C. Clarke) London, Schott Music.

Moss, P. (1986) *Child Care in the Early Months: How Child Care Arrangements are Made for Babies*, London, Thomas Coram Research Unit.

Moss, P. (1991) 'Policy issues in day care' in Moss, P. and Melhuish, E. (eds) *Current Issues in Day Care for Young Children: Research and Policy Implications*, London, HMSO.

Moss, P. (1992) 'Perspectives from Europe' in Pugh, G. (ed.), *Contemporary Issues in the Early Years: Working Collaboratively for Children*, London, Paul Chapman Publishing/National Children's Bureau.

Moss P. and Melhuish, E. (eds) (1991) *Current Issues in Day Care for Young Children: Research and Policy Implications*, London, HMSO.

Neill, A.S. (1960) *Summerhill*, London, Gollancz.

New, C. and David, M. (1986) *For the Children's Sake*, Harmondsworth, Penguin.

Newell, P. (1991) *The UN Convention and Children's Rights in the UK*, National Children's Bureau in collaboration with the Calouste Gulbenkian Foundation.

Newson, J. and Newson, E. (1989) *The Extent of Parental Physical Punishment in the UK*, APPROACH.

Opie, I. and Opie, P. (1955) *The Oxford Nursery Rhyme Book*, Oxford, Oxford University Press.

Osborn, A. and Milbank, J. (1987) *The Effects of Early Education*, Oxford, Clarendon Press.

Parker, R., Ward H., Jackson, S., Aldgate, J. and Wedge, P. (1991) (eds) *Looking After Children: Assessing Outcomes in Child Care*, London, HMSO.

Parsloe, P. (1981) *Social Services Teams*, London, Allen & Unwin.

Parsloe, P. and Williams, R. (1993) *Volunteering Through a Bureau*, University of Bristol, School of Applied Social Studies.

Parton, N. (1985) *The Politics of Child Abuse*, London, Macmillan.

Phillips, D., Howes, C. and Whitebrook, M. (1991) 'Child care as an adult work environment', *Journal of Social Issues*, 47, (2), 49–70.

Pugh, G. (ed.) (1992a) *Contemporary Issues in the Early Years: Working Collaboratively for Children*, London, Paul Chapman Publishing in association with the National Children's Bureau.

Pugh, G. (1992b) *An Equal Start for All Our Children*, London, Times Educational Supplement.

Pugh, G. and De'Ath, E. (1989) *Working Towards Partnership in the Early Years*, London, National Children's Bureau.

Richman, N. and McGuire, J. (1988) 'Institutional characteristics and staff behaviour in day nurseries', *Children and Society* 2, 138–51.

Richman, N., Stevenson, J. and Graham, P. (1982) *Preschool to School: a Behavioural Study*, London, Academic Press.

Rouse, D. and Griffin, S. (1992) 'Quality for the under threes', in Pugh, G. (ed.) *Contemporary Issues in the Early Years: Working Collaboratively for Children*, London, Paul Chapman Publishing in association with the National Children's Bureau.

Rutter, M. (1972) *Maternal Deprivation Reassessed*, Harmondsworth, Penguin.

Ryan, P. (1988) 'The context of care: staff', in Stonehouse, A. (ed.) *Trusting Toddlers*, Melbourne, Australian Early Childhood Association.

Schaffer, R. (1977) *Mothering*, London, Fontana.

Shaw, M., Masson J. and Brocklesby, E. (1990) *Children in Need and their Families: a New Approach*, A guide to Part III of the Children Act, 1989, University of Leicester School of Social Work and Faculty of Law with Department of Health.

Sherborne, V. (1990) *Developmental Movement for Children: Mainstream, Special Needs and Pre-school*, Cambridge, Cambridge University Press.

Siraj-Blatchford, I. (1992) 'Why understanding cultural differences is not enough', in Pugh, G. (ed.) *Contemporary Issues in the Early Years: Working Collaboratively for Children*, Paul Chapman Publishing in association with National Children's Bureau.

Smith P.K. (ed.) (1984) *Play in Animals and Humans*, Oxford, Blackwell.

Smith P.K. and Cowie H. (1991) *Understanding Children's Development* (2nd edn), Oxford, Blackwell.

Stein, M. (1992) *Leaving Care*, Ilford, Barnardo's.

Stonehouse, A. (1988) *Trusting Toddlers: Programming for One to Three Year Olds in Child Care Centres*, Melbourne, Australian Early Childhood Association.

Stuart, F. (1992) *Early Child Development Through Music*, Gloucester, Gloucestershire County Council Professional Development Consultancy.

Sylva, K. (1991) 'Educational aspects of day care in England and Wales', in

Moss, P. and Melhuish, E. (eds) *Current Issues in Day Care for Young Children: Research and Policy Implications*, London, Thomas Coram Research Unit/HMSO.

Sylva, K. and Moss, P. (1992) *Learning Before School*, NCE Briefing No. 8, London, National Commission on Education.

Sylva, K., Roy C. and Painter, M. (1980) *Childwatching in Playgroup and Nursery School*, London, Grant McIntyre.

Tizard, B. (1984) *Young Children Learning*, London, Fontana.

Tizard, B. (1991) 'Introduction' in Moss P. and Melhuish, E. (eds) *Current Issues in Day Care for Young Children*, London, Thomas Coram Research Unit/HMSO.

Tizard, B. and Phoenix, A. (1993) *Black, White or Mixed Race: Race and Racism in the Lives of Young People of Mixed Parentage*, London, Routledge.

Tyson, K. (1991) 'The understanding and treatment of childhood hyper activity: old problems and new approaches', *Smith College Studies in Social Work* 61 March 1991, 1.

Van der Eyken (1982) *Home Start: a Four Year Evaluation*, Leicester, Home Start Consultancy.

Van der Eyken (1984) *Day Nurseries in Action: a National Study of Local Authority Day Nurseries in England 1975-1983*, Bristol, Department of Child Health, University of Bristol.

Walsh, P. (1988) *Early Childhood Playgrounds: Planning an Outside Learning Environment*, Melbourne, Martin Educational in association with Robert Andersen Associates, Australian Early Childhood Association/Child Accident Prevention Foundation of Australia.

Wells, C.G. (1985) *Language Development in the Pre-school Years*, Cambridge, Cambridge University Press.

West, J. (1992) *Child-centred Play Therapy*, London, Edward Arnold.

Whalley, M. (1992) 'Working as a team' in Pugh G. (ed.) *Contemporary Issues in the Early Years*, London, Paul Chapman/National Children's Bureau.

Wolfe, D. (1991) *Preventing Physical and Emotional Abuse of Children*, New York/London, The Guilford Press.

Worden, J. [1983] (1991) *Grief Counselling and Grief Therapy: a Handbook for the Mental Health Practitioner* (2nd edn), London, Routledge.

Organizations concerned with young children and families

Association of Advisers for the Under 8s and their families (AAUEF)
The Secretary, Cherrystone House, Church Road, Worth, Crawley, Sussex RH10 4RT.
Aims to provide opportunities for research, information exchange and liaison among professionals concerned with under fives.

Association for Improvement of Maternity Services (AIMS)
163 Liverpool Road, London N1 0RE. Tel: 081 960 5585.

Association of Nursery Training Colleges
The Chilterns Nursery Training College, 16 Peppard Road, Caversham, Reading RG4 8LA. Tel: 0734 471847.

British Association for Early Childhood Education (BAECE)
111 City View House, 463 Bethnal Green Road, London E1. Tel: 071 739 7594.
Campaigns for provision of nursery schools and day care, and promotes the interests of young children generally. There are local groups.

Building Blocks
40 Tabard Street, London SE1 4JU. Tel: 071 403 8264.
Resources for training teachers and carers about multi-cultural care and education and information about suppliers.

Child Accident Prevention Trust
40 Portland Place, London W1N 3AL. Tel: 071 636 2545.
Carries out research into the causes of child accidents and aims to educate parents, carers and public authorities on ways of preventing them from happening.

Child Care Association
1 Floral Place, Northampton Grove, London N1 2PL. Tel: 071 354 9943.
An organization for consultants to, or providers of, privately run child care facilities. Provides information and support services and negotiates with other bodies on behalf of members.

Council for Early Years Awards (formerly National Nursery Examination Board)
8 Chequer Street, St Albans, Herts AL1 3XZ. Tel: 0727 47636.

Countrywide Workshops Charitable Trust
47 Fisherton Street, Salisbury, Wiltshire SP2 7SU. Tel: 0722 326886.
Very high quality wooden toys, jigsaws, babywalkers, slides, etc. made by blind and disabled people. Will supply Treasure Baskets to order.

Early Years Trainers Anti-Racist Network (EYTARN)
1 The Lyndens, 51 Granville Road, London N12 0JH. Tel: 081 446 7056.
Organizes conferences and training events and distributes material designed to promote anti-racist work and combat racism among staff, students and children in early childhood settings.

Fair Play for Children
Secretary Jan Cosgrove, 8A The Precinct, Wesmead, Bognor Regis PO21 5SB. Tel: 0243 869022.
Campaigns for better funding and provision for children's play. Networking organization for local groups.

Home Start Consultancy
2 Salisbury Road, Leicester LE1 7QR. Tel: 0533 554988.
Offers advice and support to people setting up Home Start schemes (volunteer home-visiting for families with children under five who are experiencing stress).

Irish Pre-school Playgroups Association
19 Wicklow Street, Dublin 2. Tel: 010 353 1 719245.

Letterbox Library
8 Bradbury Street, London N16 8JN. Tel: 071 254 1640.
Supplies multi-cultural, non-sexist, environmentally aware books for children and publishes newsletter for subscribers.

Meet a Mum Association (MAMA)
Ms Bryony Hallam, 58 Malden Avenue, S.Norwood, London SE25 4HS. Tel: 081 656 7318.
Support groups for mothers with post-natal depression

National Association of Hospital Play Staff
Thomas Coram Foundation, 40 Brunswick Square, London WC1N 1AZ. Tel: 071 278 2424.

National Association for Maternal and Child Welfare
40/42 Osnaburgh Street, London NW1 3ND. Tel: 071 383 4117.
Runs courses on child care and child development and publishes illustrated advisory booklets for parents, professional workers and teachers.

National Association of Nursery and Family Care
Dr Johnston Children and Family Centre, Catesby Street, Off Hinckley Road, Leicester LE3 5PP. Tel: 0533 59992.
Professional association for nursery workers with commitment to promoting high quality group care for children and support for families.

National Association of Nursery Nurses (NANN)
Membership Secretary, 162 Langdale Road, Thornton Heath, Surrey CH4 7PR. Tel: 0255 476 707.
Works to improve the status of all nursery nurses by encouraging a good standard of training, consulting and liaising with local authorities on all aspects of child care and development and working along with Unions at all levels.

National Campaign for Nursery Education
23 Albert Street, London NW1 7LU. Tel: 071 387 6582.
Campaigns to increase provision of nursery education by local authorities.

National Childbirth Trust
Alexandra House, Oldham Terrace, Acton, London W3 6WH. Tel: 081 992 8637.
Offers information and support in pregnancy, childbirth and early parenthood, runs antenatal classes and provides information on breastfeeding and local support groups through branches all over the country.

National Child Care Campaign/Daycare Trust
Wesley House, 4 Wild Court, London WC2B 5AU. Tel: 071 405 5617/8.
Campaigns for child care provision nationally and co-ordinates local pressure groups. Publishes excellant magazine.

National Children's Centre
The Brian Jackson Centre, New North Parade, Huddersfield HD1 5JP. Tel: 0484 519988.
Explores new ideas in family and child care through practical, locally based projects and disseminates the outcomes nationally. Provides advice and information on child-related subjects.

National Childminding Association
8 Masons Hill, Bromley, Kent BR2 9EY. Tel: 081 464 6164.
Promotes the interests of child minders and works to improve the quality of home-based day care. Also runs Advice Line for child minders 081 466 0200, Mon, Tues, Thurs 2–7 p.m.

National Children's Bureau
8 Wakley Street, London EC1V 7QE. Tel: 071 278 9441.
Promotes children's interests and wellbeing through research, co-ordination, training and dissemination of information. Invaluable Library/Information service. Early Childhood Unit produces publications, training materials and provides information for caregivers and managers in day care and preschool settings.

National Children's Play and Recreation Unit
359–361 Euston Road, London NW1 3AL. Tel: 071 383 5455 (also National Play Information Centre).
Pioneers national qualifications for play workers. The main policy-making and advisory body for children's play.

National Council for One Parent Families
255 Kentish Town Road, London NW5 2LX. Tel: 071 287 1361.

National Federation of City Farms
66 Fraser Street, Bedminster, Bristol BS3 4LY. Tel: 0272 660663.

National Information for Parents of Prematures (NIPPERS)
P.O.Box 1553, Wedmore, Somerset BS28 46Z. Tel: 0934 733123.

National Playbus Association
Unit G, Arnos Castle Estate, Junction Road, Brislington, Bristol BS4 3JP.
Tel: 0272 775375.

National Toy Libraries Association
68 Churchway, London NW1 1LT. Tel: 071 387 9592.
Provides advice and guidance on setting up and running toy libraries and publishes annual Good Toy Guide.

National Voluntary Council for Children's Play
8 Wakley Street, London EC1V 7QE. Tel: 071 278 9441.
Forum for voluntary organizations concerned with play.

Newpin (New Parent Infant Network)
Sutherland House, Sutherland Square, Walworth, London SE17 3EE. Tel:
071 703 5271.
Resource centre, information service and support programme for young families.

Northern Ireland Pre-school Playgroups Association
Boucher Crescent, Boucher Road, Belfast BT12 6HU. Tel: Belfast 662825.

Parentline
Westbury House, 57 Hart Lane, Thundersley, Essex SS7 3PD. Tel: 0268
757077.
National network of phone-in services for parents experiencing problems with their children.

Pre-School Playgroups Association
61–63 Kings Cross Road, London WC1X 9LL. Tel: 071 833 0991.

Priority Area Playgroups & Day Care Centres
117 Pershore Road, Birmingham B5 7NX. Tel: 021 440 1320.

Professional Association of Nursery Nurses (PANN)
The Secretary, 2 St James's Court, Friar Gate, Derby DE1 1BT. Tel: 0332
43029.
Aims to promote professional standards which emphasize the wellbeing of children and service to the community. Functions as a Trade Union (with a Certificate of Independence) for nursery nurses, especially those employed as nannies in private families, whether at home or abroad.

Scottish Child and Family Alliance
55 Albany Street, Edinburgh EH1 3QR. Tel: 031 557 2780.
Works with voluntary organizations to develop family and child care services on both a national and local level.

Scottish Pre-School Playgroups Association
14 Elliott Place, Glasgow G3 8EP. Tel: 041 221 4148/9.

Step by Step
Unit 4, Brunel Way, Thornbury Industrial Estate, Thornbury, Bristol BS12 2NR. Tel: 0454 281200.
Mail-order supplier of pre-school equipment and materials. Multi-cultural resource collection includes dolls, puppets, playpeople, tray puzzles, cards, books and posters.

Thomas Coram Research Unit
27–28 Woburn Square, London WC1. Tel: 071 612 6957.
Carries out research on education and care of children with special emphasis on under fives and day care.

Twins and Multiple Births Association (TAMBA)
51 Thicknall Drive, Pedmore, Stourbridge, West Midlands DY9 0YH. Tel: 051 348 0020.

Voluntary Organisations' Liaison Council for the Under-Fives (VOLCUF)
77 Holloway Road, London N7 8SZ. Tel: 071 607 9573.
Provides a forum for the development of ideas on provision for young children and for the dissemination of information.

Working Group Against Racism in Children's Resources
460 Wandsworth Road, London SW8 3LX. Tel: 071 627 4594.
Newsletter and guidelines for the evaluation of early years facilities. Also runs seminars and training days and gives information on resources and suppliers.

Name index

Subject index